Lecture Notes in Economics and Mathematical Systems

For information about Vols. 1–100, please contact your bookseller or Springer-Verlag

Vol. 101: W. M. Wonham, Linear Multivariable Control. A Geometric Approach. X, 344 pages. 1974.

Vol. 102: Analyse Convexe et Ses Applications. Comptes Rendus, Janvier 1974. Edited by J.-P. Aubin. IV, 244 pages. 1974.

Vol. 103: D. E. Boyce, A. Farhi, R. Weischedel, Optimal Subset Selection. Multiple Regression, Interdependence and Optimal Network Algorithms. XIII, 187 pages. 1974.

Vol. 104: S. Fujino, A Neo-Keynesian Theory of Inflation and Economic Growth. V, 96 pages. 1974.

Vol. 105: Optimal Control Theory and its Applications. Part I. Proceedings 1973. Edited by B. J. Kirby. VI, 425 pages. 1974.

Vol. 106: Optimal Control Theory and its Applications. Part II. Proceedings 1973. Edited by B. J. Kirby. VI, 403 pages. 1974.

Vol. 107: Control Theory, Numerical Methods and Computer Systems Modeling. International Symposium, Rocquencourt, June 17–21, 1974. Edited by A. Bensoussan and J. L. Lions. VIII, 757 pages. 1975.

Vol. 108: F. Bauer et al., Supercritical Wing Sections II. A Handbook. V, 296 pages. 1975.

Vol. 109: R. von Randow, Introduction to the Theory of Matroids. IX, 102 pages. 1975.

Vol. 110: C. Striebel, Optimal Control of Discrete Time Stochastic Systems. III. 208 pages. 1975.

Vol. 111: Variable Structure Systems with Application to Economics and Biology. Proceedings 1974. Edited by A. Ruberti and R. R. Mohler. VI, 321 pages. 1975.

Vol. 112: J. Wilhelm, Objectives and Multi-Objective Decision Making Under Uncertainty. IV, 111 pages. 1975.

Vol. 113: G. A. Aschinger, Stabilitätsaussagen über Klassen von Matrizen mit verschwindenden Zeilensummen. V, 102 Seiten. 1975.

Vol. 114: G. Uebe, Produktionstheorie. XVII, 301 Seiten. 1976.

Vol. 115: Anderson et al., Foundations of System Theory: Finitary and Infinitary Conditions. VII, 93 pages. 1976

Vol. 116: K. Miyazawa, Input-Output Analysis and the Structure of Income Distribution. IX, 135 pages. 1976.

Vol. 117: Optimization and Operations Research. Proceedings 1975. Edited by W. Oettli and K. Ritter. IV, 316 pages. 1976.

Vol. 118: Traffic Equilibrium Methods, Proceedings 1974. Edited by M. A. Florian. XXIII, 432 pages. 1976.

Vol. 119: Inflation in Small Countries. Proceedings 1974. Edited by H. Frisch. VI, 356 pages. 1976.

Vol. 120: G. Hasenkamp, Specification and Estimation of Multiple-Output Production Functions. VII, 151 pages. 1976.

Vol. 121: J. W. Cohen, On Regenerative Processes in Queueing Theory. IX, 93 pages. 1976.

Vol. 122: M. S. Bazaraa, Shetty, Foundations of Optimization VI. 193 pages. 1976

Vol. 123: Multiple Criteria Decision Making. Kyoto 1975. Edited by M. Zeleny. XXVII, 345 pages. 1976.

Vol. 124: M. J. Todd. The Computation of Fixed Points and Applications. VII, 129 pages. 1976.

Vol. 125: Karl C. Mosler. Optimale Transportnetze. Zur Bestimmung ihres kostengünstigsten Standorts bei gegebener Nachfrage. VI, 142 Seiten. 1976.

Vol. 126: Energy, Regional Science and Public Policy. Energy and Environment I. Proceedings 1975. Edited by M. Chatterji and P. Van Rompuy. VIII, 316 pages. 1976.

Vol. 127: Environment, Regional Science and Interregional Modeling. Energy and Environment II. Proceedings 1975. Edited by M. Chatterji and P. Van Rompuy. IX, 211 pages. 1976.

Vol. 128: Integer Programming and Related Areas. A Classified Bibliography. Edited by C. Kastning. XII, 495 pages. 1976.

Vol. 129: H.-J. Lüthi, Komplementaritäts- und Fixpunktalgorithmen in der mathematischen Programmierung. Spieltheorie und Ökonomie. VII, 145 Seiten. 1976.

Vol. 130: Multiple Criteria Decision Making, Jouy-en-Josas, France. Proceedings 1975. Edited by H. Thiriez and S. Zionts. VI, 409 pages. 1976.

Vol. 131: Mathematical Systems Theory. Proceedings 1975. Edited by G. Marchesini and S. K. Mitter. X, 408 pages. 1976.

Vol. 132: U. H. Funke, Mathematical Models in Marketing. A Collection of Abstracts. XX, 514 pages. 1976.

Vol. 133: Warsaw Fall Seminars in Mathematical Economics 1975. Edited by M. W. Łoś, J. Łoś, and A. Wieczorek. V. 159 pages. 1976.

Vol. 134: Computing Methods in Applied Sciences and Engineering. Proceedings 1975. VIII, 390 pages. 1976.

Vol. 135: H. Haga, A Disequilibrium – Equilibrium Model with Money and Bonds. A Keynesian – Walrasian Synthesis. VI, 119 pages. 1976.

Vol. 136: E. Kofler und G. Menges, Entscheidungen bei unvollständiger Information. XII, 357 Seiten. 1976.

Vol. 137: R. Wets, Grundlagen Konvexer Optimierung. VI, 146 Seiten. 1976.

Vol. 138: K. Okuguchi, Expectations and Stability in Oligopoly Models. VI, 103 pages. 1976.

Vol. 139: Production Theory and Its Applications. Proceedings. Edited by H. Albach and G. Bergendahl. VIII, 193 pages. 1977.

Vol. 140: W. Eichhorn and J. Voeller, Theory of the Price Index. Fisher's Test Approach and Generalizations. VII, 95 pages. 1976.

Vol. 141: Mathematical Economics and Game Theory. Essays in Honor of Oskar Morgenstern. Edited by R. Henn and O. Moeschlin. XIV, 703 pages. 1977.

Vol. 142: J. S. Lane, On Optimal Population Paths. V, 123 pages. 1977.

Vol. 143: B. Näslund, An Analysis of Economic Size Distributions. XV, 100 pages. 1977.

Vol. 144: Convex Analysis and Its Applications. Proceedings 1976. Edited by A. Auslender. VI, 219 pages. 1977.

Vol. 145: J. Rosenmüller, Extreme Games and Their Solutions. IV, 126 pages. 1977.

Vol. 146: In Search of Economic Indicators. Edited by W. H. Strigel. XVI, 198 pages. 1977.

Vol. 147: Resource Allocation and Division of Space. Proceedings. Edited by T. Fujii and R. Sato. VIII, 184 pages. 1977.

Vol. 148: C. E. Mandl, Simulationstechnik und Simulationsmodelle in den Sozial- und Wirtschaftswissenschaften. IX, 173 Seiten. 1977.

Vol. 149: Stationäre und schrumpfende Bevölkerungen: Demographisches Null- und Negativwachstum in Österreich. Herausgegeben von G. Feichtinger. VI, 262 Seiten. 1977.

Vol. 150: Bauer et al., Supercritical Wing Sections III. VI, 179 pages. 1977.

Vol. 151: C. A. Schneeweiß, Inventory-Production Theory. VI, 116 pages. 1977.

Vol. 152: Kirsch et al., Notwendige Optimalitätsbedingungen und ihre Anwendung. VI, 157 Seiten. 1978.

Vol. 153: Kombinatorische Entscheidungsprobleme: Methoden und Anwendungen. Herausgegeben von T. M. Liebling und M. Rössler. VIII, 206 Seiten. 1978.

Vol. 154: Problems and Instruments of Business Cycle Analysis. Proceedings 1977. Edited by W. H. Strigel. VI, 442 pages. 1978.

Vol. 155: Multiple Criteria Problem Solving. Proceedings 1977. Edited by S. Zionts. VIII, 567 pages. 1978.

Vol. 156: B. Näslund and B. Sellstedt, Neo-Ricardian Theory. With Applications to Some Current Economic Problems. VI, 165 pages. 1978.

continuation on page 153

Lecture Notes
in Economics and
Mathematical Systems

Managing Editors: M. Beckmann and W. Krelle

219

Eric van Damme

Refinements of the Nash Equilibrium Concept

Springer-Verlag
Berlin Heidelberg New York Tokyo 1983

Managing Editors

Prof. Dr. M. Beckmann
Brown University
Providence, RI 02912, USA

Prof. Dr. W. Krelle
Institut für Gesellschafts- und Wirtschaftswissenschaften
der Universität Bonn
Adenauerallee 24–42, D-5300 Bonn, FRG

Author

Prof. Eric van Damme
Department of Mathematics and Computing Science
University of Technology
Julianalaan 132, 2628 BL Delft, The Netherlands

ISBN 978-3-540-12690-4 ISBN 978-3-642-49970-8 (eBook)
DOI 10.1007/978-3-642-49970-8

2142/3140-543210

PREFACE

In this monograph, noncooperative games are studied. Since in a noncooperative game binding agreements are not possible, the solution of such a game has to be self-enforcing, i.e. a Nash equilibrium (NASH [1950,1951]). In general, however, a game may possess many equilibria and so the problem arises which one of these should be chosen as the solution. It was first pointed out explicitly in SELTEN [1965] that not all Nash equilibria of an extensive form game are qualified to be selected as the solution, since an equilibrium may prescribe irrational behavior at unreached parts of the game tree. Moreover, also for normal form games not all Nash equilibria are eligible, since an equilibrium need not be robust with respect to slight perturbations in the data of the game. These observations lead to the conclusion that the Nash equilibrium concept has to be refined in order to obtain sensible solutions for every game.

In the monograph, various refinements of the Nash equilibrium concept are studied. Some of these have been proposed in the literature, but others are presented here for the first time. The objective is to study the relations between these refinements, to derive characterizations and to discuss the underlying assumptions. The greater part of the monograph (the chapters 2-5) is devoted to the study of normal form games. Extensive form games are considered in chapter 6.

In chapter 1, the reasons why the Nash equilibrium concept has to be refined are reviewed and, by means of a series of examples, various refined concepts are illustrated.

In chapter 2, we study n-person normal form games. Some concepts which are considered are: perfect equilibria (SELTEN [1975]), proper equilibria (MYERSON [1978]), essential equilibria (WU WEN-TSÜN AND JIANG JIA-HE [1962]) and regular equilibria (HARSANYI [1973b]). An important result is that regular equilibria possess all robustness properties one can hope for, and that generically all Nash equilibria are regular.

Matrix and bimatrix games are studied in chapter 3. The relative simplicity of such games enables us to give characterizations of perfect equilibria (in terms of undominated strategies), of proper equilibria (by means of optimal strategies in the sense of DRESHER [1961]) and of regular equilibria.

In chapter 4, it is shown that the basic assumption underlying the properness concept (viz. that a more costly mistake is chosen with an order smaller probability than a less costly one) cannot be justified if one takes into account that a player actually has to put some effort in trying to prevent mistakes.

In chapter 5, we study how the strategy choice of a player is influenced by his uncertainty about the payoffs of his opponents. It is shown that slight uncertainty leads to perfect equilibria and that specific slight uncertainty leads to weakly proper equilibria.

In the concluding chapter 6, it is investigated to what extend the insights obtained from the study of normal form games are also valuable for games in extensive form.

It turns out that there is a big difference between these two classes of games and, in fact, even the most stringent refinement of the Nash equilibrium concept proposed to date still does not exclude all intuitively unreasonable equilibria of an extensive form game.

The research for this monograph was carried out during the years 1979-1983 at the department of mathematics and computing science of the Eindhoven University of Technology in the Netherlands under the supervision of prof. dr. Jaap Wessels. I wish to express my sincere thanks to him as well as to prof. dr. Reinhard Selten, dr. Stef Tijs and dr. Jan van der Wal for many helpful and stimulating discussions on this subject. I am most grateful to my wife, Suzan, for her continual moral support and for her excellent typing of the manuscript.

Eindhoven, The Netherlands, Eric E.C. van Damme.
June, 1983.

CONTENTS

CHAPTER 1

GENERAL INTRODUCTION

In this chapter, we illustrate, by means of a series of examples, why the Nash equilibrium concept has to be refined and several refinements which have been proposed in the literature are introduced in an informal way (No formal definitions are given in this chapter). First, in section 1.1, it is motivated why the solution of a noncooperative game has to be a Nash equilibrium. In the sections 1.2 - 1.4, we consider games in extensive form and discuss the following refinements of the Nash equilibrium concept: subgame perfect equilibria, sequential equilibria and perfect equilibria. In the sections 1.5 and 1.6, we consider refinements of the Nash equilibrium concept for normal form games, such as perfect equilibria, proper equilibria, essential equilibria and regular equilibria. The contents of the monograph are summarized in section 1.7 and, finally, in section 1.8 some notations are introduced.

1.1. INFORMAL DESCRIPTION OF GAMES AND GAME THEORY

In this section, an informal description of a (strategic) game and of Game Theory is given. For a thorough introduction to Game Theory, the reader is referred to LUCE AND RAIFFA [1957], OWEN [1968], HARSANYI [1977] or ROSENMÜLLER [1981].

Game Theory is a mathematical theory which deals with conflict situations. A conflict situation (game) is a situation in which two or more individuals (players) interact and thereby jointly determine the outcome. Each participating player can partially control the situation, but no player has full control. In addition each player has certain personal preferences over the set of possible outcomes and each player strives to obtain that outcome which is most profitable to him. Game Theory restricts itself to games with rational players. A rational player is a highly idealized person which satisfies a number of properties (see e.g. HARSANYI [1977]) of which we mention the following two:

(i) the player is sufficiently intelligent, so that he can analyse the game completely,

(ii) the player's preferences can be described by a Von Neumann/Morgenstern utility function, whose expected value this player tries to maximize (and, in fact, the player has no other objective than to maximize expected utility.

Game Theory is a normative theory: it aims to prescribe what each player in a game should do in order to promote his interests optimally, i.e. which strategy each player should play, such that his partial influence on the situation benefits him most. Hence, the aim of Game Theory is to solve each game, i.e. to prescribe a unique solution (one optimal strategy for each player) for every game.
The foundation of Game Theory was laid in an article by John von Neumann in 1928 (VON NEUMANN [1928]), but the theory received widespread attention only after the publication of the fundamental book VON NEUMANN AND MORGENSTERN [1944].

Traditionally, games have been divided into two classes: cooperative games and noncooperative games. In this monograph, we restrict ourselves to noncooperative games. By a noncooperative game, we mean a game in which the players are not able to make binding agreements (as well as other commitments), except for the ones which are explicitly allowed by the rules of the game. Since in a noncooperative game binding agreements are not possible, the solution of such game has to be self-enforcing, i.e. it must have the property that, once it is agreed upon, nobody has an incentive to deviate. This implies that the solution of a noncooperative game has to be a Nash equilibrium (NASH [1950], [1951]), i.e. a strategy combination with the property that no player can gain by unilaterally deviating from it. Let us illustrate this by means of the game of fig. 1.1.1, which is the so called prisoners' dilemma game, probably the most discussed game of the literature.

	L	R
T	10, 10	0, 11
B	11, 0	3, 3

Figure 1.1.1. Prisoners' dilemma.

The rows of the table represent the possible choices T and B for player 1, the columns represent the choices L and R of player 2. In each cell the upper left entry is the payoff to player 1, while the lower right entry is the payoff to player 2. The rules of the game are as follows: It is a one-shot game (each player has to make a choice just once), the players have to make their choices simultaneously and independently of each other, binding agreements are not possible.

The most attractive strategy combination of the game of figure 1.1.1 is (T,L). However, a sensible theory cannot prescribe this strategy pair as the solution. Namely, suppose the players have agreed to play (T,L). (So for the moment we assume the players are able to communicate, however, nothing changes if communication is not possible as we will see below). Since the game is a noncooperative one, this agreement makes sense only if it is self-enforcing which, however, is not the case. If player 1 expects that player 2 will keep to the agreement, then he himself has an incentive to violate it, since B yields him a higher payoff than T does, if player 2 plays L. Similarly, player 2 has an incentive to violate the agreement, if he expects player 1 to keep to it. Hence, the agreement to play (T,L) is self-destabilizing: each player is motivated to violate it, if he expects the other to abide it. Therefore, (T,L) cannot be the solution of the game of figure 1.1.1. In this game, the strategy pair (B,R) is the only pair with the property that no player can gain by unilaterally deviating from it. So, only an agreement to play the Nash equilibrium (B,R) is sensible and, therefore, the players will agree to play (B,R) if they are able to communicate. Sufficiently intelligent players will reach the same conclusion if communication is not possible as a consequence of the tacit principle of bargaining (SCHELLING [1960]) which states that any agreement that can be reached by explicit bargaining can also be reached by tacit understanding alone (as long as there is no coordination problem arising from equivalent equilibria). Hence, if binding agreements are not possible, only (B,R) can be chosen as the solution, whether there is communication or not.

The discussion above clearly shows that the solution of a noncooperative game has to be a Nash equilibrium,since every other strategy combination is self-destabilizing, if binding agreements are not possible. In general, however, a game may possess more than one Nash equilibrium and, therefore, the <u>core problem of noncooperative game theory</u> can be formulated as: given a game with more than one Nash equilibrium, which one of these should be chosen as the solution of the game? This core problem will not be solved in this monograph, but we will show that some Nash equilibria are better qualified to be chosen as the solution than others. Namely, we will show that not every Nash equilibrium has the property of being self-enforcing. The next 5 sections illustrate how such equilibria can arise and how one can eliminate them.

1.2. DYNAMIC PROGRAMMING

There are several ways in which a game can be described. One way is to summarize the rules of the game by indicating the choices available to each player, the information a player has when it is his turn to move, and the payoffs each player receives at the end of the game. A game described in this way is referred to as a <u>game in extensive form</u> (see section 6.1). Usually, such a game is represented by a tree, following

KUHN [1953]. Another way of representing a game is by listing all the strategies (complete plans of action) each player has available together with the payoffs associated with the various strategy combinations. A game described in this way is called a game in normal form (see section 2.1). In the sections 1.2 - 1.4, we confine ourselves to games in extensive form. Normal form games will be considered in the sections 1.5 and 1.6.

As an example of a game in extensive form, consider the game of figure 1.2.1.

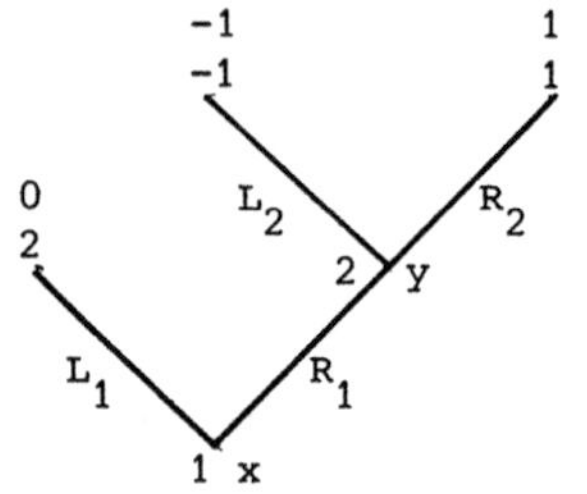

Figure 1.2.1. An extensive form game with a Nash equilibrium which is not self-enforcing.

The rules of this game are as follows. The game starts at the root x of the tree, where player 1 has to move. He can choose between L_1 and R_1. Player 2, who can choose between L_2 and R_2, has to move only after player 1 has chosen R_1. The payoffs to the players are represented at the endpoints of the tree, the upper number being the payoff to player 1. So, for example, if player 1 chooses L_1, then player 1 receives 0 and player 2 receives 2. The game is played just once.

The game of figure 1.2.1 possesses two Nash equilibria (or shortly equilibria), viz. (L_1,L_2) and (R_1,R_2). The equilibrium (L_1,L_2), however, is not self-enforcing. Namely, suppose the players have agreed to play (L_1,L_2). If player 1 expects that player 2 will keep to the agreement, then indeed it is optimal for him to play L_1. But should player 1 expect that player 2 will keep to the agreement? The answer is no: since R_2 yields player 2 a higher payoff than L_2 does, if y is reached, player 2 will play R_2, if he actually has to make a choice. Therefore, it is better for player 1 to play R_1 and so he will also violate the agreement by playing R_1. So, although (L_1,L_2) is an equilibrium, it is not self-enforcing and, therefore, it is not qualified to be chosen as the solution of the game of figure 1.2.1 .
Hence, the solution of this game is the equilibrium (R_1,R_2), which is indeed self-enforcing.

The equilibrium (L_1,L_2) of the game of figure 1.2.1 can be interpreted as a threat equilibrium: player 2 threatens player 1 that he will punish him by playing L_2, if he does not play L_1. Above we argued that this threat is not credible, since player 2 will not execute it in the event: Facing the fait accompli that player 1 has chosen R_1 it is better for player 2 to play R_2. Note that here we use the basic feature of noncooperative games: no commitments are possible, except from those explicitly allowed by the rules of the game. Notice that the situation changes drastically, if player 2 has the possibility to commit himself before the beginning of the game. In this case it is optimal for player 2 to commit himself to L_2, thereby forcing player 1 to play L_1.

To avoid misunderstandings, let us stress that we do not think that commitments are not possible in conflict situations. We merely hold the view that, if such commitments are possible, they should explicitly be incorporated in the model (also see HARSANYI AND SELTEN [1980], chapter 1). The great strategic importance of the possibilities of committing oneself in games was first pointed out in SCHELLING [1960].

The game of figure 1.2.1 is an example of what we call an extensive form game with perfect information. A game is said to have perfect information, if the following two conditions are satisfied:

(1.2.1) there are no simultaneous moves, and

(1.2.2) at each decision point it is known which choices have previously been made.

The argument used to exclude the equilibrium (L_1,L_2) in the game of figure 1.2.1 generalizes to all games with perfect information: Since in a noncooperative game there are no possibilities for commitment, once the decision point x is reached, that part of the game tree which does not come after x has become strategically irrelevant and, therefore, the decision at x should be based only on that part of the tree which comes after x. This implies that for games with perfect information only those equilibria which can be found by dynamic programming (BELLMAN [1957]), i.e. by inductively working backwards in the game tree, are sensible (i.e. self-enforcing) (cf. KUHN [1953], Corollary 1).

The game of figure 1.2.2 shows that this has the consequence that a sensible equilibrium may be payoff dominated by a non-sensible one. The unique equilibrium found by dynamic programming is (L_1r_1,R_2). i.e. player 1 plays L_1 at his first decision point, r_1 at his second, and player 2 plays R_2. Note that we require a strategy of player 1 to prescribe a choice at his second decision point also in the case in which this player chooses L_1 at his first decision point. The significance of this requirement will become clear in section 1.4. The equilibrium (L_1r_1,R_2) yields both players a payoff 1. Another equilibrium is $(R_1\ell_1,L_2)$. This equilibrium yields both players a payoff 2. This one, however, is not sensible since player 1 cannot commit himself to playing ℓ_1 at his second decision point: both players know that player 1 will play r_1, if this point is actually reached. Therefore, it is illusory of the players to think that they can get a payoff 2. If player 1 chooses R_1, he will end up with a payoff 0.

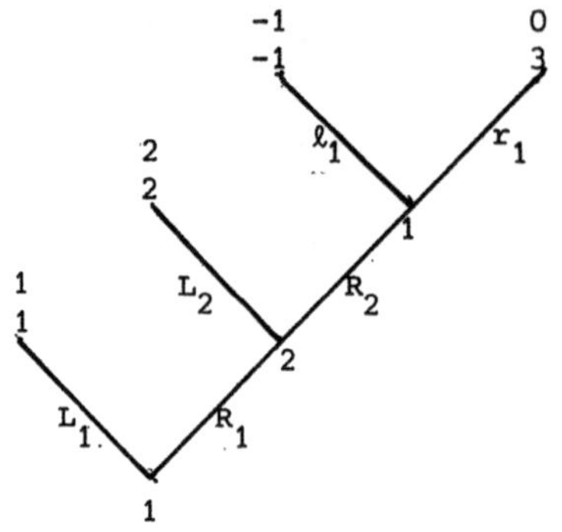

Figure 1.2.2. A sensible equilibrium may be payoff dominated by a non-sensible one.

1.3. SUBGAME PERFECT EQUILIBRIA

For games without perfect information one cannot employ the straightforward dynamic programming approach, which works so well for games with perfect information. In this section, we will illustrate a slightly more sophisticated dynamic programming approach to exclude non-sensible (i.e. not self-enforcing) equilibria of games without perfect information.

As an example of a game without perfect information, consider the game of figure 1.3.1.

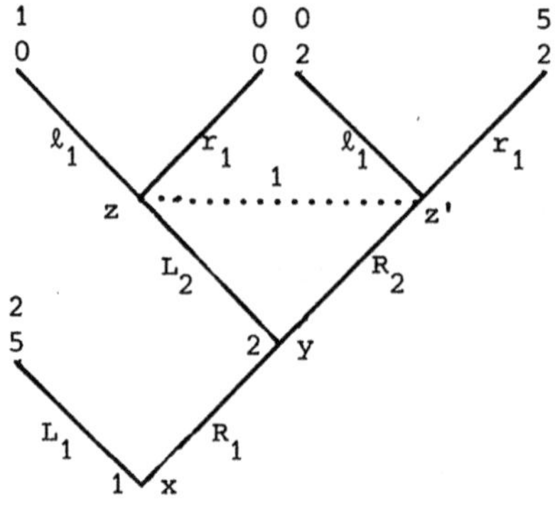

Figure 1.3.1. A game with imperfect information.

In this game player 1 cannot discriminate between z and z' (i.e. he does not get to hear whether player 2 has played L_2 of R_2), which is denoted by a dotted line connecting z and z'. The set {z,z'} is called an information set of player 1.

The straightforward dynamic programming approach fails in this example: in z player 1 should play ℓ_1 and in z' he should play r_1. Hence, he faces a dilemma, since he does not know whether he is in z or in z'. For this game, the more sophisticated approach amounts to nothing else than going one step further backwards in the game tree. Namely, notice that the subtree starting at y constitutes a game of its own, called the subgame starting at y. Since commitments are not possible, the behavior in this subgame can depend only on the subgame itself and, therefore, a sensible equilibrium of the game has to induce an equilibrium in this subgame. Otherwise at least one player would have an incentive to deviate, once the subgame is actually reached. It is easily seen, that the subgame has only one equilibrium, viz. (r_1, R_2). Hence, player 1 should play r_1 at his information set $\{z,z'\}$ and player 2 should play R_2. Once this is established, it follows that player 1 should play R_1 at x. Hence, $(R_1 r_1, R_2)$ is the only sensible equilibrium of the game of figure 1.3.1. Notice that this is not the only equilibrium: $(L_1 \ell_1, L_2)$ is also an equilibrium of this game. This equilibrium, however, is not sensible, since it involves the incredible threat of player 2 to play L_2.

It was first pointed out explicitly in SELTEN [1965] that the above argument is valid for every noncooperative game: Since commitments are not possible, behavior in a subgame can depend only on the subgame itself and, therefore, for an equilibrium to be sensible, it is necessary that this equilibrium induces an equilibrium in every subgame. Equilibria which possess this property are called subgame perfect equilibria, following SELTEN [1975].

For games with a finite time horizon and a recursive structure, the subgame perfectness criterion is very powerfull in reducing the set of equilibria which are qualified to be chosen as the solution. To demonstrate this, we will investigate a finite repetition of the game Γ of figure 1.3.2.

	L_2	M_2	R_2
L_1	10, 10	0, 11	0, 0
M_1	11, 0	3, 3	1, 0
R_1	0, 0	0, 1	0, 0

Figure 1.3.2. A normal form game Γ, which is a slight modification of the game of figure 1.1.1.

Notice that the game Γ results from the game of fig. 1.1.1 by adding for each player a dominated strategy. Also in Γ the strategy pair (L_1, L_2) is the most attractive one, but this pair is not an equilibrium. The unique equilibrium of Γ is (M_1, M_2).

Now consider the game $\Gamma(2)$, which consists of playing Γ twice in succession. In $\Gamma(2)$ each player tries to maximize the sum of the payoffs he receives at stage 1 and stage 2 and at the second stage each player gets to hear which choices have been made at the first stage.

At the second stage of $\Gamma(2)$ everything which has happened at the first stage had become strategically irrelevant and, therefore, the behavior at stage 2 can depend only on Γ. Hence, at stage 2 the players should play (M_1,M_2), the unique equilibrium of Γ. But, once this has been established, it follows that the players also should play (M_1,M_2) at the first stage. Hence, there is only one subgame perfect equilibrium of $\Gamma(2)$, which consists of playing (M_1,M_2) twice.

However, $\Gamma(2)$ has a phletora of equilibria which are not subgame perfect. An example of such an equilibrium is the strategy combination (φ_1,φ_2), where φ_i $(i \in \{1,2\})$ is given by (1.3.1):

$$(1.3.1) \qquad \varphi_i \begin{cases} \text{at stage 1: play } L_i \\ \text{at stage 2: } \begin{cases} \text{play } M_i, \text{ if } (L_1,L_2) \text{ has been played at stage 1,} \\ \text{play } R_i, \text{ otherwise.} \end{cases} \end{cases}$$

In this equilibrium, each player threatens the other one that he will punish him at the second stage, if he does not cooperate at the first stage. If both players believe the threats, the "cooperative outcome" (L_1,L_2) will result at the first stage. This equilibrium,however, is not sensible, since a player should not belief the other player's threat. If player 2 plays the strategy φ_2 of (1.3.1), then player 1, knowing that it is not optimal for player 2 to execute the threat, should play M_1 at the first stage.

In the literature a variety of examples can be found of economic situations in which the subgame perfectness concept severly reduces the set of eligible equilibria. We mention only a few: SELTEN [1965, 1973, 1977, 1978], STÅHL [1977], KALAI [1980] and KANEKO [1981]. Recently, the subgame perfectness concept received also considerable attention for games of infinite length, especially in relation to bargaining problems (cf. RUBINSTEIN [1980, 1982], FUDENBERG AND LEVINE [1981], MOULIN [1982]).

1.4. SEQUENTIAL EQUILIBRIA AND PERFECT EQUILIBRIA

It was first pointed out in SELTEN [1975] that a subgame perfect equilibrium may prescribe irrational (non maximizing) behavior at information sets which are not reached when the equilibrium is played. Consequently a subgame perfect equilibrium need not be sensible. The 3-person game of figure 1.4.1, which is taken from SELTEN [1975], section 6, can illustrate this fact.

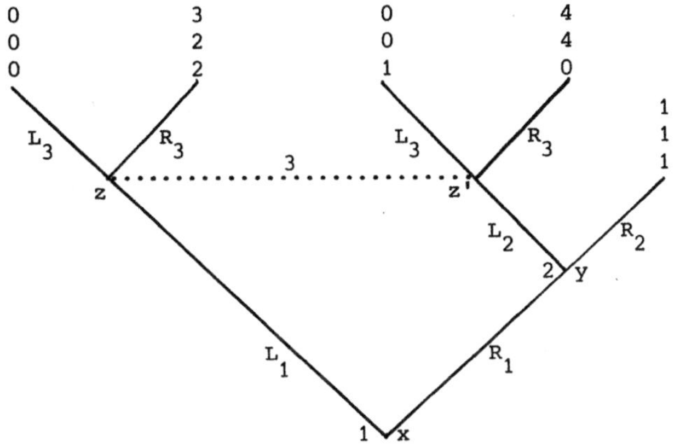

Figure 1.4.1. A subgame perfect equilibrium need not to be sensible. The numbers at the endpoints of the tree represent the payoffs to the players; the upper number is the payoff to player 1, the second one is the payoff to player 2, etc.

Since there are no subgames in the game of figure 1.4.1, every equilibrium is subgame perfect (for the formal definition of a subgame see (6.1.16)). One equilibrium of this game is (L_1,R_2,R_3). However, this equilibrium is not sensible, since player 2 will violate an agreement to play (L_1,R_2,R_3) in case his information set is actually reached. Namely, if player 2 plays L_2, then player 3 will not find out that the agreement is violated (he cannot discriminate between z and z') and, therefore, this player will still play R_3. Hence, playing L_2 yields player 2 a payoff 4, which is more than R_2 yields and therefore, this player will play L_2 if his information set is actually reached. Realizing this, player 1 will play R_1 (which yields him a payoff 4), rather than L_1 (which yields only 3). Hence, an agreement to play (L_1,R_2,R_3) is not self-enforcing and, therefore, the equilibrium (L_1,R_2,R_3) is not sensible. (It can be shown that any sensible equilibrium has player 1 playing R_1, player 2 playing R_2, and player 3 playing L_3 with a probability at least 3/4, see SELTEN [1975]).

The Nash equilibrium concept requires that each player chooses a strategy which maximizes his expected payoff, assuming that the other players will play in accordance with the equilibrium. The reason that the equilibrium (L_1,R_2,R_3) in the game of figure 1.4.1 is not sensible is the following: If (L_1,R_2,R_3) is played, the information set of player 2 is not reached and, therefore, the expected payoff of this player does not depend on his own strategy, which obviously implies that every strategy maximizes his expected payoff. However, since player 2 has to move only if the point y is actually reached, he should not let himself be guided by his <u>a priori</u> expected payoff, but by his <u>expected payoff after</u> y. The a priori expected payoff is based on the assumption that player 1 plays L_1, but, if y is reached this has shown to be wrong and player 2 should incorporate this is computing his expected payoff.

The discussion above shows that, for a subgame perfect equilibrium to be sensible, it is necessary that this equilibrium prescribes, at each information set which is a singleton, a choice which maximizes the expected payoff after that information set. Note that the restriction to singleton information sets is necessary to ensure that the expected payoff after the information set is well-defined. This restriction, however, has the consequence that not all subgame perfect equilibria which satisfy this additional condition are sensible. This is illustrated by means of the game of figure 1.4.2.

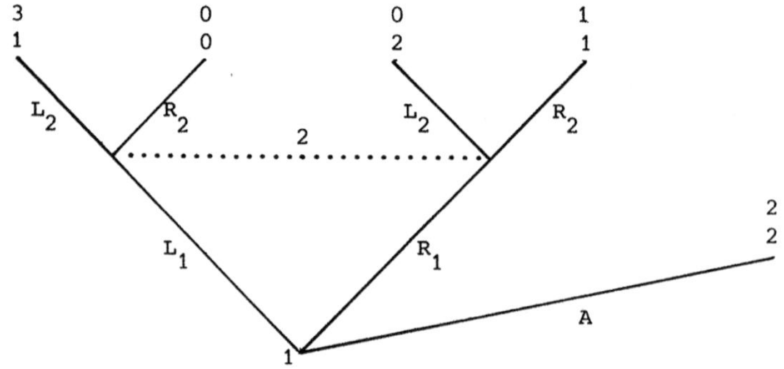

Figure 1.4.2. An unreasonable subgame perfect equilibrium.

A subgame perfect equilibrium of this game which, moreover, satisfies the above condition is (A,R_2). This equilibrium is not sensible, since it is always better for player 2 to play L_2 if his information set is reached. (Note that we can draw this conclusion without being able to compute the expected payoff of player 2 after his information set). Player 1, realizing this, should play L_1 and therefore (L_1,L_2) is the only sensible equilibrium of the game of figure 1.4.2.

The examples in this section illustrate that a sensible (self-enforcing) equilibrium has to prescribe rational (maximizing) behavior at every information set, also at the information sets which can be reached only after a deviation from the equilibrium. The problem, however, is: what is rational behavior at an information set with prior probability zero. In the literature two related solutions to this problem have been proposed, one in SELTEN [1975] (the concept of perfect equilibria) and one in KREPS AND WILSON [1982a] (the concept of sequential equilibria). Let us first explain the concept of sequential equilibria.
The basic assumption underlying the sequential equilibrium concept is, that the players are rational in the sense of SAVAGE [1954], i.e. that a player who has to

make a choice in the face of uncertainty will construct a personal probability for every event of which he is uncertain and maximize his expected utility with respect to these probabilities. To be more precise, suppose the players in an extensive form have agreed to play an equilibrium φ and assume that a player nevertheless finds himself in an information set which could not be reached when φ is actually played. In this case, the player will try to reconstruct what has gone wrong, i.e. where a deviation from the equilibrium has occurred. In general, this player will not be able to reconstruct completely what has gone wrong and, therefore, he will not be able to tell in which point of his information set he actually is. However, he will represent his uncertainty by a posterior probability distribution on the nodes in this information set (his so called beliefs at the information set) and having constructed these beliefs, he will take a choice, which maximizes his expected utility with respect to these beliefs, assuming that in the remainder of the game the players will play according to φ. A sequential equilibrium is then defined as an equilibrium φ which has the property that, if the players behave as indicated above, no player has an incentive to deviate from φ at any of his information sets. To be more precise: a strategy combination is a sequential equilibrium if there exist (consistent) beliefs such that each player's strategy prescribes at every information set a choice which is optimal with respect to these beliefs (see Definition 6.3.1).
In the game of figure 1.4.2 only the equilibrium (L_1,L_2) is a sequential equilibrium. No, matter which beliefs player 2 has, it is always optimal for him to play L_2.
Note that for an equilibrium to be sequential it is only necessary that it is optimal with respect to some beliefs, and that it does not have to be optimal with respect to all beliefs or even with respect to the most plausible ones. We will return to the role of the beliefs in chapter 6, also see KREPS AND WILSON [1982a, 1982b] and FUDENBERG AND TIROLE [1981].

In SELTEN [1975] a somewhat different approach is followed to eliminate unreasonable subgame perfect equilibria. Selten assumes, that there is always a small probability, that a player will take a choice by mistake, which has the consequence that every choice will be taken with a positive probability. Therefore, in an extensive form game with mistakes (a so called perturbed game) every information set will be reached with a positive probability, which implies that an equilibrium of such a game will prescribe rational behavior at every information set. The assumption that mistakes occur only with a very small probability, leads Selten to define a perfect equilibrium as an equilibrium which can be obtained as a limit point of a sequence of equilibria of disturbed games in which the mistake probabilities go to zero. Hence, an equilibrium is perfect if each player's equilibrium strategy is not only optimal against the equilibrium strategies of his opponents, but if it is also optimal against some slight perturbations of these strategies (see Definition 6.4.2).
In the game of figure 1.4.2 only the equilibrium (L_1,L_2) is perfect. Namely, in a perturbed game associated with this game, player 1 will take the choices L_1 and R_1

with a positive probability (if only by mistake) and, therefore, the information set of player 2 will actually be reached, which forces player 2 to play L_2.

It can be proved that every game possesses at least one perfect equilibrium (Theorem 6.4.4) and that every perfect equilibrium is a sequential equilibrium (see Theorem 6.4.3). However, not every sequential equilibrium is perfect. To illustrate the difference between the two concepts, consider the following slight modification of the game of figure 1.4.2: Player 1 receives 3 if he plays A, all other payoffs remain as in figure 1.4.2. As before, one can see that player 2 has to play L_2. For player 1, both L_1 and A are best replies against L_2 and, therefore, in a sequential equilibrium player 1 can play any combination of L_1 and A. The only perfect equilibrium, however, is (A,L_2). The reason is that if player 1 plays A he is sure of getting 3, whereas if he plays L_1 he can expect only slightly less than 3, since player 2 with a small probability will make a mistake and play R_2.
In KREPS AND WILSON [1982a] it is shown that there is not much difference between the solutions generated by the sequential equilibrium concept and the solutions generated by the perfectness concept. They proved that almost all sequential equilibria are perfect (KREPS AND WILSON [1982a] Theorem 3; for a more exact formulation of this result, see Theorem 6.4.3). However, verifying whether a given equilibrium is sequential is much easier than to verify whether it is perfect.

Two questions concerning the concepts of sequential and perfect equilibria remain to be answered:

(i) Don't we exclude any sensible equilibria by restricting ourselves to sequential (resp. perfect) equilibria?

(ii) Is every sequential (resp. perfect) equilibrium sensible?

In our view, the first question certainly has to be answered affirmatively for sequential equilibria: if an equilibrium is not sequential, then at least one player has an incentive to deviate from the equilibrium at some of his information sets and, therefore, this equilibrium is not self-enforcing. Whether this question should be answered affirmatively for perfect equilibria depends on one's personal viewpoint of how seriously the possibility of mistakes should be taken.
The second question, however, has to be answered negatively: many perfect (and, hence, sequential) equilibria are not sensible. Loosely speaking this is caused by the fact that some sequential (resp. perfect) equilibria are sustained only by implausible beliefs (resp. implausible mistake probabilities). Therefore, the equilibrium concept has to be refined further in order to yield sensible solutions for every game. In chapter 6, we will return to the question of why a perfect equilibrium of an extensive form game need not be sensible and how the equilibrium concept can be refined further.

1.5. PERFECT EQUILIBRIA AND PROPER EQUILIBRIA

If we have a game in which each player has to make a choice just once and if, moreover, the players make their choices simultaneously and independently of each other, then we speak of a <u>normal form game</u>. An example of such a game is the prisoners' dilemma game of figure 1.1.1. A normal form game can be considered as a special kind of extensive form game, but, on the other hand, with each extensive form game, one can associate a game in normal form (VON NEUMANN AND MORGENSTERN [1944], KUHN [1953]). In the next two sections, it will be shown that also for normal form games it is necessary to refine the Nash equilibrium concept in order to obtain sensible solutions and in several examples the refinements which have been proposed for this class of games will be illustrated. These refinements will be of a slightly different kind than the ones we considered for games in extensive form. Namely, for extensive form games, the basic reason why one has to refine the equilibrium concept is, that a Nash equilibrium may prescribe irrational behavior at unreached parts of the game tree. In a normal form game, however, every player has to make a choice, so that there are no unreached information sets. Yet, we will see that it is necessary to refine the equilibrium concept for normal form games, due to the fact that <u>an equilibrium</u> of such a game <u>need not be robust</u>. As an example of an equilibrium, which is not robust, consider the game of figure 1.5.1.

	L_2	R_2
L_1	1, 1	0, 0
R_1	0, 0	0, 0

<u>Figure 1.5.1.</u> The equilibrium (R_1,R_2) is not robust.

This game has two equilibria: the strategy combinations (L_1,L_2) and (R_1,R_2). In our view, the latter equilibrium is not a sensible one. This strategy combination satisfies Nash's equilibrium condition only since this condition presumes that each player will completely ignore all parts of the payoff matrix to which his opponent's strategy assigns zero probability. We feel, however, that a player should not ignore this information and that he, therefore, should play L. To be sure, if player 2 plays R_2, then player 1 cannot gain by playing L_1. However, by doing so, he cannot lose either and, as a matter of fact, if player 2 by mistake would play L_2, then player 1 is actually better off by playing L_1. Similarly, we have that player 2 can only gain by playing L_2. Therefore, even if the players have agreed to play (R_1,R_2), both players have an incentive to deviate from this equilibrium. So, an agreement to play (R_1,R_2)

is self-destabilizing and, therefore, this equilibrium is not sensible. The only sensible equilibrium of the game of figure 1.5.1 is the perfect equilibrium (L_1,L_2). If the players have agreed to play this equilibrium, no player has an incentive whatever to violate the agreement.

If one takes the possibility of the players making mistakes seriously, then, for normal form games, one can only consider perfect equilibria as being reasonable. If an equilibrium fails to be perfect, it is unstable with respect to small perturbations of the equilibrium and, therefore, at least one player will have an incentive to deviate from it.
By restricting oneself to perfect equilibria, however, one may eliminate equilibria with attractive payoffs, as is shown by the game of figure 1.5.2.

	L_2	R_2
L_1	1 1	10 0
R_1	0 10	10 10

Figure 1.5.2. A perfect equilibrium may be payoff dominated by a non-perfect one.

This game has two equilibria, viz. (L_1,L_2) and (R_1,R_2). The equilibrium (R_1,R_2) yields both players the highest payoff. The game of figure 1.5.2 has exactly the same structure as the game of figure 1.5.1 (each player can only gain by playing L) and, therefore, in this game, the equilibrium (R_1,R_2) is as unstable as it is in the game of figure 1.5.1. If the players expect mistakes to occur with a small probability, then no player can really expect a payoff 10: the only stable (perfect) equilibrium is (L_1,L_2).

It was first pointed out in MYERSON [1978] that the perfectness concept does not eliminate all intuitively unreasonable equilibria. The game of figure 1.5.3, which is a slight modification of the example given by Myerson, can serve to demonstrate this. Notice that this game results from the game of figure 1.5.1 by adding for each player a strategy A. One might argue that, since A is strictly dominated by both L and R, this strategy is strategically irrelevant and that, therefore, the games of the figures 1.5.1. and 1.5.3 have the same sets of reasonable equilibria. Hence, since (L_1,L_2) is the only reasonable equilibrium of the game of figure 1.5.1, this equilibrium is also the unique reasonable equilibrium of the game of figure 1.5.3. However, the sets of perfect equilibria do not coincide for these games: in the game of figure 1.5.3 also the equilibrium (R_1,R_2) is perfect. Namely, if the players have agreed to play (R_1,R_2) and if each player expects that the mistake A will occur with a larger probability than the mistake L, then it is indeed optimal for each player to play R. Hence, adding strictly dominated strategies may change the set of perfect equilibria.

	L_2	R_2	A_2
L_1	1, 1	0, 0	-1, -2
R_1	0, 0	0, 0	0, -2
A_1	-2, -1	-2, 0	-2, -2

Figure 1.5.3. Adding dominated strategies may enlarge the set of perfect equilibria.

Myerson considers it to be an undesirable property of the perfectness concept, that adding strictly dominated strategies may change the set of perfect equilibria and, therefore, he introduced a further refinement of the perfectness concept: the proper equilibrium (MYERSON [1978], see Definition 2.3.1). The basic idea underlying the properness concept is, that a player will make his mistakes in a more or less rational way, i.e. that he will make a more costly mistake with a much smaller probability than a less costly one, as a consequence of the fact that he will try much harder to prevent a more costly mistake.
According to the philosophy of the properness concept, in the game of figure 1.5.3, the players should not expect the mistake A to occur with a larger probability than the mistake L: since A is strictly dominated by L, each player will try harder to prevent the mistake A, than he will try to prevent the mistake L and as a result A will occur with a smaller probability than L (in Myerson's view, the probability of A will even be of smaller order than the probability of L (cf. Definition 2.3.1)). Therefore, an agreement to play (R_1,R_2) is self-destabilizing: each player will prefer to play L, and so the equilibrium (R_1,R_2) is not proper. The only proper equilibrium of the game of figure 1.5.3 is (L_1,L_2): Once the players have agreed to play (L_1,L_2), no player has an incentive whatever to deviate from the equilibrium.

Myerson has shown that every normal form game possesses at least one proper equilibrium and that every proper equilibrium is perfect (MYERSON [1978], see Theorem 2.3.3). A problem concerning this concept is, that it is not clear whether the basic assumption underlying it (a more costly mistake is chosen with a probability which is of smaller order than the probability of a less costly one) can be justified. Myerson himself did not give a justification for this assumption. In the chapters 4 and 5, we will investigate whether this assumption can be justified.

The game of figure 1.5.4 shows that not all proper equilibria possess the same degree of robustness:

	L_2	M_2	R_2
L_1	2, 2	1, 1	0, 0
M_1	1, 1	1, 1	1, 1
R_1	0, 0	1, 1	1, 1

Figure 1.5.4. Not all proper equilibria are equally robust.

This game has several equilibria. Three of these are (L_1,L_2), (M_1,M_2) and (R_1,R_2). It is easily seen, that the equilibrium (R_1,R_2) is not perfect: if mistakes might occur, each player will prefer M to R. The equilibria (L_1,L_2) and (M_1,M_2) are both perfect and even proper, but, the equilibrium (L_1,L_2) is much more robust than the equilibrium (M_1,M_2). Namely, once the players have agreed to play (L_1,L_2), as long as mistakes occur with a probability smaller than $\frac{1}{2}$, each player is still willing to choose L. However, if the players have agreed to play (M_1,M_2), then each player is willing to keep to the agreement only, if he expects that the mistake R will occur with a probability at least as big as the probability of the mistake L.

In OKADA [1981] a refinement of the perfectness concept, the strictly perfect equilibrium, is introduced, which is based on the idea that a sensible equilibrium should be stable against arbitrary slight perturbations of the equilibrium (see Definition 2.2.7). Obviously, for the game of figure 1.5.4, the equilibrium (L_1,L_2) is a strictly perfect equilibrium, whereas (M_1,M_2) is not strictly perfect. At first sight, it does not seem to be unreasonable to require that the solution of a game should be a strictly perfect equilibrium. The game of figure 1.5.5 shows that this cannot always be required, since there exist games without strictly perfect equilibria.

	L_2	M_2	R_2
L_1	1, 1	1, 0	0, 0
R_1	1, 1	0, 0	1, 0

Figure 1.5.5. A game without strictly perfect equilibria.

Every strategy pair in which player 2 plays L_2 is an equilibrium. None of these equilibria is strictly perfect: if player 1 expects that the mistake M_2 will occur more often than the mistake R_2, he should play L_1; if he expects this mistake to occur with a smaller probability, he should play R_1.

We close this section by noting that recently Kalai and Samet have introduced another refinement of the perfectness concept: the persistent equilibrium (KALAI AND SAMET [1982]). This concept will not be considered in this monograph.

1.6. ESSENTIAL EQUILIBRIA AND REGULAR EQUILIBRIA

In the previous section, we considered refinements of the Nash equilibrium concept which are based on the idea that a sensible equilibrium should be stable against slight perturbations of the equilibrium strategies. One could also argue that a sensible equilibrium should be stable against slight perturbations in the payoffs of the game. Namely, one can maintain that these payoffs can be determined only somewhat inaccurately. A refinement of the equilibrium concept, based on this idea is the essential equilibrium concept, introduced in WU WEN-TSÜN AND JIANG JIA-HE [1962]. An equilibrium φ of a game Γ is said to be essential, if every game near to Γ has an equilibrium near to φ. Intuitively, it will be clear that an essential equilibrium is very stable. This indeed will be proved in chapter 2, where we will, for instance, show that every essential equilibrium is strictly perfect. Notice that, therefore, not every game possesses an essential equilibrium. Indeed the payoffs in the game of figure 1.5.5 can be perturbed in such a way that either L_1 or R_1 is the unique best reply against L_2 and, therefore, this game does not have an essential equilibrium. Hence, we cannot require that a sensible equilibrium should be essential. Moreover, even in games which posses essential equilibria, it is not always true that an essential equilibrium should be preferred to a non-essential one, as is illustrated by the game of figure 1.6.1.

	L_2	M_2	R_2
L_1	1, 1	0, 0	0, 0
M_1	0, 0	2, 2	2, 2
R_1	0, 0	2, 2	2, 2

Figure 1.6.1. An essential equilibrium is not necessarily preferable to a non-essential equilibrium.

The unique essential equilibrium of this game is (L_1,L_2). However, if each player plays some combination of M and R, then a stable outcome results which is, moreover, preferred to (L_1,L_2) by both players. Therefore, rational players will indeed agree to play some combination of M and R: once such an agreement is reached no player has an incentive to deviate. Once again we conclude that a sensible equilibrium need not be essential. However, from a theoretical point of view, the essential equilibrium concept will prove to be very useful.

In this chapter, it was forcibly argued, that the solution of a noncooperative game has to be self-enforcing and, therefore, a Nash equilibrium. In many examples we have however seen that not all Nash equilibria are self-enforcing: there exist equilibria at which at least one player has an incentive to deviate. Now suppose we have an equilibrium at which no player has an incentive to deviate. Is this equilibrium necessarily self-enforcing? The answer is no: although no player may have an incentive to deviate, it may be the case that no player has an incentive to play his equilibrium strategy either. This situation occurs for equilibria in mixed strategies as is illustrated by means of the game of figure 1.6.2.

	L_2	R_2
L_1	2, 2	4, 1
R_1	4, 1	3, 3

Figure 1.6.2. Instability of equilibria in mixed strategies.

This game has a unique equilibrium, which is in mixed strategies. The equilibrium strategy of player 1 is $(2/3\,L_1, 1/3\,R_1)$ and the equilibrium strategy of player 2 is $(1/3\,L_2, 2/3\,R_2)$. The equilibrium yields player 1 a payoff 10/3 and player 2 a payoff 5/3. This equilibrium seems unstable, since, if player 2 plays $(1/3\,L_2, 2/3\,R_2)$, then player 1 receives a payoff of 10/3, no matter what he does and, therefore, he can shift to any other strategy without penalty. So, what is his incentive to play his equilibrium strategy? The same remark applies to player 2: if player 1 plays his equilibrium strategy, player 2 receives 5/3 no matter what he does and, therefore, he can also shift to any strategy without penalty.

One could even argue (as is done in AUMANN AND MASCHLER [1972], section 2) that, in the game of figure 1.6.2, the players could have an incentive to deviate from their equilibrium strategies. Namely, if the equilibrium is played, player 1 receives 10/3, which is just the maximin value of this game for player 1, i.e. the payoff which

player 1 can guarantee himself. However, the equilibrium strategy of player 1 does not guarantee 10/3, it only yields 10/3 if player 2 plays his equilibrium strategy. In order to guarantee 10/3 player 1 should play his maximin strategy, which is $(1/3L_1, 2/3R_1)$. So, if player 1 knows that he cannot obtain more that 10/3, why should not he play his maximin strategy which guarantees 10/3? The same remark applies to player 2 and so he also could have an incentive to play his maximin strategy, rather than his equilibrium strategy.
It should be noted that Aumann and Maschler do not know what to recommend in this situation, since the maximin strategies are not in equilibrium, but that they prefer the maximin strategies (AUMANN AND MASCHLER [1972], section 2). In HARSANYI [1977] (especially in section 7.7.) it is argued that the players indeed should play their maximin strategies in this game (also see VAN DAMME [1980a]), but Harsanyi has changed his position in favour of the equilibrium strategies (HARSANYI AND SELTEN [1980], chapter 1).

From the discussion above it will be clear that the instability of equilibria in mixed strategies poses serious problems. This problem is serious indeed, since many games possess only equilibria in mixed strategies. In HARSANYI [1973a] it is shown that this instability, however, is only a seeming instability. Harsanyi argues that in a game a player can never know the payoffs (utilities) of another player exactly, since these payoffs are subject to random disturbances, due to stochastic fluctuations in this player's mood or taste. Therefore, a conflict situation, rather than by an ordinary game, is more adequately modelled by a so called disturbed game, i.e. a game in which each player, although knowing his own payoffs exactly, knows the payoffs of the other players only somewhat inexactly. Harsanyi shows that for such a disturbed game every equilibrium is essentially in pure strategies and is, therefore, stable (also see Theorem 5.4.2.) . Harsanyi, moreover, shows that almost every equilibrium of an ordinary game (whether in pure or in mixed strategies) can be obtained as the limit of equilibria of disturbed games, in which the disturbances go to zero, i.e. in which each player's information about the other players' payoffs becomes better and better. Hence, for almost all equilibria in mixed strategies the instability disappears if we take account of the actual uncertainty each player has about the other players' payoffs. Upon a closer investigation (see Theorem 5.6.2) it turns out that the equilibria which are stable in this sense are the regular equilibria, which have been introduced in HARSANYI [1973b]. A regular equilibrium is defined as an equilibrium which has the property that the Jacobian of a certain mapping associated with the game evaluated at this equilibrium is nonsingular (see Definition 2.5.1). These regular equilibria will play a prominent role in the monograph. It will be shown that regular equilibria possess all robustness properties one reasonably can expect equilibria to possess: they are perfect, proper and even strictly perfect and essential.

Unfortunately not all normal form games possess regular equilibria, but it can be shown that for almost all normal form games all equilibria are indeed regular (Theorem 2.6.2). These results indicate that for generic normal form games there is actually little need to refine the Nash equilibrium concept. For extensive form games, however, the situation is quite different, as we will see in chapter 6.

1.7. SUMMARY OF THE FOLLOWING CHAPTERS

We have seen that, to obtain sensible solutions for noncooperative games, the Nash equilibrium concept has to be refined, both for games in extensive form and for games in normal form. In this monograph a systematic study of the refinements of the equilibrium concept which have been proposed in the literature is presented and also some new refinements are introduced. Our objective is to derive characterizations of these refinements, to establish relations between them and to discuss the plausibility of the assumptions underlying them.

In chapter 2, we consider n-person games in normal form. Among the refinements we consider for this class there are: perfect equilibria (SELTEN [1975]), proper equilibria (MYERSON [1978]), strictly perfect equilibria (OKADA [1981]) and essential equilibria (WU WEN-TSÜN AND JIANG JIA-HE [1962]). All these refinements require an equilibrium to satisfy some particular robustness condition. It is shown that an essential equilibrium is strictly perfect, which means that an equilibrium which is stable against slight perturbations in the payoffs of the game is also stable against slight perturbations in the equilibrium strategies. It turns out that the concept of regular equilibria (HARSANYI [1973b]) is very important, since a regular equilibrium possesses all robustness properties one can hope for. Furthermore, it is shown that generically all Nash equilibria are regular.

In chapter 3 we specialize the results of chapter 2 to 2-person games, i.e. matrix and bimatrix games. The relative simplicity of 2-person games enables us to give characterizations of various refinements, which elucidate their basic features. For instance, it is shown that an equilibrium of a bimatrix game is perfect if and only if both equilibrium strategies are undominated, a result which implies that verifying whether an equilibrium is perfect can be executed by solving a linear programming problem. Also several characterizations of regular equilibria are derived. For instance, an equilibrium is regular if and only if it is isolated and quasi-strong, which implies that all equilibria of a game which is nondegenerate in the sense of LEMKE AND HOWSON [1964] are regular. Furthermore, it is shown that an equilibrium of a matrix game is proper if and only if both equilibrium strategies are optimal in the sense of DRESHER [1961].

In chapter 4, we elaborate the idea that the reason that the players make mistakes lies in the fact that it is too costly to prevent them. The basic idea is that a player can reduce the probability of making mistakes by being extra careful, but that being extra careful requires an effort which involves some costs. This conception is modelled by means of a so called game with control costs, i.e. a game in which each player, in addition to receiving his ordinary payoff, incurs costs depending on how well he wants to control his actions. In an ordinary game the control costs are infinitesimally and, therefore, we view an ordinary game as a limiting case of a game with control costs and we investigate which equilibria of an ordinary game can be approximated by equilibria of games with control costs, as these costs go to zero. It turns out that the basic assumption underlying the properness concept cannot be justified if control costs are incorporated in the model and that only very specific control costs will force the players to play a perfect equilibrium.

In chapter 5, it is investigated how the strategy choice of a player is influenced by slight uncertainty about the payoffs of his opponents. Following HARSANYI [1973a], we model the situation in which each player knows the payoffs of his opponents only somewhat imprecisely by a so called disturbed game, i.e. a game in which there are random fluctuations in the payoffs. An ordinary game is viewed as a limiting case of a disturbed game, and it is investigated which equilibria of an ordinary game can be approximated by equilibria of disturbed games, as the disturbances go to zero, i.e. if the information each player has about the other players' payoffs becomes better and better. Such equilibria are called stable equilibria and it is shown that, if disturbances occur only with a small probability, every stable equilibrium is perfect. Moreover, if the disturbances have an additional property, then every stable equilibrium is weakly proper, which shows that the assumption that a considerably more costly mistake occurs with an order smaller probability can be justified.

In chapter 6, extensive form games are considered. We study the relation between sequential equilibria (KREPS AND WILSON [1982a]) and perfect equilibria (SELTEN [1975]), as well as the difference between perfectness in the extensive form and perfectness in the normal form. Furthermore, it is shown that a proper equilibrium of the normal form of a game induces a sequential equilibrium in the extensive form of this game. Several examples in this chapter illustrate that all refinements of the Nash equilibrium concept which have been proposed for extensive form games still do not exclude many intuitively unreasonable equilibria.

1.8. NOTATIONAL CONVENTIONS

This introductory chapter is concluded with a number of notations and conventions. As usual $\mathbb{N}$ denotes the set of the positive integers $\{1,2,...\}$ (positive will always mean strictly greater than 0). When dealing with an n-person game we will frequently write N for $\{1,...,n\}$.

$\mathbb{R}$ denotes the set of real numbers and $\mathbb{R}^m$ is the m dimensional Euclidean space. For

$x,y \in \mathbb{R}^m$, we write $x \leq y$ if $x_i \leq y_i$ for all i. Furthermore, $x < y$ means $x_i < y_i$ for all i. We write $\mathbb{R}^m_+$ for the set of all $x \in \mathbb{R}^m$ which satisfy $0 \leq x$ and $\mathbb{R}^m_{++}$ for the set of all $x \in \mathbb{R}^m$ for which $0 < x$. Euclidean distance on $\mathbb{R}^m$ is denoted by ρ and λ denotes Lebesgue measure on $\mathbb{R}^m$.

The set of all mappings from A to B is denoted by $F(A,B)$. If $f \in F(\mathbb{R}^m_{++}, \mathbb{R}^\ell)$, then "y is a limit point of a sequence $\{f(x)\}_{x \downarrow 0}$" is used as an abbreviation for "there exists a sequence $\{x(t)\}_{t \in \mathbb{N}}$ such that $x(t)$ converges to 0 and $f(x_t)$ converges to y as t tends to infinity".

If A is a subset of some Euclidean space, then conv A denotes its convex hull and 2^A denotes the powerset of this set.

Let A and B be subsets of Euclidean spaces. A correspondence from A to B is an element of $F(A, 2^B)$. The correspondence F from A to B is said to be upper semi-continuous if it has a closed graph, i.e. if $\{(x,F(x)); x \in A\}$ is closed.

The number of elements of a finite set A is denoted by $|A|$. If A is finite, and $f \in F(A,\mathbb{R})$ then $f(A) := \sum_{a \in A} f(a)$.

Indices can occur as subscripts or superscripts. Lower indices usually refer to players. Upper indices usually stem from a certain numbering. For instance, when dealing with an n-person normal form game, we write s_i^k for the probability which the mixed strategy s_i of player i assigns to the kth pure strategy of this player. To avoid misunderstandings between exponents and indices, we will write the basis of a power between brackets. Hence, $(s_i^k)^2$ denotes the square of s_i^k.

Definitions are indicated by using italics. The symbol := is used to define quantities. The symbol □ denotes the end of a proof.

For more specific notation concerning normal form games, we refer to section 2.1. The notation which will be used with respect to extensive form games is introduced in section 6.1.

CHAPTER 2

GAMES IN NORMAL FORM

For normal form games the Nash equilibrium concept has to be refined, since a Nash equilibrium of such a game need not be robust, i.e. may be unstable against small perturbations in the data of the game. In this chapter, we will consider various refinements of the Nash equilibrium concept for this class of games, all of which require an equilibrium to satisfy some particular robustness condition.

In section 2.2, perfect equilibria (SELTEN [1975]) are considered. These are equilibria which are stable against some slight perturbations in the equilibrium strategies. It is shown that every normal form game possesses at least one perfect equilibrium and several properties of such equilibria are derived. In this section also strictly perfect equilibria (OKADA [1981]), i.e. equilibria which are stable against arbitrary slight perturbations in the equilibrium strategies, are considered.

In section 2.3, the concepts of proper equilibria (MYERSON [1978]) and weakly proper equilibria are studied. These concepts require an equilibrium to be stable against perturbations of the equilibrium strategies which are more or less rational, i.e. which assign the preponderance of weight to the better strategies. Both concepts are refinements of the perfectness concept. Furthermore, the concept of strictly proper equilibria is introduced. This concept is a refinement of the strict perfectness concept.

In section 2.4, we consider essential equilibria (WU WEN-TSÜN AND JIANG JIA-HE [1962]), i.e. equilibria which are stable against arbitrary slight perturbations in the payoffs of the game and we show that every essential equilibrium is strictly perfect.

In section 2.5, the concept of regular equilibria (HARSANYI [1973b]) is introduced and it is shown that every regular equilibrium possesses all robustness properties one possibly could hope for.

The main result of section 2.6 states that for almost all normal form games all equilibria are regular, which means that for "nondegenerate" normal form games all equilibria possess all robustness properties one can hope for.

This chapter is based upon the references mentioned above and on VAN DAMME [1981c].

2.1. PRELIMINARIES

A *finite n-person normal form game* is a 2n-tuple $\Gamma = (\Phi_1,\dots,\Phi_n,R_1,\dots,R_n)$, where Φ_i is a finite nonempty set and R_i is a mapping $R_i : \prod_{j=1}^{n} \Phi_j \to \mathbb{R}$, for $i \in N$ $(=\{1,\dots,n\})$. The set Φ_i is the set of *pure strategies* of player i and R_i is the *payoff function* of this player.

Usually, we will just speak of a normal form game, rather than of a finite normal form game. Next, let us introduce the notation and terminology which will be used throughout the chapters 2-5 with respect to these games. Let $\Gamma = (\Phi_1,\dots,\Phi_n,R_1,\dots R_n)$ be fixed. We write:

(2.1.1) $$m_i := |\Phi_i| \quad , \quad m := \sum_{i=1}^{n} m_i \quad , \quad m^* := \prod_{i=1}^{n} m_i \ .$$

A generic element of Φ_i will be denoted by φ_i. We assume that the elements of Φ_i are numbered and, consequently, we will speak about the kth pure strategy of player i. Therefore, and even more often, a generic element of Φ_i will also be denoted by k. A *mixed strategy* s_i of player i is a probability distribution on Φ_i. We denote the probability which s_i assigns to the pure strategy k of player i by s_i^k and write S_i for the set of all mixed strategies of player i, hence

(2.1.2) $$S_i := \{s_i \in \mathcal{F}(\Phi_i,\mathbb{R}) \ ; \ \sum_k s_i^k = 1, \ s_i^k \geq 0 \text{ for all } k \in \Phi_i\}.$$

If $s_i \in S_i$, then $C(s_i)$ denotes the *Carrier* of s_i, i.e.

(2.1.3) $$C(s_i) := \{k \in \Phi_i ; \ s_i^k > 0\}.$$

s_i is said to be *completely mixed* if $C(s_i) = \Phi_i$. The pure strategy k of player i is identified with the mixed strategy which assigns probability 1 to k.
We define the sets Φ and S by:

(2.1.4) $$\Phi := \prod_{i=1}^{n} \Phi_i \quad \text{and} \quad S := \prod_{i=1}^{n} S_i \ .$$

Φ (resp. S) is the set of pure (resp. mixed) *strategy combinations* of Γ. A generic element of Φ (resp. S) is denoted by φ (resp. s). In a normal form game, the players make their choices independently of each other, therefore, the probability $s(\varphi)$ that $\varphi = (k_1,\dots,k_n)$ occurs if $s = (s_1,\dots,s_n)$ is played, is given by:

(2.1.5) $$s(\varphi) := \prod_{i=1}^{n} s_i^{k_i} \ .$$

The *Carrier* of s, which is denoted by C(s), is defined by:

$$(2.1.6)\qquad C(s) := \{\varphi;\ s(\varphi) > 0\} = \prod_{i=1}^{n} C(s_i),$$

and s is said to be *completely mixed*, if C(s) = Φ.
If s is played, the *expected payoff* $R_i(s)$ for player i is given by:

$$(2.1.7)\qquad R_i(s) := \sum_{\varphi} s(\varphi)R_i(\varphi).$$

Let $s = (s_1,\dots,s_n) \in S$ and let $\bar{s}_i \in S_i$. We denote by $s\backslash_i \bar{s}_i$ (or simply by $s\backslash\bar{s}_i$) that strategy combination which results from s by replacing the strategy s_i of player i by the strategy $\bar{s}_i$ of this player. Hence, $s\backslash\bar{s}_i$ is the strategy combination $(s_1,\dots,s_{i-1},\bar{s}_i,s_{i+1},\dots,s_n)$. We say that $\bar{s}_i$ is a *best reply* of player i against s if

$$(2.1.8)\qquad R_i(s\backslash\bar{s}_i) = \max_{s_i'\in S_i} R_i(s\backslash s_i') .$$

The set of all *pure best replies* of player i against s (i.e. the best replies of player i which are in Φ_i) is denoted by $B_i(s)$. It is easily seen that $\bar{s}_i$ is a best reply against s if and only if we have

$$(2.1.9)\qquad \text{if } R_i(s\backslash_i k) < R_i(s\backslash_i \ell),\ \text{then } \bar{s}_i^k = 0 \quad \text{for all } k,\ell \in \Phi_i,$$

which is equivalent to

$$(2.1.10)\qquad C(\bar{s}_i) \subset B_i(s) .$$

Hence, $\bar{s}_i$ is a best reply of player i against s if and only if $\bar{s}_i$ assigns a positive probability only to the pure best replies of player i against s.
In this monograph, the expression $R_i(s\backslash_j k)$ will occur only with i = j (and, hence, with $k \in \Phi_i$) and, therefore, we can simplify our notation by writing $R_i(s\backslash k)$ for $R_i(s\backslash_i k)$.
Let $s,\bar{s} \in S$. We say that $\bar{s}$ is a *best reply* against s if $\bar{s}_i$ is a best reply against s for all i, and we denote the set of all *pure best replies* against s by B(s), hence

$$(2.1.11)\qquad B(s) := \prod_{i=1}^{n} B_i(s) .$$

A strategy combination s is a *Nash equilibrium* (NASH [1950, 1951]) of Γ, if s is a best reply against itself. It follows from (2.1.10) that s is a Nash equilibrium if and only if

$$(2.1.12)\qquad C(s) \subset B(s) .$$

Usually, we will speak of *equilibria* instead of Nash equilibria. We denote the set of equilibria of Γ by E(Γ). Nash has shown that every finite normal form game possesses at least one equilibrium (NASH [1950, 1951]).
Formula (2.1.12) expresses that in an equilibrium each player only uses best replies. By requiring that each player should use all his best replies, a refinement of the Nash equilibrium concept, the so called quasi-strong equilibrium (HARSANYI [1973a]). is obtained. Hence, formally a *quasi-strong equilibrium* is defined as a strategy combination s which satisfies C(s) = B(s). In section 3.4 (figure 3.4.1), we show that not every game possesses a quasi-strong equilibrium. The game of figure 2.1.1 illustrates another drawback of the quasi-strongness concept: a quasi-strong equilibrium may be unreasonable:

	1	2
1	1 / 1	1 / 0
2	1 / 1	0 / 0

Figure 2.1.1 A quasi-strong equilibrium need not be reasonable (the rows represent player 1's choices, the columns those of player 2, in each cell the upper left entry is the payoff to player 1, while the lower right entry is the payoff to player 2).

The set of equilibria of this game is $\{(s_1, 1);\ s_1 \in S_1\}$. All equilibria are quasi-strong, except for (1, 1), but this latter equilibrium is the most stable one, since the first strategy of player 1 dominates all his other strategies.

In HARSANYI [1973a] the concept of quasi-strong equilibria is introduced as a generalization of the concept of strong equilibria. A *strong equilibrium*[1)] is a strategy combination s which is the only best reply against itself, i.e. it satisfies {s} = B(s). Hence, a strong equilibrium is a quasi-strong equilibrium in pure strategies. This nomenclature might give the impression that quasi-strong equilibria possess similar properties as strong equilibria. This, however, is not true. As one can expect, strong equilibria possess all nice properties one can hope for, but, as the example in this section shows, quasi-strong equilibria need not be nice at all. In this chapter, it will be shown that regular equilibria (section 2.5) possess similar robustness properties as strong equilibria.

1) This notion of strong equilibrium is different from the notion of strong equilibrium as it occurs in AUMANN [1959].

Let $G(\Phi_1,\ldots,\Phi_n)$ be the set of all games $\Gamma = (\Phi_1,\ldots,\Phi_n,R_1,\ldots,R_n)$, with pure strategy spaces $\Phi_1,\ldots,\Phi_n$. For $\Gamma \in G(\Phi_1,\ldots,\Phi_n)$, let r_i be the vector of payoffs of player i associated with pure strategies in Γ, i.e.

(2.1.13) $$r_i := \langle R_i(\varphi)\rangle_{\varphi \in \Phi}$$

We can view r_i as an element of $\mathbb{R}^{m^*}$, where $m^* = |\Phi|$. Therefore r_i is called the *payoff vector* of player i in Γ. The *payoff vector* of the game Γ is the vector

(2.1.14) $$r = (r_1,\ldots,r_n) \in \mathbb{R}^{nm^*}.$$

Hence, by imposing a fixed ordening on Φ, we obtain a one-to-one correspondence between $G(\Phi_1,\ldots,\Phi_n)$ and $\mathbb{R}^{nm^*}$. We will denote the game $\Gamma \in G(\Phi_1,\ldots,\Phi_n)$ which corresponds to $r \in \mathbb{R}^{nm^*}$ by $\Gamma(r)$. So $G(\Phi_1,\ldots,\Phi_n)$ can be viewed as an nm^*-dimensional Euclidian space and we speak about the (Euclidian) distance $\rho(\Gamma,\Gamma')$ between two games and about the Lebesgue measure of a (measurable) set of games.
Let S be a statement about normal form games. We say that S is true for *almost all* games if for any $n \in \mathbb{N}$ and any n-tuple of finite nonempty sets $\Phi_1,\ldots,\Phi_n$, we have that

(2.1.15) $$\lambda(c\ell\{\Gamma \in G(\Phi_1,\ldots,\Phi_n);\ S \text{ is false}\}) = 0,$$

i.e. that the closure of the set of games for which S is false has Lebesgue measure zero. Notice that, if S is true for almost all games, then for any n-tuple $\Phi_1,\ldots,\Phi_n$, the set of games in $G(\Phi_1,\ldots,\Phi_n)$ for which S is true contains an open and everywhere dense set (and, hence, the subset for which S is false is nowhere dense).

In this monograph, we are mainly interested in finite normal form games. However, at some instances such games will be approximated by infinite normal form games. An infinite normal form game is a 2n-tuple $G = (S_1,\ldots,S_n,R_1,\ldots,R_n)$, where S_i is an infinite set and R_i is a mapping from S to $\mathbb{R}$, for $i \in N$, where $S := \prod_{i=1}^{n} S_i$. We will only be dealing with concave infinite games, i.e. infinite games which satisfy the conditions of Theorem 2.1.1 below. In such games, there is no need for the players to randomize and, consequently, an equilibrium of such a game is a strategy combination $s \in S$ which is a best reply against itself. We denote the set of equilibria of G by $E(G)$. Rosen has proved the following generalization of Nash's theorem on the existence of equilibria:

<u>THEOREM 2.1.1</u> (ROSEN [1965]). Let $G = (S_1,\ldots,S_n,R_1,\ldots,R_n)$ be an infinite n-person normal form game such that the following 3 conditions are satisfied for each $i \in N$:

i) S_i is a nonempty, compact and convex subset of some finite dimensional Euclidian space,

ii) the mapping R_i is continuous, and

iii) for fixed $s \in S$, the mapping $s'_i \to R_i(s \backslash s'_i)$ is concave.

Then G possesses at least one equilibrium.

2.2 PERFECT EQUILIBRIA

In chapter 1 we saw that, to obtain sensible solutions for every game, the Nash equilibrium concept has to be refined. In this section we will consider one such refinement, the perfect equilibrium, which has been introduced in SELTEN [1975]. It will be shown that every normal form game possesses at least one perfect equilibrium and some properties of such equilibria will be derived.

The basic idea behind the perfectness concept is, that each player with a small probability makes mistakes, which has the consequence that every pure strategy is chosen with a positive (although possibly small) probability. Mathematically, this idea is modelled via a perturbed game, i.e. a game in which each player is only allowed to use completely mixed strategies.

DEFINITION 2.2.1. Let $\Gamma = (\Phi_1,\ldots,\Phi_n,R_1,\ldots,R_n)$ be an n-person normal form game. For $i \in N$, let η_i and $S_i(\eta_i)$ be defined by:

(2.2.1) $\quad \eta_i \in F(\Phi_i,\mathbb{R})$ with $\eta_i^k > 0$ for all $k \in \Phi_i$ and $\sum_k \eta_i^k < 1$,

(2.2.2) $\quad S_i(\eta_i) := \{s_i \in S_i;\ s_i^k \geq \eta_i^k$ for all $k \in \Phi_i\}$.

Furthermore, let $\eta = (\eta_1,\ldots,\eta_n)$ and $S(\eta) = \prod_{i=1}^{n} S_i(\eta_i)$. The *perturbed game* (Γ,η) is the infinite normal form game $(S_1(\eta_1),\ldots,S_n(\eta_n),R_1,\ldots R_n)$.

It is easily seen that a perturbed game (Γ,η) satisfies the conditions of Theorem 2.1.1 and so such a game possesses at least one equilibrium. It is clear that in such an equilibrium a pure strategy which is not a best reply has to be chosen with a minimum probability. Therefore, we have (cf. (2.1.9)).

LEMMA 2.2.2. A strategy combination $s \in S(\eta)$ is an equilibrium of (Γ,η) if and only if the following condition is satisfied:

(2.2.3) $\quad$ if $R_i(s\backslash k) < R_i(s\backslash \ell)$, then $s_i^k = \eta_i^k$ $\quad$ for all i,k,ℓ.

The assumption that rational players will make mistakes only with a very small probability leads to the following definition:

DEFINITION 2.2.3. Let Γ be a normal form game. An equilibrium s of Γ is a *perfect equilibrium* of Γ, if s is a limit point of a sequence $\{s(\eta)\}_{\eta \downarrow 0}$, with $s(\eta) \in E(\Gamma,\eta)$ for all η, i.e. s is perfect if there exist sequences $\{s(t)\}_{t \in \mathbb{N}}$ and $\{\eta(t)\}_{t \in \mathbb{N}}$ with $s(t) \in E(\Gamma,\eta(t))$ for all $t \in \mathbb{N}$, and such that s(t) converges to s and $\eta(t)$ converges to zero, as t tends to infinity.

Note that for an equilibrium s of Γ to be perfect it is sufficient that some perturbed games (Γ,η) with η close to zero possess an equilibrium close to s and that it is not required that all perturbed games (Γ,η) with η close to zero possess an equilibrium close to s. Hence, requiring that an equilibrium is perfect is a weak requirement and, consequently, if an equilibrium fails to be perfect, it is very unstable.
Let $\{(\Gamma,\eta(t))\}_{t \in \mathbb{N}}$ be a sequence of perturbed games, for which $\eta(t)$ converges to zero, as t tends to infinity. Since every game $(\Gamma,\eta(t))$ possesses at least one equilibrium s(t), and since each s(t) is an element of the compact set S, there exists at least one limit point of $\{s(t)\}_{t\to\infty}$. It easily follows from (2.2.2) that such a limit point is, in fact, an equilibrium of Γ. Hence, we have proved:

THEOREM 2.2.4. (SELTEN [1975]). Every normal form game possesses at least one perfect equilibrium.

By considering the game of figure 1.5.1, it is seen that not every Nash equilibrium is a perfect equilibrium (the equilibrium (R_1,R_2) of that game is not perfect), and so we have that the perfectness concept is a strict refinement of the Nash equilibrium concept.
Next, two characterizations of perfect equilibria will be derived. One of these characterizations uses the concept of ε-perfect equilibria, which has been introduced in MYERSON [1978]. Let $\Gamma = (\Phi_1,\ldots,\Phi_n,R_1,\ldots,R_n)$ be a normal form game and let $\varepsilon > 0$. A strategy combination $s \in S$ is an *ε-perfect equilibrium* of Γ, if it is completely mixed and satisfies:

(2.2.4) $\quad$ if $R_i(s\backslash k) < R_i(s\backslash \ell)$, then $s_i^k \leq \varepsilon$ $\quad$ for all i,k,ℓ.

An ε-perfect equilibrium of Γ need not be an equilibrium of Γ, but if ε is small, then an ε-perfect equilibrium is close to an equilibrium (Theorem 2.2.5). An ε-perfect equilibrium is another way of modelling the idea that rational players make mistakes (choose non-optimal strategies) only with a small probability (viz. a probability of at most ε) and, therefore, one expects that an equilibrium is perfect if and only if it is a limit point of ε-perfect equilibria. In Theorem 2.2.5 we prove that this is indeed the case. The second characterization of perfect equilibria given in Theorem 2.2.5 has first been obtained in SELTEN [1975]. This characterization is the most advantageous one from the viewpoint of mathematical simplicity.

THEOREM 2.2.5. Let $\Gamma = (\Phi_1,\ldots,\Phi_n,R_1,\ldots,R_n)$ be an n-person normal form game and let $s \in S$. The following assertions are equivalent:

(i) s is a perfect equilibrium of Γ,

(ii) s is a limit point of a sequence $\{s(\varepsilon)\}_{\varepsilon\downarrow 0}$, where $s(\varepsilon)$ is an ε-perfect equilibrium of Γ, for all ε, and

(iii) s is a limit point of a sequence $\{s(\varepsilon)\}_{\varepsilon\downarrow 0}$ of completely mixed strategy combinations, with the property that s is a best reply against every element $s(\varepsilon)$ in this sequence.

PROOF. (i) → (ii). Let s be a limit point of a sequence $\{s(\eta)\}_{\eta\downarrow 0}$, with $s(\eta) \in E(\Gamma,\eta)$ for all η. Define $\varepsilon(\eta) \in \mathbb{R}_{++}$ by:

$$\varepsilon(\eta) := \max_{i,k} \eta_i^k \quad .$$

Then $s(\eta)$ is an $\varepsilon(\eta)$-perfect equilibrium of Γ, which establishes (ii).
(ii) → (iii). Let $\{s(\varepsilon)\}_{\varepsilon\downarrow 0}$ be as in (ii) and, without loss of generality, assume $s(\varepsilon)$ converges to s, as ε tends to zero. It immediately follows from (2.2.4) that every element of $C(s)$ is a best reply against $s(\varepsilon)$ if ε is sufficiently small. Therefore, s is a best reply against $s(\varepsilon)$, if ε is sufficiently small.
(iii) → (i). Let $\{s(\varepsilon)\}_{\varepsilon\downarrow 0}$ be as in (iii) and without loss of generality assume that s is the unique limit of this sequence. Define $\eta(\varepsilon) \in \mathbb{R}^m_{++}$ by:

$$(2.2.5) \qquad \eta_i^k(\varepsilon) = \begin{cases} s_i^k(\varepsilon) & \text{if } k \notin C(s_i) \\ \varepsilon & \text{otherwise} \end{cases} \qquad \text{for all } i,k.$$

Then $\eta(\varepsilon)$ converges to zero, as ε tends to zero and so, for sufficiently small ε, the perturbed game $(\Gamma,\eta(\varepsilon))$ is well-defined. For ε sufficiently small we have that $s(\varepsilon) \in S(\eta(\varepsilon))$ and it follows from (2.2.3) that in this case $s(\varepsilon)$ is actually an equilibrium of $(\Gamma,\eta(\varepsilon))$. □

In the examples of section 1.5 we saw that the equilibria in dominated strategies were eliminated by the perfectness concept. For a normal form game $\Gamma = (\Phi_1,\ldots,\Phi_n,R_1,\ldots,R_n)$ we say that the strategy s_i' of player i is *dominated* by the strategy s_i'' if

$$(2.2.6) \qquad \begin{aligned} R_i(s\backslash s_i') &\leq R_i(s\backslash s_i'') && \text{for all } s \in S, \text{ and} \\ R_i(s\backslash s_i') &< R_i(s\backslash s_i'') && \text{for some } s \in S. \end{aligned}$$

Notice that, to check whether s_i' is dominated by s_i'', it is sufficient to check whether (2.2.6) is satisfied for all $\varphi \in \Phi$, rather than for all $s \in S$. We say that s_i' is *strictly dominated* by s_i'' if all inequalities in (2.2.6) are strict, and we say that s_i' is *undominated*, if there is no strategy s_i'', which dominates it. Finally, a strategy combination $s \in S$ is said to be *undominated* if every component s_i of s is undominated.

It easily follows from the characterization of perfect equilibria given in Theorem 2.2.5 (iii), that we have:

<u>COROLLARY 2.2.6.</u> Every perfect equilibrium is undominated.

The reader might wonder whether the converse of this Corollary is true, i.e. whether an undominated equilibrium is perfect. We will prove that this is indeed correct for 2-person normal form games (Theorem 3.2.2). For games with more than 2 players, however, the converse is not true, as the game of figure 2.2.1 shows.

	1	2
1	1, 1, 1	1, 0, 1
2	1, 1, 1	0, 0, 1

	1	2
1	1, 1, 0	0, 0, 0
2	0, 1, 0	1, 0, 0

<u>Figure 2.2.1.</u> An undominated equilibrium is not necessarily perfect. (player 1 chooses a row, player 2 a column and player 3 a matrix; in each cell the upper left entry is the payoff to player 1, the entry in the middle the payoff to player 2, etc.).

The strategy combination (2,1,1) is an undominated equilibrium of this game, which is not perfect. The only perfect equilibrium of this game is (1,1,1).

We close this section by giving the definition of a <u>strictly perfect equilibrium</u>. This concept has been introduced in OKADA [1981].

<u>DEFINITION 2.2.7.</u> Let $\Gamma = (\Phi_1,\dots,\Phi_n,R_1,\dots,R_n)$ be an n-person normal form game. For $\hat{\eta} \in \mathbb{R}^m_{++}$, let $U_{\hat{\eta}} := \{\eta \in \mathbb{R}^m_{++};\ \eta < \hat{\eta}\}$. s is a *strictly perfect equilibrium* of Γ if there exists some $\hat{\eta} \in \mathbb{R}^m_{++}$ and for each $\eta \in U_{\hat{\eta}}$ some $s(\eta) \in E(\Gamma,\eta)$ such that $\lim_{\eta \downarrow 0} s(\eta) = s$.

Obviously, each strictly perfect equilibrium is perfect, but, as we have seen in section 1.5, there exist games without strictly perfect equilibria. In the next section we will consider another refinement of the perfectness concept: the properness concept. Contrary to the strict perfectness concept, this concept generates a nonempty set of solutions for every normal form game.

2.3. PROPER EQUILIBRIA

In chapter 1 (particularly in section 1.5), we saw that a perfect equilibrium may be unreasonable. In order to exclude these unreasonable perfect equilibria, Myerson has introduced a refinement of the perfectness concept: the proper equilibrium (MYERSON [1978]). In this section we will consider this concept, as well as the closely related concepts of weakly proper equilibria and strictly proper equilibria.

The basic idea underlying the properness concept is that a player, although making mistakes, will try much harder to prevent the more costly mistakes than he will try to prevent the less costly ones, i.e. that there is some sort of rationality in the mechanism of making mistakes. As a result of this a more costly mistake will (in Myerson's view) occur with a probability which is of smaller order than the probability of a less costly one. The formal definition of a proper equilibrium is in the same spirit as the characterization of perfect equilibria given in Theorem 2.2.5 (ii):

DEFINITION 2.3.1. Let $\Gamma = (\Phi_1,\dots,\Phi_n,R_1,\dots R_n)$ be an n-person normal form game, let $\varepsilon \in \mathbb{R}_{++}$ and $s(\varepsilon) \in S$. We say that $s(\varepsilon)$ is an *ε-proper equilibrium* of Γ if $s(\varepsilon)$ is completely mixed and satisfies:

(2.3.1) $\quad$ if $R_i(s(\varepsilon)\backslash k) < R_i(s(\varepsilon)\backslash \ell)$, then $s_i^k(\varepsilon) \le \varepsilon s_i^\ell(\varepsilon)$ for all i,k,ℓ.

$s \in S$ is a *proper equilibrium* of Γ, if s is a limit point of a sequence $\{s(\varepsilon)\}_{\varepsilon\downarrow 0}$, where $s(\varepsilon)$ is an ε-proper equilibrium of Γ.

Notice that, if s is a proper equilibrium of Γ, then for every $\varepsilon > 0$ there exists some ε-proper equilibrium of Γ such that actually $s = \lim_{\varepsilon\downarrow 0} s(\varepsilon)$, due to the fact that an ε-proper equilibrium is ε'-proper for $\varepsilon' \ge \varepsilon$. Furthermore, it is clear that a proper equilibrium is perfect, since an ε-proper equilibrium is ε-perfect.
From the proof of Theorem 2.2.5 we can deduce:

LEMMA 2.3.2. Let s be a proper equilibrium of a normal form game Γ and for $\varepsilon > 0$, let $s(\varepsilon)$ be an ε-proper equilibrium of Γ, such that $\lim_{\varepsilon\downarrow 0} s(\varepsilon) = s$. Then s is a best reply against $s(\varepsilon)$ for all ε which are sufficiently close to zero.

By considering the game of figure 1.5.3, we see that the properness concept is a strict refinement of the perfectness concept (namely (R_1, R_2) is a perfect equilibrium of this game, which is not proper). Obviously we would like a refinement of the Nash equilibrium concept to generate a nonempty set of solutions for every normal form game. It will now be shown (as in MYERSON [1978]) that this is indeed the case for the properness concept.

THEOREM 2.3.3. (MYERSON [1978]). Every normal form game possesses at least one proper equilibrium.

PROOF. Let $\Gamma = (\Phi_1, \ldots, \Phi_n, R_1, \ldots, R_n)$ be a normal form game. It suffices to show that, for $\varepsilon > 0$ sufficiently close to zero, there exists an ε-proper equilibrium of Γ. Let $\varepsilon \in (0,1)$. For $i \in N$, define $\eta_i \in F(\Phi_i, \mathbb{R})$ by:

$$\eta_i^k = \frac{(\varepsilon)^{m_i}}{m_i} \qquad \text{for all } k \in \Phi_i.$$

Furthermore, let η, $S_i(\eta_i)$ and $S(\eta)$ be as in Definition 2.2.1. For $i \in N$, define the correspondence F_i from $S(\eta)$ to $S_i(\eta_i)$ by:

$$F_i(s) = \{\sigma_i \in S_i(\eta_i) : \text{if } R_i(s\backslash k) < R_i(s\backslash \ell), \text{ then } \sigma_i^k \le \varepsilon\sigma_i^\ell, \text{ for all } k,\ell\}.$$

Then $F_i(s) \neq \emptyset$, for all $s \in S(\eta)$. Namely, let $s \in S(\eta)$ and define

$$\nu_i(s,k) = |\{\ell \in \Phi_i ; R_i(s\backslash k) < R_i(s\backslash \ell)\}| \qquad \text{for } k \in \Phi_i, \text{ and}$$

$$\sigma_i^k = (\varepsilon)^{\nu_i(s,k)} \Big/ \sum_\ell (\varepsilon)^{\nu_i(s,\ell)} \qquad \text{for } k \in \Phi_i,$$

Then $\sigma_i \in F_i(s)$. Furthermore, we have that $F_i(s)$ is a closed and convex set, for every $s \in S(\eta)$, and that the mapping F_i is upper semicontinuous. Let F be the n-tuple $(F_1, \ldots, F_n)$. Then F satisfies the conditions of the Kakutani Fixed Point Theorem (KAKUTANI [1941]) and, therefore F has a fixed point. Since every fixed point of F is an ε-proper equilibrium of Γ, the proof is complete. □

One of Myerson's motives for introducing the properness concept is, that the perfectness concept has the drawback, that adding strictly dominated strategies may enlarge the set of perfect equilibria. By means of the game of figure 2.3.1. we show that the properness concept suffers from the same drawback. In this game the second strategy of players 3 is strictly dominated and, therefore, one could consider this strategy as being strategically irrelevant. If one holds this view, then one can consider only (1,1,1) as being reasonable, since it is the unique perfect (proper) equilibrium of the game in which player 3 is restricted to his first strategy. However, this equilibrium is not the only proper equilibrium of the game of figure 2.3.1: also (2,2,1) is a proper equilibrium.

1

	1	2
1	1, 1, 1	0, 0, 1
2	0, 0, 1	0, 0, 1

2

	1	2
1	0, 0, 0	0, 0, 0
2	0, 0, 0	1, 1, 0

Figure 2.3.1. Adding strictly dominated strategies may enlarge the set of the proper equilibria.

Another aspect of proper equilibria which the reader might consider as being undesirable is, that the properness concept requires a more costly mistake to be chosen with a probability which is of smaller order than the probability of a less costly mistake, even if this mistake is only a little bit more costly. Let us, therefore, introduce the concept of weakly proper equilibria. This concept requires only that a considerably more costly mistake should be chosen with a probability which is of smaller order.

DEFINITION 2.3.4. Let $\Gamma = (\Phi_1,\ldots,\Phi_n,R_1,\ldots,R_n)$ be an n-person normal form game and let $s \in S$. We say that s is a *weakly proper equilibrium* of Γ, if there exists a sequence $\{s(\varepsilon)\}_{\varepsilon\downarrow 0}$ of completely mixed strategy combinations with limit s, such that s is a best reply against every element in this sequence and such that

$$\text{(2.3.2)} \qquad \text{if } R_i(s\backslash k) < R_i(s\backslash \ell), \text{ then } s_i^k(\varepsilon) \le \varepsilon s_i^\ell(\varepsilon) \quad \text{for all } i,k,\ell,\varepsilon\ .$$

From the characterization of perfect equilibria given in Theorem 2.2.5 (iii), it is clear that every weakly proper equilibrium is perfect. The weakly properness concept is a strict refinement of the perfectness concept, since the perfect equilibrium (R_1,R_2) of the game of figure 1.5.3. is not weakly proper. Furthermore, it is clear from lemma 2.3.2 that every proper equilibrium is weakly proper. By means of the game of figure 2.3.3, we show that a weakly proper equilibrium is not necessarily proper. The unique proper equilibrium of this game is (1,1), since according to this concept player 2 chooses his third strategy with an order smaller probability than his second one. According to the weakly properness concept, player 2 does not have to choose his third strategy with a much smaller probability than his second one, since the third strategy is only a little bit worse (player 1 chooses his third strategy only with small probability). Consequently also the equilibrium (2,1) is weakly proper.

	1	2	3
1	2, 2	1, 1	1, 1
2	2, 2	0, 1	3, 1
3	0, 2	0, 1	0, 0

Figure 2.3.2. A weakly proper equilibrium need not be proper.

From the above discussion, it follows that we have:

THEOREM 2.3.5. Every proper equilibrium is weakly proper and every weakly proper equilibrium is perfect. Both inclusions may be strict.

Furthermore, we have:

THEOREM 2.3.6. Every strictly perfect equilibrium is weakly proper.

PROOF. Assume s is a strictly perfect equilibrium of a normal form game $\Gamma = (\Phi_1,\ldots,\Phi_n,R_1,\ldots,R_n)$. For $\varepsilon > 0$, define $\eta(\varepsilon)$ by

$$\begin{aligned} \nu_i(k) &:= \{\ell \in \Phi_i ;\ R_i(s\backslash k) \leq R_i(s\backslash \ell)\} \\ \eta_i^k(\varepsilon) &:= (\varepsilon)^{\nu_i(k)} \end{aligned} \qquad \text{for } i \in N,\ k \in \Phi_i.$$

If ε is small, $\eta(\varepsilon)$ is close to zero, which implies that $(\Gamma,\eta(\varepsilon))$ has an equilibrium $s(\varepsilon)$ which is close to s. It follows from (2.2.3) that $s(\varepsilon)$ satisfies (2.3.2) and that s is a best reply against $s(\varepsilon)$ if ε is sufficiently small. Hence, s is a weakly proper equilibrium. □

The reader might conjecture that every strictly perfect equilibrium is even proper. In trying to prove this conjecture, the author has run into difficulties, caused by the fact that the correspondence $\eta \to E(\Gamma,\eta)$ may (possibly) be ill-behaved in the neighborhood of $\eta = 0$. To circumvent these difficulties, we will introduce a refinement of the strictly perfectness concept, the strict properness concept and we will prove that every strictly proper equilibrium is proper.

DEFINITION 2.3.7. Let $\Gamma = (\Phi_1,\ldots,\Phi_n,R_1,\ldots,R_n)$ be a normal form game. For $\hat{\eta} \in \mathbb{R}^m_{++}$, let $U_{\hat{\eta}}$ be as in Definition 2.2.7. s is a *strictly proper equilibrium* of Γ, if there exists some $\hat{\eta} \in \mathbb{R}^m_{++}$ and a continuous map $\eta \to s(\eta)$ from $U_{\hat{\eta}}$ to S such that $s(\eta) \in E(\Gamma,\eta)$ for all η and $\lim_{\eta \downarrow 0} s(\eta) = s$.

Clearly, every strictly proper equilibrium is strictly perfect, but the author does not know whether the converse is also true. We will now show, that the strict properness concept is indeed a refinement of the properness concept:

THEOREM 2.3.8. Every strictly proper equilibrium is proper.

PROOF. Let $\Gamma = (\Phi_1,\ldots,\Phi_n,R_1,\ldots,R_n)$ be an n-person normal form game and assume s is a strictly proper equilibrium of Γ. Let $\hat{\eta}$ and $s(\eta)$ (for $\eta \in U_{\hat{\eta}}$) be as in Definition 2.3.7. Let ε and V be given by:

$$0 < \varepsilon < \min_{i,k} \hat{\eta}^k_i \qquad V = \{\eta \in U_{\hat{\eta}};\ (\varepsilon)^m \le \eta^k_i \le \varepsilon \quad \text{for all } i,k\},$$

and define the correspondence F from S to V by:

$$F(s) = \{\eta \in V;\ \text{if } R_i(s\backslash k) < R_i(s\backslash \ell),\ \text{then } \eta^k_i \le \varepsilon\eta^\ell_i \quad \text{for all } i,k,\ell\}.$$

As in the proof of Theorem 2.3.2, one can show that F(s) is a nonempty, compact and convex set, for every $s \in S$, and that F is upper semi-continuous. Define the correspondence G from V to V by $G(\eta) = F(s(\eta))$, where $s(\eta) \in E(\Gamma,\eta)$ is as in Definition 2.3.7. Then G satisfies the conditions of the Kakutani Fixed Point Theorem (KAKUTANI [1941]) and, therefore, G possesses a fixed point. Let $\eta(\varepsilon)$ be such a fixed point and write $s(\varepsilon)$ for $s(\eta(\varepsilon))$. We have

$$\text{(2.3.3)} \qquad \text{if } R_i(s(\varepsilon)\backslash k) < R_i(s(\varepsilon)\backslash \ell),\ \text{then } \eta^k_i(\varepsilon) \le \varepsilon\eta^\ell_i(\varepsilon) \qquad \text{for all } i,k,\ell.$$

Since $s(\varepsilon)$ is an equilibrium of $(\Gamma,\eta(\varepsilon))$ we, moreover, have

$$\text{(2.3.4)} \qquad s^\ell_i(\varepsilon) \ge \eta^\ell_i(\varepsilon) \qquad \text{for all } i,\ell, \text{ and}$$

$$\text{(2.3.5)} \qquad \text{if } R_i(s(\varepsilon)\backslash k) < R_i(s(\varepsilon)\backslash \ell),\ \text{then } s^k_i(\varepsilon) = \eta^k_i(\varepsilon) \qquad \text{for all } i,k,\ell.$$

Hence, by combining the formulae (2.3.3) - (2.3.5), we see that $s(\varepsilon)$ is an ε-proper equilibrium of Γ. Since ε can be chosen arbitrarily small and since $s(\varepsilon)$ is close to s if ε is close to zero, we have that s is a proper equilibrium of Γ. □

2.4. ESSENTIAL EQUILIBRIA

In the previous sections of this chapter, we considered refinements of the Nash equilibrium concept which are based on the idea that a reasonable equilibrium should be stable against slight perturbations in the equilibrium strategies. In this section, we will consider a refinement of the equilibrium concept, the essential equilibrium concept, which is based on the idea that a reasonable equilibrium should be stable against slight perturbations in the payoffs of the game. The concept of essential equilibria has been introduced in WU WEN-TSÜN AND JIANG JIA-HE [1962]. The main result proved in this section is, that every essential equilibrium is strictly perfect.

DEFINITION 2.4.1. Let Γ be an n-person normal form game. An equilibrium s of Γ is an *essential equilibrium* of Γ, if for every $\varepsilon > 0$ there exists some $\delta > 0$, such that for every game Γ' with $\rho(\Gamma,\Gamma') < \delta$ there exists some $s' \in E(\Gamma')$ with $\rho(s,s') < \varepsilon$.

In chapter 1, we have already seen that there exist games without essential equilibria (the game of figure 1.5.5. is such a game). Wu Wen-Tsün and Jiang Jia-he, however, showed that such games are more or less exceptional. They proved:

THEOREM 2.4.2. (WU WEN-TSÜN AND JIANG JIA-HE [1962], Theorems A and B).

(i) For any n-tuple $\Phi_1,\ldots,\Phi_n$ of finite sets, the set of games in $G(\Phi_1,\ldots,\Phi_n)$, for which all equilibria are essential, is open and dense in $G(\Phi_1,\ldots,\Phi_n)$.

(ii) If a game has finitely many equilibria, then it has at least one essential equilibrium.

The proof of Theorem 2.4.2, given by Wu Wen-Tsün and Jiang Jia-He, is based on the theory of essential fixed points for continuous mappings (cf. FORT [1950]). For the special case of a bimatrix game a different proof of Theorem 2.4.2, only using game theoretic arguments, was given in JANSEN [1981b]. Jansen's proof of part (ii) of the theorem can easily be generalized to the n-person case, but his proof of the first part essentially uses the 2-person character of the game. In section 6 of this chapter, we will prove a slightly stronger assertion than the one of Theorem 2.4.2. (i), by using properties of regular equilibria.

In the remainder of this section, it is proved that stability against perturbations in payoffs implies stability against perturbations in strategies:

THEOREM 2.4.3. Every essential equilibrium is strictly perfect.

PROOF. Let $\Gamma = (\Phi_1,\ldots,\Phi_n,R_1,\ldots,R_n)$ be an n-person normal form game and assume $\tilde{s}$ is an essential equilibrium of Γ. Let $\eta = (\eta_1,\ldots,\eta_n)$ be such that (2.2.1) is satisfied. We will construct a normal form game Γ^η whose equilibria induce equilibria in (Γ,η). If η is small, Γ^η will be close to Γ and therefore Γ^η has an equilibrium close to $\tilde{s}$. In this case, the equilibrium induced in (Γ,η) will also be close to $\tilde{s}$ and this will establish the proof.

It will be convenient to denote a generic element of Φ_i by φ_i rather than by k. If $s_i \in S_i$, then we write $s_i(\varphi_i)$ for the probability which s_i assigns to φ_i. We also write $\eta_i(\varphi_i)$ for the minimum probability of φ_i in the perturbed game (Γ,η). For $i \in N$ and $s_i \in S_i$, define $\lambda_i \in (0,1)$ and $s_i * \eta_i$ by

$$\lambda_i := \sum_{\varphi_i} \eta_i(\varphi_i) \quad \text{and} \quad s_i * \eta_i := (1 - \lambda_i)s_i + \eta_i .$$

Notice that $s_i * \eta_i$ can be viewed as a mixture of mixed strategies: s_i is chosen with probability $1 - \lambda_i$ and η_i/λ_i is chosen with probability λ_i. The interpretation of $s_i * \eta_i$ is: if the mistake probabilities of player i are determined by η_i, then this player will actually play $s_i * \eta_i$ if he intends to play s_i. For $s \in S$, let $s * \eta$ be defined by:

$$(s * \eta)_i = s_i * \eta_i \qquad \text{for } i \in N,$$

and let the game $\Gamma^\eta = (\Phi_1,\ldots,\Phi_n,R_1^\eta,\ldots,R_n^\eta)$ be defined by

$$R_i^\eta(\varphi) = R_i(\varphi * \eta) \qquad \text{for } i \in N,\ \varphi \in \Phi. \tag{2.4.1}$$

Hence, $R_i^\eta(\varphi)$ is the expected payoff to player i, if the players intend to play φ and make mistakes according to η. We claim that

$$R_i^\eta(s) = R_i(s * \eta) \qquad \text{for all } i \in N \text{ and } s \in S. \tag{2.4.2}$$

Namely, for $i \in N$ and $s \in S$, we have

$$R_i^\eta(s) = \sum_{\varphi} s(\varphi)R_i(\varphi * \eta) = \sum_{\varphi}\sum_{\varphi'} s(\varphi)(\varphi * \eta)(\varphi')R_i(\varphi') =$$

$$= \sum_{\varphi'} \left\{\sum_{\varphi} s(\varphi)(\varphi * \eta)(\varphi')\right\} R_i(\varphi') \overset{(*)}{=} \sum_{\varphi'} (s * \eta)(\varphi')R_i(\varphi')$$

$$= R_i(s * \eta),$$

where the equality marked with (*) follows from the fact that for all $i \in N$:

$$(s_i * \eta_i)(\varphi_i') = \sum_{\varphi_i} s_i(\varphi_i)(\varphi_i * \eta_i)(\varphi_i') \qquad \text{for all } s_i \in S_i,\ \varphi_i' \in \Phi_i,$$

and the fact that the players choose their strategies (and make their mistakes) independently. As a consequence of (2.4.2), we have that for all $i \in N$, $s \in S, \varphi_i \in \Phi_i$:

$$R_i^\eta(s\backslash\varphi_i') = (1-\lambda_i)R_i(s*\eta\backslash\varphi_i') + \sum_{\varphi_i}\eta_i(\varphi_i)R_i(s*\eta\backslash\varphi_i)$$

which implies

(2.4.3) $$R_i^\eta(s\backslash\varphi_i) < R_i^\eta(s\backslash\varphi_i') \text{ iff } R_i(s*\eta\backslash\varphi_i) < R_i(s*\eta\backslash\varphi_i') \qquad \text{for all } i,s,\varphi_i,\varphi_i'.$$

Next, let η be close to zero. For $\varphi \in \Phi$, we have that $\varphi * \eta$ is close to φ which implies, since R_i is continuous, that $R_i^\eta(\varphi)$ is close to $R_i(\varphi)$. Hence, if η is close to zero, Γ^η is close to Γ. Therefore, in this case, Γ^η has an equilibrium $s^\eta = (s_1^\eta,\ldots,s_n^\eta)$ which is close to the essential equilibrium $\tilde{s}$ of Γ. We have

$$\text{if } R_i^\eta(s^\eta\backslash\varphi_i) < R_i^\eta(s^\eta\backslash\varphi_i'), \text{ then } s_i^\eta(\varphi_i) = 0 \qquad \text{for all } i \in N,\ \varphi_i,\varphi_i' \in \Phi_i,$$

from which it follows, by using (2.4.3), that for all $i \in N$ and $\varphi_i,\varphi_i' \in \Phi_i$,

$$\text{if } R_i(s^\eta*\eta\backslash\varphi_i) < R_i(s^\eta*\eta\backslash\varphi_i'), \text{ then } (s^\eta*\eta)_i(\varphi_i) = \eta_i(\varphi_i)$$

which implies that $s^\eta * \eta$ is an equilibrium of (Γ,η). Since $s^\eta * \eta$ converges to $\tilde{s}$ as η tends to zero, we have that $\tilde{s}$ is a strictly perfect equilibrium of Γ. □

2.5. REGULAR EQUILIBRIA

In this section we introduce the most stringent refinement of the Nash equilibrium concept which will be considered: the concept of <u>regular equilibria</u>. This concept has been introduced in HARSANYI [1973b]. It is shown that regular equilibria possess all robustness properties one can hope for: they are both essential and strictly proper.

It should be noted that also in JANSEN [1981b] a concept of regular equilibria has been introduced. Jansen's results, however, should not be confused with ours: what he calls a regular equilibrium is what we have called a quasi-strong equilibrium, and although every regular equilibrium is quasi-strong (Corollary 2.5.3), it is definitely not true that every quasi-strong equilibrium is regular (as follows e.g. from the game of figure 2.1.1).

Before defining the concept of regular equilibria, let us introduce some notational conventions. Let $(\Phi_1,\ldots,\Phi_n,R_1,\ldots,R_n)$ be an n-person normal form game.

For $i \in N$, we write X_i for $F(\Phi_i,\mathbb{R})$, the set of all mappings from Φ_i to $\mathbb{R}$. We have $S_i \subset X_i$. A generic element of X_i is denoted by x_i and x_i^k denotes the value of x_i at k. We identify X_i with $\mathbb{R}^{m_i}$, where m_i is given by (2.1.1). X denotes $\prod_{i=1}^n X_i$ and a generic element of X is denoted by x. The set X can be identified with $\mathbb{R}^m$, where m

is given by (2.1.1). If $x \in X$ and $x_i' \in X_i$, then $x\backslash x_i' := (x_1,\dots,x_{i-1},x_i',x_{i+1},\dots,x_n)$. By means of the formulae (2.1.5) and (2.1.7), we have extended R_i from Φ to S. We can extend R_i from S to X by means of the formulae

(2.5.1) $$R_i(x) = \sum_{\varphi\in\Phi} x(\varphi)R_i(\varphi) \qquad x(\varphi) := \prod_{j=1}^{n} x_j^{k_j} \quad \text{if } \varphi = (k_1,\dots,k_n)$$

In the next two sections, it will be convenient to think of R_i as a mapping which is defined on $\mathbb{R}^m$. Notice that R_i is a polynomial and, hence, is infinitely often differentiable.

Let $\Gamma = (\Phi_1,\dots,\Phi_n,R_1\dots,R_n)$ be an n-person normal form game. From (2.1.11) we see that a strategy combination $s \in S$ is an equilibrium of Γ if and only if the following condition is fulfilled:

$$\text{if } s_i^k > 0, \text{ then } R_i(s\backslash k) = \max_{\ell\in\Phi_i} R_i(s\backslash \ell) \qquad \text{for all } i \in N,\ k \in \Phi_i.$$

Hence, $s \in \mathbb{R}^m_{++}$ is an equilibrium of Γ if and only if s is a solution to the following set of equations:

(2.5.2) $$x_i^k[R_i(x\backslash k) - \max_{\ell\in\Phi_i} R_i(x\backslash \ell)] = 0 \qquad \text{for all } i \in N,\ k \in \Phi_i \text{ and}$$

(2.5.3) $$\sum_k x_i^k - 1 = 0 \qquad \text{for all } i \in N.$$

In (2.5.2) and (2.5.3) we have m + n equations in m unknowns, but, since for each i at least one equation in (2.5.2) is trivially fulfilled, we actually have m equations in m unknowns. However, the system possesses the undesirable property that the mapping defined by the left hand side of (2.5.2) - (2.5.3) is not differentiable. Therefore, we will consider a slightly different system of equations. Namely, let $\varphi = (k_1,\dots,k_n) \in \Phi$ be fixed, and consider the system:

(2.5.4) $$x_i^k[R_i(x\backslash k) - R_i(x\backslash k_i)] = 0 \qquad \text{for all } i \in N,\ k \in \Phi_i,\ k \neq k_i,$$

(2.5.5) $$\sum_k x_i^k - 1 = 0 \qquad \text{for all } i \in N.$$

If s is an equilibrium of Γ with $\varphi \in C(s)$, then s is a solution to the system (2.5.4) - (2.5.5) and, furthermore, the mapping defined by the left hand side of these equations is infinitely often differentiable. The price we have to pay for gaining this differentiability is that not every positive solution of this system is an equilibrium and that not every equilibrium of Γ need to be solution of the system. Nevertheless, it turns out to be more convenient to work with the system (2.5.4) - (2.5.5) than to work with the system (2.5.2) - (2.5.3). Let $F(.|\varphi)$ be the mapping defined by the left hand side of (2.5.4) - (2.5.5). More precisely:

$$(2.5.6) \qquad F_i^k(x|\varphi) = x_i^k[R_i(x\backslash k) - R_i(x\backslash k_i)] \qquad \text{for } i \in N,\ k \in \Phi_i,\ k \neq k_i,$$

$$(2.5.7) \qquad F_i^{k_i}(x|\varphi) = \sum_k x_i^k - 1 \qquad \text{for } i \in N.$$

Let $J(s|\varphi)$ be the Jacobian (i.e. the matrix of first order partial derivatives) of $F(.|\varphi)$ evaluated at s, i.e.

$$(2.5.8) \qquad J(s|\varphi) = \left.\frac{\partial F(x|\varphi)}{\partial x}\right|_{x = s} .$$

If s is an equilibrium of Γ with $\varphi \in C(s)$, then $F(s|\varphi) = 0$. One can expect that an equilibrium s with $\varphi \in C(s)$ will have nice properties if $F(.|\varphi)$ is locally invertible at s, i.e. if $J(s|\varphi)$ is nonsingular. Therefore, we define:

DEFINITION 2.5.1. An equilibrium s of Γ is a *regular equilibrium* of Γ if $J(s|\varphi)$ is nonsingular for some $\varphi \in C(s)$. An equilibrium is *irregular* if it is not regular.

By considering the game of figure 1.5.5, it can easily be verified that there exist games without regular equilibria (this also follows from Corollary 2.5.6). However, in HARSANYI [1973b], it has been proved that games without regular equilibria are exceptional (also cf. Theorem 2.6.1). It should be noted that Definition 2.5.1 is slightly different from the definition of regular equilibria given by Harsanyi. Harsanyi defines a regular equilibrium as an equilibrium s for which the Jacobian $J(s|\bar{\varphi})$ is nonsingular, where $\bar{\varphi}$ is the strategy combination (1,...,1). To illustrate the difference between these definitions, consider the game of figure 2.5.1:

	1	2
1	0, 0	0, 0
2	0, 0	1, 1

Figure 2.5.1. An example to illustrate the role of the reference point φ in the definition of a regular equilibrium.

This game has two equilibria, viz. $\hat{\varphi} = (1,1)$ and $\tilde{\varphi} = (2,2)$. The equilibrium $\hat{\varphi}$ is not a reasonable one, but the equilibrium $\tilde{\varphi}$ possesses all nice properties one possibly could ask for. Therefore, the definition of a regular equilibrium should be such that $\bar{\varphi}$ is irregular and $\tilde{\varphi}$ is regular. Our definition of regular equilibria satisfies this condition. However, according to Harsanyi's definition both equilibria are irregular. This is the reason why we have modified Harsanyi's definition as in Definition 2.5.1. Actually, in the proofs in HARSANYI [1973b] it is implicitly assumed that every equilibrium s satisfies $\bar{\varphi} \in C(s)$ and so in his proofs Harsanyi actually works with our definition of regularity. Therefore, the results of HARSANYI [1973b] are correct if regularity is defined as in Definition 2.5.1.

Next, we will show that, if s is a regular equilibrium of Γ, then $J(s|\varphi)$ is nonsingular, for all $\varphi \in C(s)$. First we prove:

LEMMA 2.5.2. Let $\Gamma = (\Phi_1,\dots,\Phi_n,R_1,\dots,R_n)$ be an n-person normal form game, let $s \in E(\Gamma)$ and let $\varphi = (k_1,\dots,k_n) \in C(s)$. For $x \in \mathbb{R}^m$, let $F(x|\varphi)$ and $J(x|\varphi)$ be defined as before and let $\tilde{J}(x|\varphi)$ be the Jacobian which results from $J(s|\varphi)$ by crossing out the rows and columns corresponding to the pure strategies which do not belong to $C(s)$. Then we have[1)]

$$(2.5.9) \qquad |J(s|\varphi)| = |\tilde{J}(s|\varphi)| \prod_{i \in N} \prod_{k \notin C(s_i)} [R_i(s\backslash k) - R_i(s\backslash k_i)].$$

PROOF. For $i \in N$ and $k \in \Phi_i \backslash C(s_i)$, we have

$$\left.\frac{\partial F_i^k(x|\varphi)}{\partial x_j^\ell}\right|_s = 0 \qquad \text{for all } j \in N,\ \ell \in \Phi_j,\ \ell \neq k,$$

$$\left.\frac{\partial F_i^k(x|\varphi)}{\partial x_i^k}\right|_s = R_i(s\backslash k) - R_i(s\backslash k_i),$$

which immediately implies (2.5.9) □

If s is a strong equilibrium of Γ, then the right hand side of (2.5.9) is nonzero and, hence, a strong equilibrium is regular. On the other hand, if an equilibrium is not quasi-strong, then the right hand side is zero, and so we have:

COROLLARY 2.5.3. Every strong equilibrium is regular; every regular equilibrium is quasi-strong.

---

1) For a matrix A, we denote by $|A|$ the determinant of A.

LEMMA 2.5.4. Let $\Gamma = (\Phi_1,\dots,\Phi_n,R_1,\dots,R_n)$ be an n-person normal form game, let $s \in E(\Gamma)$ and let $\varphi = (k_1,\dots,k_n)$ and $\varphi' = (\ell_1,\dots,\ell_n)$ be in the carrier of s. Then $J(s|\varphi)$ is nonsingular if and only if $J(s|\varphi')$ is nonsingular.

PROOF. It follows from Lemma 2.5.2. that it suffices to show that $|\tilde{J}(s|\varphi)| = 0$ if and only if $|\tilde{J}(s|\varphi')| = 0$. By writing out the formulae, the reader can verify that for any $i \in N$:

$$\left.\frac{\partial F_i^{k_i}(x|\varphi)}{\partial x_j^\alpha}\right|_s = \left.\frac{\partial F_i^{\ell_i}(x|\varphi')}{\partial x_j^\alpha}\right|_s \qquad \text{for all } j \in N,\ \alpha \in C(s_j),$$

$$\left.\frac{\partial F_i^{k}(x|\varphi)}{\partial x_i^\alpha}\right|_s = \left.\frac{\partial F_i^{\ell}(x|\varphi')}{\partial x_i^\alpha}\right|_s \qquad \text{for all } k,\ell,\alpha \in C(s_i),\ k \neq k_i,\ \ell \neq \ell_i,$$

$$\left.\frac{\partial F_i^{k}(x|\varphi)}{\partial x_j^\alpha}\right|_s = \left.\frac{\partial F_i^{k}(x|\varphi')}{\partial x_j^\alpha}\right|_s - \frac{s_i^k}{s_i^{k_i}}\left.\frac{\partial F_i^{k_i}(x|\varphi')}{\partial x_j^\alpha}\right|_s \qquad \text{for all } k \in C(s_i),\ j \in N,\ \alpha \in C(s_j),\ k \neq k_i,\ j \neq i.$$

Therefore, $\tilde{J}(s|\varphi)$ results from $\tilde{J}(s|\varphi')$ by elementary algebraic operations, which preserve the value of the determinant. □

In the remainder of this section, we will prove two important properties of regular equilibria, namely that a regular equilibrium is essential and that a regular equilibrium is strictly proper. The fundamental result in proving these properties is the following Theorem 2.5.5. Recall that, via (2.1.12) - (2.1.13), we identify a game $\Gamma \in G(\Phi_1,\dots,\Phi_n)$ with a vector $r = (r_1,\dots,r_n) \in \mathbb{R}^{nm^*}$, where m^* is given by (2.1.1), so that we view $G(\Phi_1,\dots,\Phi_n)$ as an nm^*-dimensional Euclidian space.

THEOREM 2.5.5. Let $\tilde{\Gamma} = (\Phi_1,\dots,\Phi_n,\tilde{R}_1,\dots,\tilde{R}_n)$ be an n-person normal form game and assume $\tilde{s}$ is a regular equilibrium of $\tilde{\Gamma}$. Then there exist neighborhoods U of $\tilde{\Gamma}$ in $\mathbb{R}^{nm^*}$ and V of $\tilde{s}$ in $\mathbb{R}^m$, such that

(i) $|E(\Gamma) \cap V| = 1$, for all $\Gamma \in U$, and

(ii) the mapping $s: U \to V$ defined by $\{s(\Gamma)\} = E(\Gamma) \cap V$ is continuous.

PROOF. Let us denote the payoff vector of $\tilde{\Gamma}$ by $\tilde{r}$. Let $\varphi = (k_1,\dots,k_n) \in C(\tilde{s})$ be fixed and define the mapping $F : \mathbb{R}^{nm^*} \times \mathbb{R}^m \to \mathbb{R}^m$ by:

(2.5.10) $\quad F_i^k(r,x) = x_i^k\,[R_i(x\backslash k) - R_i(x\backslash k_i)] \quad$ for $i \in N$, $k \in \Phi_i$, $k \neq k_i$, and

(2.5.11) $\quad F_i^{k_i}(r,x) = \sum_k x_i^k - 1 \quad$ for $i \in N$.

Since $\tilde{s}$ is an equilibrium of $\tilde{\Gamma}$ and $\varphi \in C(\tilde{s})$, we have $F(\tilde{r},\tilde{s}) = 0$. Furthermore, since $\tilde{s}$ is a regular equilibrium of $\tilde{\Gamma}$, we have

$$(2.5.12) \qquad J(\tilde{r},\tilde{s}) = \left.\frac{\partial F(r,x)}{\partial x}\right|_{(\tilde{r},\tilde{s})} \text{ is nonsingular.}$$

By the implicit function theorem (DIEUDONNÉ [1960],p.268) there exist neighborhoods U of $\tilde{r}$ and V of $\tilde{s}$ and a differentiable mapping $s : U \rightarrow V$ such that

$$(2.5.13) \qquad \{(r,x) \in U \times V \; ; \; F(r,x) = 0\} = \{(r,s(r)) \; ; \; r \in U\} .$$

By choosing U and V sufficiently small, we can provide that for all $i \in N$ and $k \in \Phi_i$:

$$(2.5.14) \qquad \text{if } \tilde{s}_i^k > 0, \text{ then } x_i^k > 0 \text{ for all } x \in V,$$

$$(2.5.15) \qquad \text{if } \tilde{R}_i(\tilde{s}\backslash k) < \tilde{R}_i(\tilde{s}\backslash k_i), \text{ then } R_i(x\backslash k) < R_i(x\backslash k_i) \text{ for all } (r,x) \in U \times V.$$

From (2.5.13) - (2.5.15) and the fact that $\tilde{s}$ is a quasi-strong equilibrium of $\tilde{\Gamma}$ (Corollary 2.5.4), we can conclude, that for all $i \in N$ and $r \in U$:

$$s_i^k(r) > 0 \qquad \text{for all } k \in C(\tilde{s}_i),$$

$$R_i(s(r)\backslash k) = R_i(s(r)\backslash k_i) \qquad \text{for all } k \in C(\tilde{s}_i),$$

$$R_i(s(r)\backslash k) < R_i(s(r)\backslash k_i) \qquad \text{for all } k \notin C(\tilde{s}_i), \text{ and}$$

$$s_i^k(r) = 0 \qquad \text{for all } k \notin C(\tilde{s}_i).$$

Therefore, we have that $s(r) \in E(\Gamma(r))$, for all $r \in U$. Since every equilibrium s of $\Gamma(r)$ which is in V satisfies $F(s,r) = 0$, we, in fact, have that $s(r)$ is the only equilibrium of $\Gamma(r)$ which is in V. This establishes the first part of the Theorem. Furthermore, since the mapping $r \rightarrow s(r)$ is continuous, also the second assertion of the theorem is true. □

As an immediate consequence of Theorem 2.5.5, we have:

<u>COROLLARY 2.5.6.</u> Every regular equilibrium is essential.

Let us call an equilibrium s of a game Γ *isolated*, if there exists a neighborhood V of s such that $V \cap E(\Gamma) = \{s\}$. As a consequence of Theorem 2.5.5, we have

<u>COROLLARY 2.5.7.</u> Every regular equilibrium is isolated.

Finally, by using the result of Theorem 2.5.5. and the method of the proof of Theorem 2.4.3, we can show:

THEOREM 2.5.8. Every regular equilibrium is strictly proper.

2.6. AN "ALMOST ALL" THEOREM.

Intuitively, it will be clear that games with irregular equilibria are exceptional. Namely, the existence of an irregular equilibrium entails a special numerical relationship among the payoffs of the game and this relationship can be disturbed by perturbing the payoffs of the game slightly. In this section, we will prove that indeed for almost all games all equilibria are regular. This result was first proved in HARSANYI [1973b] and the proof we will give essentially follows the same lines as the proof given in that paper. It is an application of Sard's Theorem (SARD [1942] or MILNOR [1965]), in the way as initiated in DEBREU [1970].

THEOREM 2.6.1. For almost all normal form games all equilibria are regular.

PROOF. Let $\Phi_1,\dots,\Phi_n$ be an n-tuple of finite, nonempty sets and let $G(\Phi_1,\dots,\Phi_n)$ be the set of all games with pure strategy spaces $\Phi_1,\dots,\Phi_n$. We identify $G(\Phi_1,\dots,\Phi_n)$ with $\mathbb{R}^{nm^*}$ via (2.1.13). Furthermore let $I(\Phi_1,\dots,\Phi_n)$ be the set of all games in this class, which have an irregular equilibrium. We will prove that $I(\Phi_1,\dots,\Phi_n)$ is a closed set with Lebesgue measure zero.
We first prove that $I(\Phi_1,\dots,\Phi_n)$ is closed. Let $F : \mathbb{R}^{nm^*} \times \mathbb{R}^m \to \mathbb{R}^m$ be the mapping defined by (2.5.10)-(2.5.11). Since this mapping depends on which reference point $\varphi \in \Phi$ is chosen, we will write $F(r,x|\varphi)$ for the image of (r,x) under this mapping. Let $J(r,x|\varphi)$ be the Jacobian of (2.5.12). If s is an equilibrium of $\Gamma(r)$ with $\varphi \in C(s)$, then $F(r,s|\varphi) = 0$ and, in this case, s is an irregular equilibrium of $\Gamma(r)$ if and only if $J(r,s|\varphi) = 0$. Let $\{\Gamma(r(t))\}_{t\in\mathbb{N}}$ be a sequence of games in $I(\Phi_1,\dots,\Phi_n)$, such that $\lim_{t\to\infty} r(t) = r$. For $t \in \mathbb{N}$, let $s(t)$ be an irregular equilibrium of $\Gamma(r(t))$ and, without loss of generality, assume $s = \lim_{t\to\infty} s(t)$. Then s is an equilibrium of $\Gamma(r)$, since the correspondence which assigns to each game its set of equilibria is upper semi-continuous. We claim that s is an irregular equilibrium of $\Gamma(r)$. Namely, let $\varphi \in C(s)$. Then $\varphi \in C(s(t))$ for all t which are sufficiently large and therefore, $J(r(t),s(t)|\varphi) = 0$, for all sufficiently large t. Since F is infinitely often differentiable, J is continuous and so $J(r,s|\varphi) = 0$, which establishes our claim. Hence $\Gamma(r) \in I(\Phi_1,\dots\Phi_n)$ and so $I(\Phi_1,\dots,\Phi_n)$ is closed.

Next, we will show that $\lambda(I(\Phi_1,\dots,\Phi_n)) = 0$. For $i \in N$, let $C_i, B_i \subset \Phi_i$, and let $C = \prod_{i=1}^{n} C_i$ and $B = \prod_{i=1}^{n} B_i$. We write $G(C,B)$ (resp. $I(C,B)$) for the set of all games in $G(\Phi_1,\ldots,\Phi_n)$ which have an equilibrium (resp. irregular equilibrium) s with $C(s) = C$ and $B(s) = B$. We have

$$G(\Phi_1,\ldots,\Phi_n) = \bigcup_{C,B\subset\Phi} G(C,B) \qquad I(\Phi_1,\ldots,\Phi_n) = \bigcup_{C,B\subset\Phi} I(C,B),$$

hence, since Φ is finite, it suffices to show that for all $C,B \subset \Phi$:

(2.6.1) $\lambda(I(C,B)) = 0$.

Hence, let $C,B \subset \Phi$ be fixed. If $C = \emptyset$ or $C \not\subset B$, then (2.6.1) is trivially fulfilled, so assume $C \neq \emptyset$, $C \subset B$. Let $\bar{\varphi} = (k_1,\ldots,k_n) \in C$ be fixed. For $i \in N$, let $\Phi(i) \subset \Phi$ be defined by

$$\Phi(i) = \{\varphi \in \Phi \ ; \ \varphi = \bar{\varphi}\backslash k \ \text{ for some } k \in B_i\backslash\{k_i\}\} .$$

Assume that we have given r and s such that:

(2.6.2) $\Gamma(r) \in G(C,B)$, $s \in E(\Gamma(r))$, $C(s) = C$ and $B(s) = B$.

Then, to be able to compute the complete payoff vector r, we actually only have to know the collection of payoffs

(2.6.3) $\{R_i(\varphi) \ ; \ \varphi \in \Phi\backslash\Phi(i),\ i \in N\}$.

Namely, if $k \in B_i\backslash\{k_i\}$, then the payoff $R_i(\bar{\varphi}\backslash k)$ can be computed from the equation

$$R_i(s\backslash k) = R_i(s\backslash k_i),$$

since this equation (once we know (2.6.3) only contains $R_i(\bar{\varphi}\backslash k)$ as an unknown variable, and since this variable occurs in this equation with a positive coefficient. Let us denote by H the mapping, by means of which the complete payoff vector r can be computed from the data in (2.6.3). To be more precise, let

$$P := \{\rho = (\rho_1,\ldots,\rho_n) \ ; \ \rho_i : \Phi\backslash\Phi(i) \to \mathbb{R}\} \text{ , and}$$

$$S(C) := \{s \in S \ ; \ s = (s_1,\ldots,s_n),\ C(s_i) = C_i\},$$

and for $\rho \in P$, $s \in S(C)$ define $H(\rho,s)$ as the unique vector $r \in \mathbb{R}^{nm^*}$ which satisfies

$$(2.6.4) \qquad R_i(\varphi) = \rho_i(\varphi) \qquad \text{for } i \in N,\ \varphi \in \Phi\backslash\Phi(i), \text{ and}$$

$$(2.6.5) \qquad R_i(s\backslash k) = R_i(s\backslash k_i) \qquad \text{for } i \in N,\ k \in B_i\backslash\{k_i\}\ .$$

Notice that there is indeed a unique vector r satisfying (2.6.4) and (2.6.5), since for fixed $i \in N$, $k \in B_i\backslash\{k_i\}$, the equation (2.6.5) only contains the unknown $R_i(\bar{\varphi}\backslash k)$ which occurs in it with the coefficient $s_{-i}(\bar{\varphi}_{-i}) := s(\bar{\varphi})/s_i(\bar{\varphi}_i)$ (which is positive since $s \in S(C)$ and $\bar{\varphi} \in C(s)$). Futhermore, since in this case $R_i(\bar{\varphi}\backslash k)$ is computed by using multiplications, additions and substractions and only dividing by $s_{-i}(\bar{\varphi}_{-i})$, we have that H is infinitely often differentiable on $P \times S(C)$.
For $r = (r_1,\dots,r_n) \in \mathbb{R}^{nm^*}$, let $\rho(r) \in P$ be the vector $(\rho_1(r_1),\dots,\rho_n(r_n))$ where $\rho_i(r_i)$ is the restriction of r_i to $\Phi\backslash\Phi(i)$, for $i \in N$. The mapping H is constructed in such a way that $H(\rho(r),s) = r$, if r and s satisfy (2.6.2). Therefore, we have:

$$(2.6.6) \qquad G(C,B) \subset \{\Gamma(r)\ ;\ \exists_{(\bar{\rho},\bar{s}) \in P \times S(C)}[H(\bar{\rho},\bar{s}) = \bar{r}]\}\ ,$$

from which we can conclude that (2.6.1) is true, in the special case where $C \neq B$. Namely, in this case

$$\dim(P) = nm^* - |B| + n\ , \qquad \dim(S(C)) = |C| - n,$$

and, therefore, $\dim(P \times S(C)) < nm^*$, if $|C| < |B|$. This implies, by means of (2.6.6), that $\lambda(G(C,B)) = 0$, if $C \neq B$ (since we assumed that $C \subset B$). Hence, (2.6.1) is true if $C \neq B$.
Next, assume $C = B$. In this case, it easily follows from the definition of H, that, if r,s are such that (2.6.2) is satisfied, then

$$(2.6.7) \qquad \left.\frac{\partial H(\rho,\sigma)}{\partial(\rho,\sigma)}\right|_{(\rho(r),s)} \text{ is singular iff } \left.\frac{\partial F(r,x|\bar{\varphi})}{\partial x}\right|_{(r,s)} \text{ is singular.}$$

From (2.6.6) and (2.6.7) we see that I(C,C) is a subset of

$$(2.6.8) \qquad \{\Gamma(\bar{r});\ \exists_{\bar{\rho},\bar{s}}\ [H(\bar{\rho},\bar{s}) = \bar{r} \text{ and } \left.\frac{\partial H(\rho,\sigma)}{\partial(\rho,\sigma)}\right|_{(\bar{\rho},\bar{s})} \text{ is singular}]\}\ .$$

Sard's theorem (MILNOR [1965],p.10) assures us that Lebesque measure of the set in (2.6.8) is zero and, therefore, we have $\lambda(I(C,C)) = 0$. □

If all equilibria of a normal form game Γ are regular, then this game has a finite number of equilibria (Corollary 2.5.7). Harsanyi has sharpened this result and proved that a game for which all equilibria are regular, in fact has an odd number of equilibria (HARSANYI [1973b], Theorem 1; for alternative proofs that almost all games have an odd number of equilibria, see ROSENMÜLLER [1971] or WILSON [1971]). Therefore, by combining the Theorems 2.3.5, 2.3.7, 2.5.8, 2.6.1 and the Corollaries 2.5.3, 2.5.6, we can draw our main conclusion for normal form games:

<u>THEOREM 2.6.2</u>. Almost all normal form games possess an odd number of equilibria, which are all regular, quasi-strong, essential and strictly proper (and hence also proper and strictly perfect).

CHAPTER 3

MATRIX AND BIMATRIX GAMES

In this chapter, we study 2-person normal form games, zero-sum games (matrix games) as well as nonzero-sum games (bimatrix games). It is our objective to investigate whether, for the special case of a 2-person game, the results of the previous chapter can be refined and specialized.

In section 3.1, some notation and terminology is introduced, something is said about the structure of the set of equilibria of a bimatrix game and some well-known results concerning matrix games are stated.

In section 3.2, perfect equilibria are studied. The main result is, that an equilibrium of a bimatrix game is perfect if and only if it is undominated, from which it follows, that one can verify whether an equilibrium of a bimatrix game is perfect by solving a linear programming problem.

Regular equilibria are studied in section 3.3. A first characterization of such equilibria is derived and it is shown that, for a bimatrix game which is nondegenerate in the sense of LEMKE AND HOWSON [1964], all equilibria are regular.

In section 3.4, further characterizations of regular equilibria are derived. The main result is, that an equilibrium s of a bimatrix game is regular if and only if s is isolated and perfect in the s-restriction of Γ. From this result several other characterizations follow easily.

In the last section of the chapter zero-sum games are studied. Attention is focused on proper equilibria, and it is shown that an equilibrium of a matrix game is proper if and only if it is a pair of best strategies in the sense of DRESHER [1961], from which it follows that it is easy to check whether an equilibrium of such a game is proper.

The results in this chapter are based upon VAN DAMME [1980b, 1981b].

3.1. PRELIMINARIES

A 2-person normal form game $\Gamma = (\Phi_1, \Phi_2, R_1, R_2)$ is also called a *bimatrix game*, for reasons which will be clear. With respect to such a game, we will use the same notation and terminology as the one we used for general n-person normal form games (cf. section 2.1). Hence, S_i denotes the set of all mixed strategies of player i in Γ and

$S = S_1 \times S_2$. For $s \in S$, the expected payoff $R_i(s)$ to player i if s is played is defined as in (2.1.7). Furthermore, as in section 2.5, we write X_i for $F(\Phi_i, \mathbb{R})$ (the set of all functions from Φ_i to $\mathbb{R}$) and $X = X_1 \times X_2$. R_i is extended from S to X as in (2.5.1). Note that R_i is bilinear. Hence, if $x_1 \in X_1$, then R_i and x_1 determine a linear mapping from X_2 to $\mathbb{R}$, which we denote by $R_i(x_1)$. Hence, we have $(R_i(x_1))(x_2) = R_i(x_1,x_2)$ (for $x_2 \in X_2$). Similarly, R_i and $x_2 \in X_2$ determine a linear mapping $R_i(x_2)$ from X_1 to $\mathbb{R}$. The mappings $R_i(x_1)$ and $R_i(x_2)$ cannot be mixed up, since the index will always point out which mapping is meant. We say that

R_i is *row-regular*, if $R_i(x_1) \neq 0$ for all $x_1 \neq 0$,

R_i is *column-regular*, if $R_i(x_2) \neq 0$ for all $x_2 \neq 0$, and

R_i is *regular* (or nonsingular) if R_i is both row-regular and column-regular.

Let $s = (s_1,s_2) \in S$. If player 1 knows, that player 2 plays s_2, then he will assign a positive probability only to the pure strategies belonging to $B_1(s)$, and a similar remark applies to player 2. Hence, if s is played, the most relevant payoffs are the payoffs $R_i(\varphi)$ with $\varphi \in B(s)$. Therefore, we define the *s-restriction* of Γ as the game $\Gamma^s = (\Phi_1^s, \Phi_2^s, R_1^s, R_2^s)$, where $\Phi_i^s := B_i(s)$ and R_i^s is the restriction of R_i to $\Phi^s := \Phi_1^s \times \Phi_2^s$. R_i^s is called the *s-restriction* of the payoff matrix R_i. We write X_i^s for $F(\Phi_i^s, \mathbb{R})$ and we extend R_i^s bilinearly from Φ^s to $X^s := X_1^s \times X_2^s$. A generic element of X_i^s is denoted by x_i^s and the *extension* of x_i^s to Φ_i is the element $x_i \in F(\Phi_i, \mathbb{R})$, defined by

$$x_i(\varphi_i) = \begin{cases} x_i^s(\varphi_i) & \text{if } \varphi_i \in \Phi_i^s, \\ 0 & \text{otherwise.} \end{cases}$$

When no confusion can result, x_i and x_i^s are identified and, consequently, sometimes x_i is used to denote a generic element of X_i^s.

Next, let us briefly say something about the structure of the set of equilibria of a bimatrix game. If s,s' are equilibria of a bimatrix game Γ, then s and s' are said to be *interchangeable*, if (s_1,s_2') and (s_1',s_2) are also equilibria of Γ. A set of equilibria is said to be a *maximal Nash subset* (MILLHAM [1974], HEUER AND MILLHAM [1976]) or *subsolution* (NASH [1951] if it is a maximal set with the property that all its elements are interchangeable. Theorem 2.1.1, of which a proof can be found in JANSEN [1981a], shows that maximal Nash subsets are important in the study of the structure of the set of equilibria:

<u>THEOREM 3.1.1</u>. Let Γ be a bimatrix game. Then

(i) every maximal Nash subset is a closed and convex polyhedral set,

(ii) the set of equilibria of Γ is the (not necessarily disjoint) union of all maximal Nash subsets,

(iii) there are only finitely many maximal Nash subsets.

By using Theorem 3.1.1., it is straightforward to prove

COROLLARY 3.1.2. An equilibrium s of a bimatrix game is isolated if and only if $\{s\}$ is a maximal Nash subset.

For general n-person games, also interchangeability of equilibria and maximal Nash subsets can be defined. If $n \geq 3$, however, there may exist an uncountable number of maximal Nash subsets (CHIN, PARTHASARATHY AND RAGHAVAN [1974], p.3) and, therefore, in this case if $\{s\}$ is a maximal Nash subset, s is not necessarily isolated.
To conclude our preliminary discussion on bimatrix games, let us remark, that we can assume, whenever it is convenient to do so, that all payoffs in a bimatrix game are positive. Namely, let $\Gamma = (\Phi_1,\Phi_2,R_1,R_2)$ be an arbitrary bimatrix game and let Γ', result from Γ by adding a fixed amount to all payoffs in Γ, such that all payoffs in Γ' are positive. Then the strategic situation in Γ' is the same as the one in Γ, and so the equilibria of these games are the same and, hence, in order to analyse Γ, we can just as well analyse Γ'.

In the remaining part of this section, we consider *matrix games*, i.e. bimatrix games (Φ_1,Φ_2,R_1,R_2) with $R_2 = -R_1$. We denote the matrix game in which the payoff function of player 1 is R by (Φ_1,Φ_2,R). For a matrix game $\Gamma = (\Phi_1,\Phi_2,R)$ all equilibria are interchangeable, i.e. $E(\Gamma)$ is a maximal Nash subset, and all equilibria yield the same payoff to player 1. This payoff is called the *value* of the game Γ and is denoted by $v(\Gamma)$. It is easily seen, that $E(\Gamma) = O_1(\Gamma) \times O_2(\Gamma)$, where

$$(3.1.1) \qquad O_1(\Gamma) = \{s_1 \in S_1;\ R(s_1,\ell) \geq v(\Gamma) \quad \text{for all } \ell \in \Phi_2\}, \text{ and}$$

$$(3.1.2) \qquad O_2(\Gamma) = \{s_2 \in S_2;\ R(k,s_2) \leq v(\Gamma) \quad \text{for all } k \in \Phi_1\}.$$

$O_i(\Gamma)$ is a closed, convex polyhedral set (and, hence, $O_i(\Gamma)$ has a finite number of extreme points), the elements of which are called the *optimal strategies* of player i in Γ. It is easily seen, that $s_1 \in O_1(\Gamma)$ if and only if

$$\min_{s_2 \in S_2} R(s_1,s_2) = \max_{s_1' \in S_1} \min_{s_2 \in S_2} R(s_1',s_2),$$

and so in a matrix game a strategy of player 1 is an equilibrium strategy if and only if it is a so called *maximin strategy* (as we know from the game of figure 1.6.2, this is not true for nonzero-sum games). A similar property holds for the optimal strategies of player 2. From (3.1.1) and (3.1.2) it follows that $O_1(\Gamma)$ and $v(\Gamma)$ can be determined by solving the linear programming problem (3.1.3):

$$(3.1.3)\qquad \begin{cases} \text{maximize } v \\ \text{subject to } R(s_1,\ell) \geq v \text{ for all } \ell \in \Phi_2; \quad s_1 \in S_1. \end{cases}$$

To be more precise: we have that $s_1 \in O_1(\Gamma)$ and $v = v(\Gamma)$ if and only if (s_1,v) solves (3.1.3), (where "solves" means "is an optimal solution of"). Therefore, $v(\Gamma)$ and $O_1(\Gamma)$ can be determined easily (cf. BALINSKI [1961]). An important property of matrix games, which first was proved in GALE AND SHERMAN [1950] and, independently, in BOHNENBLUST, KARLIN AND SHAPLEY [1950] is, that a pure strategy is used by some optimal strategy with a positive probability, if and only if this strategy is a best reply against all optimal strategies of the opponent. Hence, for a matrix game Γ:

$$(3.1.4)\qquad \bigcup_{s_i \in O_i(\Gamma)} C(s_i) = \bigcap_{s_j \in O_j(\Gamma)} B_i(s) \qquad i,j \in \{1,2\},\ i \neq j,$$

or, to put it differently

$$(3.1.5)\qquad \bigcup_{s \in E(\Gamma)} C(s) = \bigcap_{s \in E(\Gamma)} B(s).$$

We denote the set of pure strategies which are in the Carrier of some equilibrium strategy of player i in Γ by $C_i(\Gamma)$ (hence, $C_i(\Gamma)$ is the set of (3.1.4)) and $C(\Gamma)$ denotes the set $C_1(\Gamma) \times C_2(\Gamma)$.

Finally we remark that, just as we can assume that in a bimatrix game all payoffs are positive, we can assume, whenever it is convenient to do so, that all payoffs to player 1 in a matrix game are positive (and, hence, that all payoffs to player 2 are negative).

3.2. PERFECT EQUILIBRIA

In chapter 2 (Corollary 2.2.6), we have seen that a perfect equilibrium is always undominated, but that an undominated equilibrium is not necessarily perfect. It is our objective in this section to show, that in a bimatrix game, however, an undominated equilibrium is perfect. Furthermore, it is shown that in this case one can verify whether an equilibrium is perfect, by solving a linear programming problem.

The proof of the main result of the section is based on the following lemma:

<u>LEMMA 3.2.1</u>. Let $\Gamma = (\Phi_1,\Phi_2,R_1,R_2)$ be a bimatrix game and let $s_1 \in S_1$. Define the matrix game $\Gamma(s_1) = (\Phi_1,\Phi_2,R)$ by:

$$R(k,\ell) = R_1(k,\ell) - R_1(s_1,\ell) \qquad \text{for } k \in \Phi_1 \text{ and } \ell \in \Phi_2.$$

Then s_1 is undominated in Γ, if and only if $v(\Gamma(s_1)) = 0$ and $C_2(\Gamma(s_1)) = \Phi_2$.

PROOF. It is easily verified, that the assertions (3.2.1)-(3.2.4) are all equivalent:

(3.2.1) s_1 is dominated by s_1' in Γ, for some s_1',

(3.2.2) $R_1(s_1',\ell) \geq R_1(s_1,\ell)$ for all ℓ and $R(s_1',\ell) > R_1(s_1,\ell)$ for some ℓ, for some s_1',

(3.2.3) $R(s_1',\ell) \geq 0$ for all ℓ and $R(s_1',\ell) > 0$ for some ℓ, for some s_1',

(3.2.4) $v(\Gamma(s_1)) \geq 0$ and, if $v(\Gamma(s_1)) = 0$, then $C_2(\Gamma(s_1)) \neq \Phi_2$.

Since in $\Gamma(s_1)$ player 1 can guarantee himself a payoff 0 by playing s_1, we have $v(\Gamma(s_1)) \geq 0$, hence, (3.2.4) is equivalent to

(3.2.5) if $v(\Gamma(s_1)) = 0$, then $C_2(\Gamma(s_1)) \neq \Phi_2$.

The equivalence of (3.2.1) and (3.2.5) establishes the lemma. □

THEOREM 3.2.2. An equilibrium of a bimatrix game is perfect if and only if it is undominated.

PROOF. Let $s = (s_1,s_2)$ be an equilibrium of the bimatrix game $\Gamma = (\Phi_1,\Phi_2,R_1,R_2)$. In view of Corollary 2.2.6, it suffices to show, that s is perfect if s is undominated. Assume s is undominated and let $\Gamma(s_1)$ be as in Lemma 3.2.1. Since $v(\Gamma(s_1)) = 0$, we have $s_1 \in O_1(\Gamma(s_1))$. Furthermore, let s_2' be a completely mixed element of $O_2(\Gamma(s_1))$, the existence of which is guaranteed by $C_2(\Gamma(s_1)) = \Phi_2$ and formula (3.1.4.). Then s_1 is a best reply against s_2' in $\Gamma(s_1)$, which implies that s_1 is also a best reply against s_2' in Γ. For $\varepsilon > 0$, let $s_2(\varepsilon) = (1-\varepsilon)s_2 + \varepsilon s_2'$. Then $s_2(\varepsilon)$ is completely mixed, s_1 is a best reply against $s_2(\varepsilon)$ and $s_2(\varepsilon)$ converges to s_2, as ε tends to zero. Since undominated strategies of player 2 can be characterized similarly as undominated strategies of player 1, we can follow the same procedure for this player and, hence, we can construct, for $\varepsilon > 0$, a completely mixed strategy $s_1(\varepsilon) \in S_1$, such that s_2 is a best reply against $s_1(\varepsilon)$ and such that $s_1(\varepsilon)$ converges to s_1, as ε tends to zero. Let $s(\varepsilon) = (s_1(\varepsilon),s_2(\varepsilon))$. Then $\{s(\varepsilon)\}_{\varepsilon \downarrow 0}$ satisfies the condition of Theorem 2.2.5 (iii) which shows that s is a perfect equilibrium of Γ. □

In view of the theorem above, in order to verify whether an equilibrium of a bimatrix game is perfect, it suffices to check whether both equilibrium strategies are undominated. We will now demonstrate that this is an easy task. Let us confine ourselves to the equilibrium strategy of player 1. It follows from Lemma 3.2.1, that it suffices to show that the value of a matrix game $\Gamma = (\Phi_1,\Phi_2,R)$ can be easily determined and, that it is easy to verify whether $C_2(\Gamma) = \Phi_2$. Without loss of generality, we can restrict ourselves to the case where $R(\varphi) > 0$ for all $\varphi \in \Phi$.

The value of Γ can be determined by solving the linear programming problem (3.1.3). It is convenient to make a change of variables and to write x_1 for s_1/v (this causes no troubles, since $v(\Gamma) > 0$). By this change of variables (3.1.3) is transformed into (3.2.6), in which $x_1(\Phi_1)$ denotes the sum of all x_1^k with $k \in \Phi_1$.

$$(3.2.6)\quad \begin{cases} \text{minimize} & x_1(\Phi_1), \\ \text{subject to} & R(x_1,\ell) \geq 1 \quad \text{for all } \ell \in \Phi_2 \quad ; x_1 \in X_1;\ x_1 \geq 0. \end{cases}$$

It is easily seen that:

if (s_1,v) solves (3.1.3), then s_1/v solves (3.2.6), and

if x_1 solves (3.2.6), then $(x_1(\Phi_1))^{-1}(x_1,1)$ solves (3.1.3),

which implies that

(3.2.7) $\quad \ell \in C_2(\Gamma)$ if and only if $R(x_1,\ell) = 1$, for all x_1 which solve (3.2.6).

Let us consider (3.2.6) in conjunction with its dual. We have that x_1 solves (3.2.6) and x_2 solves the dual of this problem, if and only if (x_1,x_2) is a solution to the following system of inequalities:

$$(3.2.8)\quad \begin{cases} x_1(\Phi_1) = x_2(\Phi_2), & \\ R(x_1,\ell) \geq 1 & \text{for all } \ell \in \Phi_2, \\ R(k,x_2) \leq 1 & \text{for all } k \in \Phi_1, \text{ and} \\ x_1 \in X_1,\ x_2 \in X_2,\ x_1 \geq 0,\ x_2 \geq 0. & \end{cases}$$

(3.2.7) leads us to the following linear programming problem, in which $R(x_1,\Phi_2)$ denotes the sum of all $R(x_1,\ell)$, where ℓ ranges over Φ_2:

$$(3.2.9)\quad \begin{cases} \text{maximize} & R(x_1,\Phi_2), \\ \text{subject to} & x_1(\Phi_1) = x_2(\Phi_2), \\ & R(x_1,\ell) \geq 1 \quad \text{for all } \ell \in \Phi_2, \\ & R(k,x_2) \leq 1 \quad \text{for all } k \in \Phi_1, \text{ and} \\ & x_1 \in X_1,\ x_2 \in X_2,\ x_1 \geq 0,\ x_2 \geq 0. \end{cases}$$

From (3.2.7), one can conclude that $C_2(\Gamma) = \Phi_2$ if and only if the value of the linear programming problem (3.2.9) is $m_2(=|\Phi_2|)$. Furthermore, if (x_1,x_2) solves (3.2.9), then $v(\Gamma) = (x_1(\Phi_1))^{-1}$ and so, we have proved:

<u>THEOREM 3.2.3</u>. Let $\Gamma = (\Phi_1,\Phi_2,R)$ be a matrix game with $R(\varphi) > 0$ for all $\varphi \in \Phi$. Then
(i) $v(\Gamma) = (x_1(\Phi_1))^{-1}$, where x_1 is such that (x_1,x_2) solves (3.2.9),
(ii) $C_2(\Gamma) = \Phi_2$ if and only if the value of (3.2.9) is m_2.

The linear programming problem (3.2.9) can easily be solved and so, in a bimatrix game, it can easily be checked whether a strategy of player 1 is dominated. The same holds for player 2 and, therefore, it is easy to verify whether an equilibrium of a bimatrix game is perfect.

3.3. REGULAR EQUILIBRIA

In this section, a first characterization of regular equilibria in a bimatrix game is derived. Furthermore, it is shown that, for a game which is nondegenerate in the sense of LEMKE AND HOWSON [1964] or SHAPLEY [1974], all equilibria are regular.

Let $s = (s_1, s_2)$ be an equilibrium of a bimatrix game $\Gamma = (\Phi_1, \Phi_2, R_1, R_2)$. From Corollary 2.5.3 we know that s has to be quasi-strong in order to be regular.
Let us investigate under which conditions a quasi-strong equilibrium s is regular. Without loss of generality, assume that $\bar{\varphi} = (1,1) \in \Phi^s$, where $\Phi^s = C(s) = B(s)$. Define the $|C(s_1)| \times |C(s_2)|$ matrices A_1 and A_2 by (3.3.1)-(3.3.4).

(3.3.1) $\quad A_1(1,\ell) = 1 \qquad$ for $\ell \in \Phi_2^s$,

(3.3.2) $\quad A_1(k,\ell) = R_1(k,\ell) - R_1(1,\ell) \qquad$ for $k \in \Phi_1^s$, $\ell \in \Phi_2^s$, $k \neq 1$,

(3.3.3) $\quad A_2(k,1) = 1 \qquad$ for $k \in \Phi_1^s$,

(3.3.4) $\quad A_2(k,\ell) = R_2(k,\ell) - R_2(k,1) \qquad$ for $k \in \Phi_1^s$, $\ell \in \Phi_2^s$, $\ell \neq 1$.

Let the Jacobian $\tilde{J}(s|\bar{\varphi})$ be as in Lemma 2.5.2. Since s is quasi-strong, it follows that $\tilde{J}(s|\bar{\varphi})$ is nonsingular if and only if the matrix

$$\begin{array}{|c|c|} \hline \emptyset & A_1 \\ \hline A_2^T & \emptyset \\ \hline \end{array}$$

is nonsingular. Obviously, this matrix is nonsingular, if and only if A_1 and A_2 are both nonsingular, which can be the case only if $|C(s_1)| = |C(s_2)|$. We have proved:

<u>LEMMA 3.3.1</u>. An equilibrium s of a bimatrix game is regular if and only if it is a quasi-strong equilibrium with $|C(s_1)| = |C(s_2)|$, for which the matrices A_1 and A_2 as defined in (3.3.1)-(3.3.4), are nonsingular.

Next, assume $\Gamma = (\Phi_1, \Phi_2, R_1, R_2)$ is a bimatrix game in which all payoffs are positive and assume s is a quasi-strong equilibrium of Γ with $|C(s_1)| = |C(s_2)|$. We claim that, in this case, A_i is nonsingular if and only if the s-restricted payoff matrix R_i^s is nonsingular $(i \in \{1,2\})$. Let us demonstrate this fact for $i = 1$. Assume A_1 is singular and let $x_2 \in X_2^s$ be such that $x_2 \neq 0$ and $A_1(x_2) = 0$. Then

$$\text{if } R_1^s(1,x_2) = 0, \text{ then } R_1^s(x_2) = 0, \text{ and}$$

$$\text{if } R_1^s(1,x_2) \neq 0, \text{ then } R_1^s(x_2) \text{ is a scalar multiple of } R_1^s(s_2),$$

whereas x_2 is not a scalar multiple of s_2

(since $x_2(\Phi_2^s) = 0$ and $s_2(\Phi_2^s) = 1$) .

In both cases, we can conclude that R_1^s is singular.

Next, assume R_1^s is singular and let $x_2 \in X_2^s$ be such that $x_2 \neq 0$ and $R_1^s(x_2) = 0$. Then

$$\text{if } x_2(\Phi_2^s) = 0, \quad \text{then } A_1(x_2) = 0, \text{ and}$$

$$\text{if } x_2(\Phi_2^s) \neq 0, \quad \text{then } x_2(\Phi_2^s)s_2 - x_2 \text{ is in the null space of } A_1,$$

whereas $x_2(\Phi_2^s)s_2 \neq x_2$

(since $R_1^s(x_2) = 0$ and $R_1^s(s_2) > 0$, since R_1 is positive)

In both cases, one can conclude that A_1 is singular. Similarly, it can be proved that A_2 is singular if and only if R_2^s is singular and so we have:

<u>Theorem 3.3.2</u>. Let $\Gamma = (\Phi_1,\Phi_2,R_1,R_2)$ be a bimatrix game with positive payoffs. Then s is a regular equilibrium of Γ, if and only if s is a quasi-strong equilibrium with $|C(s_1)| = |C(s_2)|$, for which the matrices R_1^s and R_2^s are nonsingular.

Up to now, nothing has been said about the actual computation of equilibria. Algorithms to compute the set of <u>all</u> equilibria of a bimatrix game have been given in VOROB'EV [1958], MILLS [1960], KUHN [1961] and WINKELS [1979], but all these algorithms are more of theoretical than of practical interest. An efficient algorithm to compute <u>one</u> equilibrium of a bimatrix game, has been proposed in LEMKE AND HOWSON [1964]. This algorithm is based on path following and can be applied to <u>nondegenerate games</u> (see below). To compute an equilibrium of a degenerate game, one first has to perturb the game slightly (e.g. by means of the scheme proposed by Lemke and Howson) in order to get a nondegenerate game to which the algorithm can be applied. In this monograph, we will not consider the question how to compute equilibria, but we will show, that a bimatrix game which satisfies the nondegeneracy condition of Lemke and Howson, possesses only regular equilibria. The following lemma is essential:

<u>LEMMA 3.3.3</u>. For a bimatrix game Γ which is such that $|B(s)| \leq |C(s)|$ for all $s \in S$, all equilibria are regular.

<u>PROOF</u>. Assume Γ satisfies the condition of the lemma and let s be an equilibrium of Γ. Then $C(s) \subset B(s)$ and, therefore $C(s) = B(s)$ by the condition of the lemma. Hence,

s is a quasi-strong equilibrium. From Lemma 3.3.1 it follows that it suffices to show that the matrices A_1 and A_2, as defined in (3.3.1)-(3.3.4) are nonsingular. Assume A_1 is column-singular and let $x_2^s \in X_2^s$ be such that $x_2^s \neq 0$ and $A_1(x_2^s) = 0$. Let x_2 be the extension from x_2^s to X_2 and, for $\varepsilon > 0$, let $s_2(\varepsilon) = s_2 + \varepsilon x_2$ and $s(\varepsilon) = (s_1, s_2(\varepsilon))$. If ε is sufficiently small, then $s(\varepsilon) \in S$, $C(s(\varepsilon)) = C(s)$ and $B(s(\varepsilon)) = B(s)$. Define $\tilde{\varepsilon}$ by

$$\tilde{\varepsilon} := \sup \{\varepsilon > 0 \; ; \; s(\varepsilon) \in S, \; C(s(\varepsilon)) = C(s), \; B(s(\varepsilon)) = B(s)\}.$$

Notice that $\tilde{\varepsilon}$ is finite, since x_2 has at least one negative component. Since s is an equilibrium of Γ, we can conclude from the definition of $\tilde{\varepsilon}$

$$C(s(\tilde{\varepsilon})) \subset C(s) = B(s) \subset B(s(\tilde{\varepsilon})), \text{ where at least one inclusion is strict.}$$

This contradicts the condition of the lemma and so A_1 is column-regular, which implies $|C(s_1)| \geq |C(s_2)|$. Similarly, it can be shown that A_2 is row-regular, and so $|C(s_1)| \leq |C(s_2)|$. Hence, $|C(s_1)| = |C(s_2)|$ and A_1 and A_2 are both nonsingular, which implies that s is a regular equilibrium of Γ. □

Next, let us turn to the nondegeneracy assumption, which is imposed in LEMKE AND HOWSON [1964]. We restrict ourselves to bimatrix games $(\Phi_1, \Phi_2, R_1, R_2)$ in which all payoffs are positive. For $s \in S$, define matrices $\tilde{R}_1^s$ and $\tilde{R}_2^s$ by

$$\tilde{R}_1^s := [R_1(k,\ell)]_{k,\ell} \qquad (k \in B_1(s), \; \ell \in C(s_2)), \text{ and}$$

$$\tilde{R}_2^s := [R_2(k,\ell)]_{k,\ell} \qquad (k \in C(s_1), \; \ell \in B_2(s)).$$

The <u>nondegeneracy assumption</u> which Lemke and Howson impose is:

the rows of $\tilde{R}_1^s$ are independent, for all $s \in S$, and

the columns of $\tilde{R}_2^s$ are independent, for all $s \in S$.

Obviously if this condition is satisfied, then for every $s \in S$:

$$|C(s_2)| \geq \text{rank } (A_1^s) = |B_1(s)|,$$

$$|C(s_1)| \geq \text{rank } (A_2^s) = |B_2(s)|,$$

from which it follows that

$$|C(s)| \geq |B(s)| \quad \text{for every } s \in S.$$

Hence, if the nondegeneracy condition of Lemke and Howson is satisfied, then the condition of Lemma 3.3.1 is fulfilled and all equilibria are regular. In SHAPLEY [1974] a similar nondegeneracy condition is imposed and, therefore, we also have that all equilibria are regular, if that condition is fulfilled.

THEOREM 3.3.4. For a bimatrix game which satisfies the nondegeneracy condition of LEMKE AND HOWSON [1964] (or SHAPLEY [1974]) all equilibria are regular.

3.4. CHARACTERIZATIONS OF REGULAR EQUILIBRIA

In this section several characterizations of regular equilibria are derived. The fundamental result of the section is, that an equilibrium s of a bimatrix game Γ is regular if and only if s is an isolated equilibrium of Γ which is perfect in the s-restriction of Γ. Once this result has been established, several other characterizations of regular equilibria follow easily. At the end of the section, an example is given to demonstrate, that the results of this section cannot be generalized to games with more than two players.
We first prove our main result:

THEOREM 3.4.1. s is a regular equilibrium of the bimatrix game $\Gamma = (\Phi_1,\Phi_2,R_1,R_2)$ if and only if s is an isolated equilibrium of Γ, which is perfect in the s-restriction Γ^s of Γ.

PROOF. If s is a regular equilibrium of Γ, then s is isolated, as we know from Corollary 2.5.7. Furthermore, if s is regular in Γ, then s is regular in Γ^s, as follows from Lemma 2.5.2 and, therefore, s is a perfect equilibrium of Γ^s (Theorem 2.5.8). Next, assume $s = (s_1,s_2)$ is an isolated equilibrium of Γ, which is perfect in Γ^s. Since s is perfect in Γ^s there exists a sequence $\{s(\varepsilon)\}_{\varepsilon\downarrow 0}$ which converges to s, such that $C(s(\varepsilon)) = B(s)$ and such that s is a best reply against $s(\varepsilon)$ for every $\varepsilon > 0$. In this case, we have that $(s_1,s_2(\varepsilon))$ and $(s_1(\varepsilon),s_2)$ are both equilibria of Γ, for any $\varepsilon > 0$. Since s is isolated, we therefore have $s_1(\varepsilon) = s_1$ and $s_2(\varepsilon) = s_2$, for all ε sufficiently close to zero, which implies that $C(s) = B(s)$. Hence, s is a quasi-strong equilibrium of Γ. In view of Lemma 3.3.1, it remains to be shown that the matrices A_1 and A_2, as defined in (3.3.1)-(3.3.4) are nonsingular. Assume $x_2^s \in X_2^s$ is such that $A_1(x_2^s) = 0$. Let x_2 be the extension of x_2^s to X_2 and, for $\varepsilon > 0$, let $\bar{s}_2(\varepsilon) = s_2 + \varepsilon x_2$. For ε sufficiently close to zero, we have that $\bar{s}_2(\varepsilon) \in S_2$ and that $(s_1,\bar{s}_2(\varepsilon))$ is an equilibrium of Γ. Since s is isolated, we have $\bar{s}_2(\varepsilon) = s_2$ for ε close to zero and, therefore, $x_2 = 0$. Hence, A_1 is column-regular. Similarly, it can be shown that A_2 is row-regular, from which it follows that both matrices are square and nonsingular. □

If s is a regular equilibrium, then s is quasi-strong, as we know from Corollary 2.5.3. Furthermore, if s is a quasi-strong equilibrium of a bimatrix game Γ, then s is a completely mixed equilibrium of Γ^s. Since every completely mixed equilibrium is perfect, we immediately deduce from Theorem 3.4.1:

COROLLARY 3.4.2. An equilibrium of a bimatrix game is regular if and only if it is isolated and quasi-strong.

The game of figure 1.5.3 shows, that a perfect equilibrium s of a bimatrix game Γ is not necessarily a perfect equilibrium of the s-restriction Γ^s of Γ (namely take $s = (M_1, M_2)$) and consequently a perfect and isolated equilibrium of a bimatrix game need not be regular (it is easily verified, that (M_1, M_2) is an isolated, though not a regular equilibrium of the game of figure 1.5.3). Next, we will show, that a weakly proper equilibrium of Γ has the property that it is perfect in Γ^s, from which it can be concluded that a weakly proper and isolated equilibrium is regular.

LEMMA 3.4.3. Let s be a weakly proper equilibrium of the bimatrix game $\Gamma = (\Phi_1, \Phi_2, R_1, R_2)$. Then s is a perfect equilibrium of the s-restriction Γ^s of Γ.

PROOF. In view of Theorem 3.2.2, it suffices to show that s is undominated in Γ^s. Assume s_1 is dominated by s_1' in Γ^s and let $\ell' \in \Phi_2^s$ $(=B_2(s))$ be such that

$$R_1(s_1', \ell') > R_1(s_1, \ell') \ .$$

Let the sequence $\{s(\varepsilon)\}_{\varepsilon \downarrow 0}$ be as in definition 2.3.4. Notice that, if $\ell \in \Phi_2 \setminus B_2(s)$, then

$$s_2^{\ell}(\varepsilon) \le \varepsilon s_2^{\ell'}(\varepsilon) \ .$$

Let M be defined by

$$M = \max\{R_1(k, \ell);\ k \in \Phi_1, \ell \in \Phi_2\} \ .$$

Then we have, for ε sufficiently close to zero

$$R_1(s_1', s_2(\varepsilon)) - R_1(s_1, s_2(\varepsilon)) = R_1(s_1' - s_1, s_2(\varepsilon))$$

$$= \sum_{\ell \in B_2(s)} R_1(s_1' - s_1, \ell) s_2^{\ell}(\varepsilon) + \sum_{\ell \notin B_2(s)} R_1(s_1' - s_1, \ell) s_2^{\ell}(\varepsilon)$$

$$\ge R_1(s_1' - s_1, \ell') s_2^{\ell'}(\varepsilon) - 2M \sum_{\ell \notin B_2(s)} s_2^{\ell}(\varepsilon)$$

$$\geq R_1(s_1' - s_1,\ell')s_2^{\ell'}(\varepsilon) - 2Mm_2\varepsilon s_2^{\ell'}(\varepsilon) > 0,$$

which contradicts the definition of $\{s(\varepsilon)\}_{\varepsilon\downarrow o}$. Hence, s_1 is undominated in Γ^s. similarly, it can be shown that s_2 is undominated in Γ^s. Hence, s is a perfect equilibrium of Γ^s. □

By combining Lemma 2.4.3 with the Theorems 3.4.1, 2.3.6, 2.4.3 and the Corollaries 2.5.6 and 2.5.7, we see that regular equilibria can be characterized as follows:

THEOREM 3.4.4. For a bimatrix game Γ, the following assertions are equivalent:

(i) s is a regular equilibrium of Γ,

(ii) s is an isolated and weakly proper equilibrium of Γ,

(iii) s is an isolated and strictly perfect equilibrium of Γ, and

(iv) s is an isolated and essential equilibrium of Γ.

The last characterization of regular equilibria which we give, is

THEOREM 3.4.5. (cf. JANSEN [1981b], Theorem 7.4). An equilibrium of a bimatrix game is regular if and only if it is essential and quasi-strong.

PROOF. The only if part of the theorem follows from Corollary 2.5.3 and Corollary 2.5.6. Next, assume $s = (s_1,s_2)$ is an essential and quasi-strong equilibrium of the bimatrix game $\Gamma = (\Phi_1,\Phi_2,R_1,R_2)$. Without loss of generality, assume that all payoffs in Γ are positive. In view of Theorem 3.3.2 it suffices to show that R_1^s and R_2^s are nonsingular. Assume R_1^s is row-singular and let $x_1 \in X_1^s$ be such that $x_1 \neq 0$ and $R_1^s(x_1) = 0$. Without loss of generality assume $x_1^1 \neq 0$ and, for $\varepsilon > 0$, define the bimatrix game $\Gamma^{s,\varepsilon} = (\Phi_1^s,\Phi_2^s,R_1^{s,\varepsilon},R_2^s)$ by:

$$R_1^{s,\varepsilon}(1,\ell) = R_1^s(1,\ell) + \varepsilon \qquad \text{for } \ell \in \Phi_2^s, \text{ and}$$

$$R_1^{s,\varepsilon}(k,\ell) = R_1^s(k,\ell) \qquad \text{for } k \in \Phi_1^s,\ \ell \in \Phi_2^s,\ k \neq 1.$$

Since s is an essential equilibrium of Γ, we have that s is an essential equilibrium of Γ^s and, therefore, if ε is sufficiently close to zero, there exists an equilibrium $s(\varepsilon)$ of $\Gamma^{s,\varepsilon}$ which is close to s. In this case we have:

$$\varepsilon x_1^1 = \varepsilon x_1^1 + R_1(x_1,s_2(\varepsilon)) = R_1^{s,\varepsilon}(x_1,s_2(\varepsilon)) = x_1(\Phi_1^s)R_1^{s,\varepsilon}(s(\varepsilon)).$$

Therefore, $x_1(\Phi_1^s) \neq 0$ and $R_1(s) = \lim_{\varepsilon\to o} R_1^{s,\varepsilon}(s(\varepsilon)) = 0,$

but this contradicts our assumption that all payoffs in Γ are positive. Hence, R_1^s is row-regular. Similarly, it can be shown that R_2^s is column-regular and, therefore, R_1^s and R_2^s are both nonsingular, which implies that s is a regular equilibrium of Γ. □

We conclude this section by presenting an example which illustrates, that the results obtained in this section are not true for games with more than two players. Consider the 3-person game of figure 3.4.1.

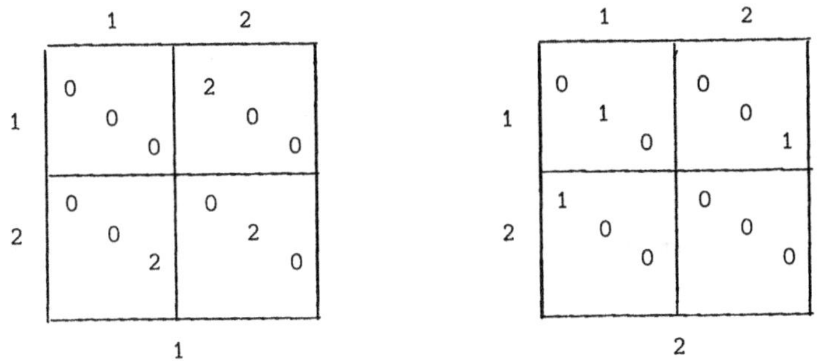

Figure 3.4.1. The results of this section cannot be generalized to games with more than two players.

The reader can verify, that this game has exactly two equilibria, viz. $\varphi = (\varphi_1,\varphi_2,\varphi_3) = (1,1,1)$ and $\bar{\varphi} = (\bar{\varphi}_1,\bar{\varphi}_2,\bar{\varphi}_3) = (2,2,2)$. We will show that the second equilibrium is not perfect. Let $s = (s_1,s_2,s_3)$ be a mixed strategy combination. Then, we have:

$\bar{\varphi}_1$ is a best reply against s if and only if $2s_2^2s_3^1 \leq s_2^1s_3^2$,

$\bar{\varphi}_2$ is a best reply against s if and only if $s_1^1s_3^2 \leq 2s_1^2s_3^1$, and

$\bar{\varphi}_3$ is a best reply against s if and only if $2s_1^2s_2^1 \leq s_1^1s_2^2$,

from which it follows that

$$\text{if } \bar{\varphi} \text{ is a best reply against s, then } s_2^1 = 0 \text{ or } s_2^2 = 0.$$

Hence, there does not exist a completely mixed strategy combination s such that $\bar{\varphi}$ is a best reply against s, and so $\bar{\varphi}$ is not perfect. Since this game possesses at least one essential equilibrium (by Theorem 2.4.2) and since $\bar{\varphi}$ is not essential (Theorem 2.4.3), we have that φ is essential. Hence, φ is also strictly perfect and weakly proper. Moreover, φ is even proper, since in a game in which each player has just 2 pure strategies, every perfect equilibrium is proper. So, φ is an isolated, essential,

strictly perfect and proper equilibrium. This equilibrium, however, is not regular, since it is not quasi-strong.
Notice that this example shows, that a game with finitely many equilibria need not possess a regular equilibrium and that there exist games without quasi-strong equilibria (the latter phenomenon has also been observed in OKADA [1982]).

3.5. MATRIX GAMES

In this section, we consider matrix games, i.e. 2-person zero-sum games in normal form. We concentrate on proper equilibria and show that an equilibrium is proper if and only if both equilibrium strategies are optimal in the sense of DRESHER [1961].

Let us first briefly consider the question which conditions an equilibrium has to satisfy in order to be regular. In section 3.1, we have seen that the set of equilibria of a matrix game is convex and, therefore, we can conclude from Corollary 2.5.7 that, if s is a regular equilibrium of a matrix game Γ, then s is the unique equilibrium of Γ. Conversely, if s is the unique equilibrium of Γ, then s is isolated and proper (since every game has a proper equilibrium) and, therefore, in view of Theorem 3.4.4, regular. So, we have proved:

<u>THEOREM 3.5.1</u>. s is a regular equilibrium of a matrix game Γ if and only if s is the unique equilibrium of Γ.

In BOHNENBLUST, KARLIN AND SHAPLEY [1950] it is shown, that the set of all matrix games with a unique equilibrium is open and dense in the set of all matrix games. By similar methods as the ones used in the proof of Theorem 2.6.1, we can prove the slightly stronger result, that, within the set of all matrix games, the set of games with an irregular equilibrium is closed and has Lebesque measure zero. Hence, we have:

<u>THEOREM 3.5.2</u>. Almost all matrix games have a unique equilibrium.

Hence, if a matrix game is "nondegenerate", it has a unique equilibrium. However, in practice one almost always encounters degenerate games with more than one equilibrium and so the result of Theorem 3.5.2 is not as strong as it might look at first sight. Therefore, in the remainder of this section, we will consider matrix games with more than one equilibrium and we will investigate whether there exists an equilibrium which should be preferred to all others.
If, in a matix game Γ, player 1 has more than one optimal (i.e. equilibrium, maximin) strategy, then by using any of these he can guarantee himself a payoff of at least $v(\Gamma)$. If, moreover, his opponent also uses an optimal strategy, then every optimal strategy of player 1 yields exactly $v(\Gamma)$ and so, if both players play optimally, there

is no reason to prefer one optimal strategy to another. However, if player 1 considers the possibility, that his opponent may make a mistake and may, therefore, fail to choose an optimal strategy, then by playing a specific optimal strategy he can perhaps take maximal advantage of such a mistake. Hence, the question which has to be considered is: which strategy should be chosen in order to exploit the potential mistakes of the opponent optimally?[1] One approach in trying to solve this problem, is to restrict oneself to perfect equilibria. The game of figure 3.5.1 shows that this approach does not always lead to a definite answer:

	1	2	3
1	1	2	3
2	1	1	4

Figure 3.5.1. Which strategy should be chosen by player 1 in order to exploit the mistakes of player 2 optimally?

In this game all equilibria are perfect: if player 1 expects that player 2 will choose his second pure strategy with a greater probability than his third, then he should play his first strategy; if he expects the third pure strategy of player 2 to occur with the greater probability, then he should play his second strategy; and if he expects both mistakes to occur with the same probability, then all his strategies are equally good. Hence, if one follows this approach, one has to know how the opponent makes his mistakes, in order to obtain a definite answer.

If one expects that the opponent will make a more costly mistake with a much smaller probability than a less costly one and, hence, that the opponent makes his mistakes in a more or less rational way, one is led to proper equilibria. According to the properness concept in the game of figure 3.5.1, player 2 will mistakenly choose his second strategy with a much greater probability than his third strategy and, therefore, player 1 should play his first strategy. Hence, in this example, the properness concept leads to a definite answer. Below, we will prove that the same is the case for any matrix game. To be more precise, we will prove that proper equilibria of a matrix game Γ are equivalent, where two strategy pairs s and s' are said to be *equivalent* in Γ if

$$R(s_1,\ell) = R(s_1',\ell) \text{ for all } \ell \in \Phi_2, \text{ and}$$

$$R(k,s_2) = R(k,s_2') \text{ for all } k \in \Phi_1.$$

1) This question has also been considered in PONSSARD [1976].

A slightly different approach to solve the problem has been proposed in DRESHER [1961]. This approach amounts to a lexicographic application of the maximin criterion. The idea underlying it is, that, since one does not know beforehand which mistake will be made by the opponent, one should follow a conservative plan of action and maximize the minimum gain resulting from the opponent's mistakes. If, in the game of figure 3.5.1, player 1 behaves in this way, then he will play his first strategy, since this strategy guarantees a payoff 2 if player 2 makes a mistake, whereas his second strategy guarantees only 1 in this case. Hence, in this example, Dresher's approach yields a definite answer, which is the same as the one given by the properness concept (which is no coincidence, as we will see in Theorem 3.5.5).

For a matrix game $\Gamma = (\Phi_1,\Phi_2,R)$ Dresher's procedure to select a particular optimal strategy of player 1 is described as follows:

(i) Set t := 0, write $\Phi_1^t := \Phi_1$, $\Phi_2^t := \Phi_2$ and $\Gamma^t := (\Phi_1^t,\Phi_2^t,R)$. Compute $O_1(\Gamma^t)$, i.e. the set of optimal strategies of player 1 in the game Γ^t.

(ii) If all elements of $O_1(\Gamma^t)$ are equivalent in Γ^t, then go to (v), otherwise go to (iii).

(iii) Assume that player 2 makes a mistake in Γ^t, i.e. that he assigns a positive probability only to the pure strategies which yield player 1 a payoff greater than $v(\Gamma^t)$. Hence, restrict his pure strategy set to $\Phi_2^t \backslash C_2(\Gamma^t)$.

(iv) Determine the optimal strategies of player 1 which maximize the minimum gain resulting from mistakes of player 2. Hence, compute the optimal strategies of player 1 in the game $\Gamma^{t+1} := (\Phi_1^{t+1},\Phi_2^{t+1},R)$, where $\Phi_1^{t+1} := \text{ext } O_1(\Gamma^t)$ is the (finite) set of extreme optimal strategies of player 1 in Γ^t and $\Phi_2^{t+1} := \Phi_2^t \backslash C_2(\Gamma^t)$. Replace t by t+1 and repeat step (ii).

(v) The set of *Dresher-optimal* (or shortly *D-optimal strategies*) of player 1 in Γ is the set $D_1(\Gamma) := O_1(\Gamma^t)$.

Note that $D_1(\Gamma)$ is well-defined, since in each iteration the number of permissible pure strategies of player 2 decreases with at least one, such that, eventually, all remaining optimal strategies of player 1 must be equivalent in Γ^t. We claim that all D-optimal strategies of player 1 in Γ are, in fact, equivalent in Γ. Let $s_1, s_1' \in D_1(\Gamma)$ and let $\Gamma^0,\dots,\Gamma^\tau$ be the sequence of games generated by the above procedure. Then s_1, s_1' are equivalent in Γ^τ, by the definition of $D_1(\Gamma)$. But then s_1 and s_1' are also equivalent in $\Gamma^{\tau-1}$ since every element ℓ of $\Phi_2^{\tau-1}$ is either an element of $C_2(\Gamma^{\tau-1})$, in which case s_1 and s_1' both yield $v(\Gamma^{\tau-1})$ against ℓ, or an element of Φ_2^τ, in which case s_1 and s_1' yield the same against ℓ, since s_1 and s_1' are equivalent in Γ^τ. Hence, inductively it can be proved that s_1 and s_1' are equivalent in Γ^t for all $t \in \{0,\dots,\tau\}$, which shows, that s_1 and s_1' are equivalent in Γ.

It will be clear that by reversing the roles of the players one obtains a procedure for selecting a particular optimal strategy (or more precisely a particular class of equivalent optimal strategies) of player 2. The set of all D-optimal strategies of player 2 in Γ will be denoted by $D_2(\Gamma)$, and the product $D_1(\Gamma) \times D_2(\Gamma)$ will be denoted by $D(\Gamma)$. We have already seen:

LEMMA 3.5.3. If $s,s' \in D(\Gamma)$, then s and s' are equivalent.

From the description of Dresher's procedure it will be clear that a D-optimal strategy cannot be dominated. Hence, by Theorem 3.2.2, we have

THEOREM 3.5.4. A pair of D-optimal strategies constitutes a perfect equilibrium.

We have already seen, that the converse of Theorem 3.5.4 is false: in the game of figure 3.5.1 only (1,1) is D-optimal, whereas all equilibria are perfect. This is not really surprising, since the perfectness concept allows all kinds of mistakes, whereas player 1 assumes, if he plays a D-optimal strategy, that his opponent makes his mistakes as if he actually wishes to minimize player 1's gain resulting from his mistakes. Hence, by playing a D-optimal strategy you optimally exploit the mistakes of your opponent only if he makes his mistakes in a rational way. Based on this observation, one might conjecture that D-optimal strategies are related to proper equilibria. In the following theorem, we prove that this conjecture is correct.

THEOREM 3.5.5. For matrix games, the following assertions are equivalent:

(i) s is a proper equilibrium,

(ii) s is a weakly proper equilibrium,

(iii) s is a D-optimal strategy pair.

PROOF. Let $\Gamma = (\Phi_1,\Phi_2,R)$ be a matrix game. It suffices to show that (ii) implies (iii) and that (iii) implies (i).

(ii) $\rightarrow$ (iii). Let $s = (s_1,s_2)$ be a weakly proper equilibrium of Γ and let $\{s(\varepsilon)\}_{\varepsilon \downarrow 0}$ be as in Definition 2.3.4. We will show that $s_1 \in D_1(\Gamma)$. Let $\Gamma^0,\ldots,\Gamma^\tau$ be the sequence of games generated by Dresher's procedure for player 1. We have that $s_1 \in D_1(\Gamma)$ if and only if $s_1 \in O_1(\Gamma^t)$ for all $t \in \{0,\ldots,\tau\}$. We will show, by using induction with respect to t, that s_1 has the latter property.

First of all, $s_1 \in O_1(\Gamma^0)$, since s is an equilibrium of Γ.

Next, assume $t \in \{1,\ldots,\tau\}$ is such that

$$s_1 \in O_1(\Gamma^{t'}) \text{ for all } t' \in \{0,\ldots,t-1\}, s_1 \notin O_1(\Gamma^t).$$

Let $\bar{s}_1 \in O_1(\Gamma^t)$. Then $\bar{s}_1 \in O_1(\Gamma^{t'})$ for all $t' \in \{0,\ldots,t\}$ and, therefore

$$(3.5.1) \qquad R(s_1,\ell) = R(\bar{s}_1,\ell) \qquad \text{for all } \ell \in \Phi_2 \backslash \Phi_2^t .$$

Since $s_1 \notin O_1(\Gamma^t)$, there exists some $\ell \in \Phi_2^t$ such that

(3.5.2) $$R(s_1,\ell) < v(\Gamma^t) .$$

Let Ψ_2^t be the set of all $\ell \in \Phi_2^t$ for which (3.5.2) is satisfied. Since $\bar{s}_1 \in O_1(\Gamma^t)$, we have

(3.5.3) $$R(s_1,\ell) < v(\Gamma^t) \le R(\bar{s}_1,\ell) \qquad \text{for all } \ell \in \Psi_2^t .$$

Furthermore, if $k \in \Phi_2^t \backslash \Psi_2^t$ and $\ell \in \Psi_2^t$, then

$$R(s_1,\ell) < v(\Gamma^t) \le R(s_1,k).$$

from which it follows, by definition of $s(\varepsilon)$, that

(3.5.4) $$s_2^k(\varepsilon) \le \varepsilon s_2^\ell(\varepsilon) \qquad \text{for all } k \in \Phi_2^t \backslash \Psi_2^t \text{ and } \ell \in \Psi_2^t .$$

By using (3.5.1), (3.5.3) and (3.5.4) one can show, similarly as in the proof of Lemma 3.4.3, that

$$R(\bar{s}_1,s_2(\varepsilon)) > R(s_1,s_2(\varepsilon)) \qquad \text{for all } \varepsilon \text{ sufficiently close to zero,}$$

but this contradicts the definition of $\{s(\varepsilon)\}_{\varepsilon\downarrow 0}$. This establishes the induction step, and so $s_1 \in O_1(\Gamma^t)$, for all $t \in \{0,\ldots\tau\}$. Hence, $s_1 \in D_1(\Gamma)$. Similarly, it can be shown, that $s_2 \in D_2(\Gamma)$.

<u>(iii) → (i)</u>. Assume $s \doteq (s_1,s_2) \in D(\Gamma)$ and let $\bar{s} = (\bar{s}_1,\bar{s}_2)$ be a proper equilibrium of Γ. From the first part of the theorem, it follows that $\bar{s} \in D(\Gamma)$, hence, by Lemma 3.5.3, we have that s and $\bar{s}$ are equivalent. For $\varepsilon > 0$, let $\bar{s}(\varepsilon)$ be an ε-proper equilibrium of Γ such that $\bar{s}(\varepsilon)$ converges to $\bar{s}$, as ε tends to zero. Define $s(\varepsilon)$ by:

$$s_i(\varepsilon) = (1-\varepsilon)s_i + \varepsilon\bar{s}_i(\varepsilon) \qquad \text{for } i \in \{1,2\} .$$

We will show that $s(\varepsilon)$ is an ε-proper equilibrium of Γ, if ε is sufficiently close to zero. It is clear that $s(\varepsilon)$ is completely mixed. Assume $k,\ell \in \Phi_1$ and $\varepsilon > 0$ are such that

$$R(k,s_2(\varepsilon)) < R(\ell,s_2(\varepsilon)) .$$

Then we have, if ε is sufficiently close to zero

(3.5.6) $$R(k,s_2) < R(\ell,s_2) \text{ or } [R(k,s_2) = R(\ell,s_2) \text{ and } R(k,\bar{s}_2(\varepsilon)) < R(\ell,\bar{s}_2(\varepsilon))] .$$

Since s_2 is equivalent to $\bar{s}_2$, formula (3.5.6) is equivalent to

(3.5.7) $$R(k,\bar{s}_2) < R(\ell,\bar{s}_2) \text{ or } [R(k,\bar{s}_2) = R(\ell,\bar{s}_2) \text{ and } R(k,\bar{s}_2(\varepsilon)) < R(\ell,\bar{s}_2(\varepsilon))] .$$

If ε is sufficiently close to zero, (3.5.7) implies

(3.5.8) $$R(k,\bar{s}_2(\varepsilon)) < R(\ell,\bar{s}_2(\varepsilon)) ,$$

and, therefore, if (3.5.5) is satisfied, we have

$$\bar{s}_1^k(\varepsilon) \leq \varepsilon\bar{s}_1^\ell(\varepsilon),$$

since $\bar{s}(\varepsilon)$ is an ε-proper equilibrium of Γ. From Lemma 2.3.2 we know that $\bar{s}_1$ is a best reply against $\bar{s}_2(\varepsilon)$, if ε is small, which implies, since s_1 is equivalent to $\bar{s}_1$, that s_1 is a best reply against $\bar{s}_2(\varepsilon)$, if ε is small. Hence, if (3.5.8) is satisfied and ε is small, then $s_1^k = 0$. Therefore we have, if ε is sufficiently small and if (3.5.5) is satisfied

$$s_1^k(\varepsilon) = (1-\varepsilon)s_1^k + \varepsilon\bar{s}_1^k(\varepsilon) = \varepsilon\bar{s}_1^k(\varepsilon) \leq (\varepsilon)^2\bar{s}_1^\ell(\varepsilon) \leq \varepsilon s_1^\ell(\varepsilon) .$$

Similarly, we can prove, that for all ε sufficiently close to zero

$$\text{if } R(s_1(\varepsilon),k) > R(s_1(\varepsilon),\ell), \text{ then } s_2^k(\varepsilon) \leq \varepsilon s_2^\ell(\varepsilon) \qquad \text{for all } k,\ell \in \Phi_2,$$

and, therefore, $s(\varepsilon)$ is an ε-proper equilibrium of Γ, if ε is sufficiently close to zero. Hence, s is a proper equilibrium of Γ. □

Since the set of D-optimal strategies of a matrix game can easily be determined (the only thing one has to do is to compute the optimal strategy sets of a finite number of matrix games, which is an easy task, cf. BALINSKI [1961]), we have, as a consequence of the theorem above, that a proper equilibrium of a matrix game can be computed easily. Furthermore, as a consequence of Lemma 3.5.3 and Theorem 3.5.5 we have

<u>COROLLARY 3.5.6</u>. If s,s' are weakly proper equilibria of a matrix game , then s and s' are equivalent.

So, a matrix game has essentially one (weakly) proper equilibrium and, therefore if one expects the opponent to make his mistakes in a rational way, there is a unique way to exploit these mistakes optimally.

CHAPTER 4

CONTROL COSTS

In this chapter, games with control costs[1] are studied. These are normal form games in which each player, in addition to receiving his payoff from the game, incurs costs depending on how well he chooses to control his actions. Such a game models the idea that a player can reduce the probability of making mistakes, but that he can only do so by being extra prudent, hence, by spending an extra effort, which involves some costs. The goal of the chapter is to investigate what the consequences are of viewing an ordinary normal form game as a limiting case of a game with control costs, i.e. it is examined which equilibria are still viable when infinitesimally control costs are incorporated into the analysis of normal form games.

In section 4.1, the motives for studying games with control costs are discussed and the formal definition of such a game is given, while it is shown in section 4.2, that a game with control costs always possesses at least one equilibrium. In this section, also a characterization of equilibria of such a game is derived.

In section 4.3, a first analysis is performed on the question of which equilibria of an ordinary normal form game are still viable when control costs are taken into account, i.e. it is investigated which equilibria can be approximated by equilibria of games with control costs as these costs go to zero. It is shown that the set of equilibria which are approximated may depend on the control costs and that there exist equilibria (even perfect ones) which cannot be approximated.

In section 4.4, it is shown that the basic assumption underlying the properness concept, viz. that a more costly mistake is made with a probability which is of smaller order, cannot be justified by the control cost approach. Namely, if the players incur control costs, then a non-optimal strategy is chosen with a probability which is inversely proportional to the loss which is incurred if this strategy is played.

In section 4.5, it is investigated whether control costs result in playing a perfect equilibrium. It is shown that this is the case only if the control costs are sufficiently high. For the special case of a bimatrix game, an exact formulation of

1) The idea to study such games was raised by R.Selten.

the control costs being sufficiently high is given.
Finally, it is shown in section 4.6, that a regular equilibrium is always approximated by equilibria of games with control costs as these costs go to zero.
The material in this chapter is based on VAN DAMME [1982].

4.1. INTRODUCTION

Consider the 2-person normal form game of figure 4.1.1, in which M is some positive real number.

	1	2	3
1	2, 2	1, 1	0, 0
2	2, 2	0, 1	M, 0

Figure 4.1.1. A bimatrix game to illustrate undesirable properties of the perfectness concept and the properness concept.

The equilibria of this game are the strategy pairs in which player 2 plays his first strategy. What player 1 should do depends on how player 2 makes his mistakes. If we write p_k for the probability that player 2 mistakenly chooses k ($k \in \{2,3\}$), then

if $p_2 > Mp_3$, player 1 should play his first strategy,

if $p_2 = Mp_3$, player 1 can play anything, and

if $p_2 < Mp_3$, player 1 should play his second strategy.

The perfectness concept does not give an opinion on which of these cases will prevail and, consequently, all equilibria are perfect. If player 1 believes in the properness concept (or weakly properness concept), however, then he should always (no matter what the value of M is) choose his first strategy, since, according to this concept, p_3 is of smaller order than p_2, as a consequence of the fact that player 2 tries much harder to prevent playing his third strategy by mistake.
In this game both the perfectness concept and the properness concept yield unsatisfactory answers: the perfectness concept does not discriminate between the Nash equilibria and the properness concept yields a solution which is independent of M, whereas, intuitively, one would say that player 1 should choose his first strategy for small values of M and his second strategy for large values of M.

The game of figure 4.1.1 illustrates a phenomenon which occurs for many games: Since the perfectness concept allows for all kinds of mistakes, there exists a plethora of perfect equilibria, some of which are unreasonable; Contrary to this, the properness concept severely restricts the possibilities for making mistakes, such that some unreasonable perfect equilibria are excluded. However, it is unclear whether it is appropriate to restrict oneself to proper equilibria, since the basic assumption underlying this concept (viz. that more costly mistakes occur with a probability which is of smaller order) is questionable. In this chapter, as well as in the next one, we investigate whether this assumption can be justified. It will be clear that, in order to judge the reasonableness of this assumption and in order to be able to refine the perfectness concept in a well-founded way, one needs a model in which the mistake probabilities are endogenously determined, rather than a model in which these probabilities can be chosen in some ad hoc way. In this chapter, one such model is developed. A second model will be considered in the next chapter.

Obviously, the reason that the players make mistakes, lies in the fact that they are not as careful as is needed to prevent these mistakes. In this chapter, we elaborate the idea that the players are not as careful as is needed simply because it is too costly to be so careful. The basic idea behind the approach of this chapter is that a player can reduce his probability of making mistakes, but that this probability can be reduced only by being extra careful. If a player wants to be extra careful, this means that he actually has to do something, i.e. that he has to spend an extra effort which involves some costs. Hence, in this chapter, we assume that a player can reduce his probability of making mistakes, but that he incurs costs in doing so. Obviously, the more a player wants to reduce his mistake probability, the more effort he has to spend and, hence, the higher the cost he incurs. Furthermore, it will be clear that, if it becomes increasingly difficult (i.e. increasingly costly) to reduce the mistake probability further and further, then a player will choose to prevent mistakes only to a certain level and, hence, each player will make mistakes with a positive probability. In this chapter, this is viewed as the basic reason why mistakes occur and it is investigated what the consequences of this view are, i.e. it is investigated whether this view leads to a refinement of the perfectness concept, whether it leads to a justification of the properness concept, etc.

Next, let us state the ideas outlined above more precisely. For the remainder of this section, let an n-person normal form game $\Gamma = (\Phi_1,\ldots,\Phi_n,R_1,\ldots,R_n)$ be fixed. Let s_i be a mixed strategy of player i in Γ. We will assume that player i incurs control costs $\sum_k f_i^k(s_i^k)$ if he wants to play s_i in Γ, where f_i^k represents the cost player i incurs due to his special attention to the strategy k. We will assume that player i can control all his pure strategies equally good (or equally bad), which implies that all f_i^k are equal to some function f_i. Hence, we assume (although the theory could as well be developed without this assumption, however, see the end of section 4.3):

ASSUMPTION 4.1.1. $f_i^1 = \ldots = f_i^k \ldots = f_i^{m_i} =: f_i$.

The function f_i is called the control cost function of player i.
The following assumption has been motivated above.

ASSUMPTION 4.1.2. $f_i : [0,1] \to \mathbb{R} \cup \{\infty\}$ is a decreasing function with $f_i(0) = \infty$.

Notice that we allow a control cost function to take the value ∞. From the fact that f_i is decreasing it follows, however, that $f_i(x) < \infty$ if $x > 0$. The conventions which will be used with respect to $-\infty$ and ∞ are the same as in ROCKEFELLAR [1970].
The exact formulation of the assumption, that it becomes increasingly difficult for player i to decrease his mistake probability further and further, is

$$\text{if } 0 < \varepsilon < x < y, \quad \text{then} \quad f_i(x - \varepsilon) - f_i(x) > f_i(y - \varepsilon) - f_i(y),$$

which is equivalent to saying that f_i is strictly convex.

ASSUMPTION 4.1.3. f_i is a strictly convex function.

Finally, we make an additional assumption for mathematical convenience.

ASSUMPTION 4.1.4. f_i is at least twice differentiable.

From now on, a *control cost function*, is a function for which the Assumptions 4.1.2 - 4.1.4 are satisfied. Let $f = (f_1, \ldots f_n)$ be an n-tuple of such functions. If, in the game Γ, each player i, in addition to receiving a payoff as described by R_i, incurs a cost as determined by f_i, then the strategic situation is more adequately described by the infinite normal form game $\Gamma^f = (S_1, \ldots S_n, R_1^f, \ldots, R_n^f)$, where

$$R_i^f(s) := R_i(s) - \sum_k f_i(s_i^k) \qquad \text{for } i \in N,\ s \in S.$$

The game Γ^f is called a *game with control costs*. Note that in such a game a payoff of $-\infty$ can occur. Strategically, however, this is irrelevant, since each player can guarantee a finite payoff by playing a completely mixed strategy.

If control costs are present in an ordinary normal form game, these costs will be of much less importance than the ordinary payoffs of the game. This can be modelled by considering infinitesimally small control costs, i.e. by approximating an ordinary normal form game Γ with games $\Gamma^{\varepsilon f}$ by letting ε go to zero. In this chapter, it is investigated what the consequences are of doing so. Hence, we examine which equilibria of Γ are approximated by equilibria of $\Gamma^{\varepsilon f}$ as ε goes to zero. Such equilibria are called f-approachable equilibria, and we are particularly interested in aspects as:

(i) How does the set of f-approachable equilibria depend on f?

(ii) Is an f-approachable equilibrium perfect (resp. proper)?

(iii) Is a perfect (resp. proper) equilibrium f-approachable?

Before considering these questions, let us first study games with control cost in somewhat greater detail.

4.2. GAMES WITH CONTROL COSTS

In this section, we prove some elementary properties of games with control costs. In particular it is shown, that any such game possesses at least one equilibrium. Furthermore, a condition which is necessary and sufficient for a strategy combination to be an equilibrium is derived.

Throughout the section we consider a fixed n-person normal form game $\Gamma = (\Phi_1,\ldots,\Phi_n,R_1,\ldots,R_n)$ and a fixed n-tuple of control cost functions $f = (f_1,\ldots,f_n)$. We write S_i for the set of mixed strategies of player i and, if $\varepsilon > 0$, then

$$(4.2.1) \qquad S_i(\varepsilon) := \{s_i \in S_i \;;\; s_i^k \geq \varepsilon \text{ for all } k\}, \quad S(\varepsilon) = \prod_{i=n}^{n} S_i(\varepsilon).$$

The object of study is the game Γ^f, defined as in the previous section. Throughout the section, when we speak of a best reply, we will mean a best reply in Γ^f.

LEMMA 4.2.1. There exists some $\varepsilon > 0$, such that for all $\bar{s} \in S$: if s is a best reply against $\bar{s}$, then $s \in S(\varepsilon)$.

PROOF. Let s' be an arbitrary completely mixed strategy combination. Since $f_i(0) = \infty$, we have for each $i \in N$ and $k \in \Phi_i$,

$$\lim_{s_i^k \to 0} R_i^f(\bar{s}\backslash s_i) < R_i^f(\bar{s}\backslash s_i'),$$

which proves the lemma. □

LEMMA 4.2.2. Every strategy combination has a unique best reply. The mapping which assigns to each strategy combination its best reply is continuous.

PROOF. Let $\bar{s} \in S$, let $\varepsilon > 0$ be as in Lemma 4.2.1 and let $i \in N$. From Lemma 4.2.1, we know that every best reply of player i against $\bar{s}$ is an element of $S_i(\varepsilon)$. Since

$S_i(\varepsilon)$ is compact and since $s_i \to R_i^f(\bar{s}\backslash s_i)$ is continuous on $S_i(\varepsilon)$, we have that a best reply of player i against $\bar{s}$ exists. The best reply of player i must be unique, since the mapping $s_i \to R_i^f(\bar{s}\backslash s_i)$ is strictly concave. Continuity follows in a standard way. □

The unique best reply against $\bar{s} \in S$ in the game Γ^f will be denoted by $b(\bar{s},f) = (b_1(\bar{s},f),\ldots,b_n(\bar{s},f))$. We have

LEMMA 4.2.3. If $s,\bar{s} \in S$, then $s = b(\bar{s},f)$ if and only if s is a solution to the following set of equations:

(4.2.2) $$R_i(\bar{s}\backslash k) - R_i(\bar{s}\backslash \ell) = f_i'(s_i^k) - f_i'(s_i^\ell) \qquad \text{for all } i \in N,\ k,\ell \in \Phi_i.$$

PROOF. $s = b(\bar{s},f)$ if and only if for each $i \in N$ we have that s_i is a solution of the convex programming problem.

(4.2.3) $$\text{maximize } R_i^f(\bar{s}\backslash s_i)\ , \text{ subject to } s_i \in S_i.$$

Since every solution of (4.2.3) is in the interior of S_i, we have that $s_i \in S_i$ solves (4.2.3) if and only if

(4.2.4) $$\frac{\partial R_i^f(\bar{s}\backslash s_i)}{\partial s_i^k} = \lambda_i \qquad \text{for all } k \in \Phi_i\ ,$$

where $\lambda_i \in \mathbb{R}$ is a Lagrange multiplier. This completes the proof, since (4.2.2) is nothing else than a restatement of (4.2.4) □

Let $\bar{s} \in S$ and let $s = b(\bar{s},f)$. Formula (4.2.2) shows that

$$\text{if } R_i(\bar{s}\backslash k) < R_i(\bar{s}\backslash \ell)\ , \text{ then } f_i'(s_i^k) < f_i'(s_i^\ell) \qquad \text{for all } i \in N,\ k,\ell \in \Phi_i\ .$$

Since f_i is convex, f_i' is increasing and, therefore, we have

COROLLARY 4.2.4. Let $\bar{s} \in S$ and $s = b(\bar{s},f)$. Then

$$\text{if } R_i(\bar{s}\backslash k) < R_i(\bar{s},\ell)\ , \text{ then } s_i^k < s_i^\ell \qquad \text{for all } i \in N,\ k,\ell \in \Phi_i.$$

The following corollary of Lemma 4.2.3, will turn out to be useful in section 4.6:

LEMMA 4.2.5. Let $\bar{s} \in S$, $i \in N$, $\Psi_i \subset \Phi_i$ and $s_i \in S_i$. If s_i is such that

(4.2.5) $$R_i(\bar{s}\backslash k) - R_i(\bar{s}\backslash \ell) = f_i'(s_i^k) - f_i'(s_i^\ell) \qquad \text{for all } k,\ell \in \Psi_i, \text{ and}$$

(4.2.6) $$s_i^k = b_i^k(\bar{s},f) \qquad \text{for all } k \notin \Psi_i .$$

Then $s_i = b_i(\bar{s},f)$.

PROOF. From Lemma 4.2.3 we see that for all $k,\ell \in \Psi_i$:

$$f_i'(s_i^k) - f_i'(s_i^\ell) = R_i(\bar{s}\backslash k) - R_i(\bar{s}\backslash \ell) = f_i'(b_i^k(\bar{s},f)) - f_i'(b_i^\ell(\bar{s},f)) ,$$

from which it follows, by using the monotonicity of f_i', that

(4.2.7) $$\text{if } s_i^k < b_i^k(\bar{s},f) \text{ for some } k \in \Psi_i, \text{ then } s_i^k < b_i^k(\bar{s},f) \text{ for all } k \in \Psi_i.$$

Formula (4.2.6) has the consequence that

(4.2.8) $$\sum_{k\in\Psi_i} s_i^k = \sum_{k\in\Psi_i} b_i^k(\bar{s},f),$$

and so, by combining (4.2.7) and (4.2.8), we see that $s_i^k = b_i^k(\bar{s},f)$ for all $k \in \Psi_i$. □

By combining the results of the Lemmas 4.2.1 and 4.2.3, we obtain the main result of this section:

THEOREM 4.2.6. The game Γ^f possesses at least one equilibrium. All equilibria of Γ^f are completely mixed. A strategy combination $s \in S$ is an equilibrium of Γ^f if and only if s is a solution to the following set of equations

(4.2.9) $$R_i(s\backslash k) - R_i(s\backslash \ell) = f_i'(s_i^k) - f_i'(s_i^\ell) \qquad \text{for all } i \in N,\ k,\ell \in \Phi_i.$$

PROOF. Let ε be as in Lemma 4.2.1. It follows from that lemma, that s is an equilibrium of Γ^f if and only if s is an equilibrium of the game $(S_1(\varepsilon),\dots,S_n(\varepsilon),R_1^f,\dots,R_n^f)$. In view of Theorem 2.1.1, the latter game has an equilibrium and, hence, also Γ^f has an equilibrium. The other assertions of the theorem follow directly from Lemma 4.2.1 and Lemma 4.2.3. □

4.3. APPROACHABLE EQUILIBRIA

In this section, we start investigating the consequences of viewing an ordinary normal form game as a limiting case of a game with control costs. Hence, for an n-person normal form game Γ and an n-tuple of control cost functions f, we consider the question which strategy combinations of Γ are approached by equilibria of $\Gamma^{\varepsilon f}$ as ε tends to zero. Theorem 4.3.1 shows that only equilibria of Γ can be approached in this way.

Theorem 4.3.1. Let $\Gamma = (\Phi_1,\ldots,\Phi_n,R_1,\ldots,R_n)$ be an n-person normal form game and let $f = (f_1,\ldots,f_n)$ be an n-tuple of control cost functions. If $s \in S$ is the limit of a sequence $\{s(\varepsilon)\}_{\varepsilon \downarrow 0}$ with $s(\varepsilon) \in E(\Gamma^{\varepsilon f})$ for all ε, then s is an equilibrium of Γ.

PROOF. Assume s is the limit of such a sequence $\{s(\varepsilon)\}_{\varepsilon \downarrow 0}$. Let $i \in N$ and $k \in \Phi_i$. We have to prove that $s_i^k = 0$ if k is not a best reply against s in Γ. For $\varepsilon > 0$ and $\ell \in \Phi_i$, we have, by (4.2.9)

(4.3.1) $$R_i(s(\varepsilon)\backslash k) - R_i(s(\varepsilon)\backslash \ell) = \varepsilon[f_i'(s_i^k(\varepsilon)) - f_i'(s_i^\ell(\varepsilon))] .$$

If k is not a best reply against s in Γ, while ℓ is a best reply against s, then the limit (as ε tends to zero) of the left hand side of (4.3.1) is negative, hence, in this case we have

$$\lim_{\varepsilon \downarrow 0}[f_i'(s_i^k(\varepsilon)) - f_i'(s_i^\ell(\varepsilon))] = -\infty,$$

which implies, since f_i is decreasing, that $s_i^k(\varepsilon)$ converges to zero, as ε tends to zero. Hence, $s_i^k = 0$, if k is not a best reply against s in Γ. □

If one holds the view, that the players in a normal form game always incur some infinitely small control costs, then one can consider as being reasonable only those equilibria which can be obtained as a limit in the way of Theorem 4.3.1. The fact that, in general, such a limit need not exist (see below), motivates the different approachability concepts introduced in Definition 4.3.2.

DEFINITION 4.3.2. Let Γ be an n-person normal form game and let $f = (f_1,\ldots,f_n)$ be an n-tuple of control cost functions. A strategy combination $s \in S$ is said to be *weakly f-approachable*, if s is a limit point of a collection $\{s(\varepsilon)\}_{\varepsilon \downarrow 0}$ with $s(\varepsilon) \in E(\Gamma^{\varepsilon f})$ for all ε; if s is actually the limit of such collection, then s is said to be *f-approachable*, and s is said to be *continuously f-approachable* if s is the limit of such a collection $\{s(\varepsilon)\}_{\varepsilon \downarrow 0}$ with the property that the mapping $\varepsilon \to s(\varepsilon)$ is continuous in a neighborhood of zero.

We have the following:

THEOREM 4.3.3. Let Γ and f be as in Definition 4.3.2. Then

(i) if s is weakly f-approachable, then $s \in E(\Gamma)$,

(ii) there exists at least one weakly f-approachable equilibrium of Γ,

(iii) if f is such that the equations in (4.2.9) are algebraic, then there exists at least one continuously f-approachable equilibrium of Γ.

PROOF. (i) follows in the same way as in the proof of Theorem 4.3.1, and (ii) follows from Theorem 4.2.6 and the compactness of S. The assertion in (iii) can be proved in the same way as in HARSANYI [1973b] (Lemmas 2,3 and 4). □

In the remainder of this section, we elucidate the concepts introduced above by computing the set of approachable equilibria in a simple example (the game of figure 4.3.1). This example will serve to demonstrate the following properties of the approachability concepts:

(4.3.2) the set of weakly f-approachable equilibria may depend upon the choice of f,

(4.3.3) there exist equilibria which fail to be weakly f-approachable for any choice of f, and

(4.3.4) f-approachable equilibria need not exist.

	1	2
1	1, 1	1, 0
2	1, 1	0, 0

Figure 4.3.1. A bimatrix game to illustrate the approachability concepts.

The equilibria of the game Γ of figure 4.3.1 are the strategy pairs in which player 2 plays his first strategy. Let $f = (f_1, f_2)$ be a pair of control cost functions and, for $\varepsilon > 0$, let $(s_1(\varepsilon), s_2(\varepsilon))$ be an equilibrium of $\Gamma^{\varepsilon f}$. Because of Corollary 4.2.4, we have $s_1^1(\varepsilon) > \frac{1}{2}$ for all $\varepsilon > 0$ and, therefore, the equilibria with $s_1^1 < \frac{1}{2}$ fail to be weakly f-approachable for any choice of f.

Next, let us show that every equilibrium with $s_1^1 \geq \frac{1}{2}$ is continuously f-approachable for some choice of f. Let us write $p(\varepsilon)$ for $s_1^2(\varepsilon)$ and $q(\varepsilon)$ for $s_2^2(\varepsilon)$. From (4.2.9) we know that $p(\varepsilon)$ and $q(\varepsilon)$ satisfy:

(4.3.5) $$f_1'(1 - p(\varepsilon)) - f_1'(p(\varepsilon)) = q(\varepsilon)/\varepsilon ,$$

(4.3.6) $$f_2'(1 - q(\varepsilon)) - f_2'(q(\varepsilon)) = 1/\varepsilon .$$

For $i \in \{1,2\}$, define the mapping $g_i : [0,\frac{1}{2}] \to [0,\infty]$ by

$$g_i(x) = f_i'(1 - x) - f_i'(x) .$$

Then (4.3.5) and (4.3.6) are equivalent to

(4.3.7) $g_1(p(\varepsilon)) = q(\varepsilon)/\varepsilon$, $g_2(q(\varepsilon)) = 1/\varepsilon$.

Since, f_i is convex, g_i is decreasing and, hence, g_i has an inverse $h_i : [0,\infty] \to [0,\tfrac{1}{2}]$, which is continuous (as follows e.g. from the implicit function theorem). Formula (4.3.7) is equivalent to

(4.3.8) $p(\varepsilon) = h_1(q(\varepsilon)/\varepsilon)$ $q(\varepsilon) = h_2(1/\varepsilon)$,

From which it follows that $\Gamma^{\varepsilon f}$ has a unique equilibrium and that this equilibrium depends continuously on ε. Substituting the expression for $1/\varepsilon$ of (4.3.7) in the expression for $p(\varepsilon)$ in (4.3.8), yields

(4.3.9) $p(\varepsilon) = h_1[q(\varepsilon)g_2(q(\varepsilon))]$.

Next, assume f_2 is such that

$$L(f_2) := \lim_{x \downarrow 0} x\, f_2'(x) \quad \text{exists,}$$

where we allow the possibility that $L(f_2) = -\infty$. Since $q(\varepsilon)$ converges to zero as ε tends to zero, we have

$$s_1^2 = \lim_{\varepsilon \downarrow 0} p(\varepsilon) = h_1(-L(f_2)) ,$$

from which it follows that every equilibrium with $s_1^2 \leq \tfrac{1}{2}$ is continuously f-approachable for some f. Namely, choosing

$f_2(x) = 1/x$, yields $L(f_2) = -\infty$ and, hence, $s_1^2 = 0$,

$f_2(x) = a\log x$ with $a < 0$, yields $L(f_2) = a$ and, hence, $0 < s_1^2 < \tfrac{1}{2}$,

$f_2(x) = \log|\log x|$, yields $L(f_2) = 0$ and, hence, $s_1^2 = \tfrac{1}{2}$.

Furthermore, it follows from (4.3.9) that f-approachable equilibria may not exist, if f_2 is not nice. Namely, if f_2 is such that

$$\liminf_{x \downarrow 0} x\, f_2'(x) = -\infty \quad \text{and} \quad \limsup_{x \downarrow 0} x\, f_2'(x) = 0$$

(indeed some f_2 which also satisfies the Assumptions 4.1.1 - 4.1.4 can be constructed), then all equilibria with $s_1^2 \leq \tfrac{1}{2}$ will be weakly f-approachable, but none of them is f-approachable.

Notice that, in the game of figure 4.3.1, the perfect equilibrium is obtained only if $L(f_2) = -\infty$. Intuitively this can be explained as follows. If this condition is fulfilled, the costs of player 2 increase very fast if this player tries to reduce his mistake probability, which means that player 2 has great trouble in controlling his actions. In this case, player 2 will play his second strategy with a relatively large probability, with the consequence that the second strategy of player 1 is much worse than his first strategy, which implies that player 1 will choose his second strategy with a small probability. If, however, $L(f_2) > -\infty$, then player 2 is capable of choosing his second strategy with a relatively small probability, which implies that the second strategy of player 1 is only a little bit worse than his first one, in which case the control costs force player 1 to choose his second strategy with a relatively large probability.
In section 4.5, we will see that, if both players in a bimatrix game have great trouble in controlling their actions, then the control costs will result in a perfect equilibrium being played (Theorem 4.5.1).

We conclude this section by presenting an example which shows that there exist perfect equilibria which fail to be weakly f-approachable for any choice of f. Namely, consider the game of figure 4.1.1 with $M = 1$. All equilibria of this game are perfect, however, the equilibria in which player 1 assigns a probability greater than ½ to his second strategy can never be weakly f-approachable, as follows from Corollary 4.2.4.
As a consequence of Corollary 4.2.4, the unreasonable perfect equilibria in which a player chooses a more costly mistake with a greater probability than a less costly one are excluded by the approachability concept. Notice, however, that Corollary 4.2.4 essentially uses Assumption 4.1.1. If this assumption would not be satisfied and if, for instance, in the game of figure 4.1.1 (with $M = 1$) player 2 could control his second strategy much better than his third, then it might be optimal for player 1 to choose his second strategy. Hence, to reach the conclusion that there exist perfect equilibria which fail to be weakly f-approachable for any choice of f, one essentially needs the assumption that a player can control all his strategies equally good. The assertion in (4.3.3), however, remains true for non-identical control costs. Namely, it is easily seen that the equilibrium (R_1,R_2) of the game of figure 1.5.1 fails to be weakly f-approachable for any choice of f, even if Assumption 4.1.1 is dropped.

4.4. PROPER EQUILIBRIA

The basic assumption underlying the concepts of proper and weakly proper equilibria is that, if a pure strategy k is worse than a pure strategy ℓ, then k will be mistakenly chosen with a probability which is an order smaller than the probability with which ℓ is mistakenly chosen. Our objective in this section is to show that this assumption cannot be justified by means of the control cost approach as set forth in this chapter.

To make the above statement more precise, consider an n-person normal form game $\Gamma = (\Phi_1,\dots,\Phi_n,R_1,\dots,R_n)$. If s is a weakly proper equilibrium of Γ and if $\{s(\varepsilon)\}_{\varepsilon\downarrow 0}$ is as in Definition 2.3.4, then for all i,k,ℓ

$$\text{(4.4.1)}\qquad \text{if } R_i(s\backslash k) < R_i(s\backslash \ell)\text{ , then } \lim_{\varepsilon\downarrow 0} s_i^k(\varepsilon)/s_i^\ell(\varepsilon) = 0\ .$$

In this section, however, it will be shown that, if f is an n-tuple of control cost functions and if the equilibrium s of Γ is continuously approached by $s(\varepsilon) \in E(\Gamma^{\varepsilon f})$, then for all i,k,$\ell$

$$\text{(4.4.2)}\qquad \text{if } R_i(s\backslash k) < R_i(s\backslash \ell) < \max_{k'\in\Phi_i} R_i(s\backslash k')\text{, then } \limsup_{\varepsilon\downarrow 0} s_i^k(\varepsilon)/s_i^\ell(\varepsilon) > 0.$$

Hence, if a player incurs control costs, then he will not make a more costly mistake with a probability which is an order smaller than the probability of a less costly one.

This section is devoted to the proof of (4.4.2), as well as several specializations of it for cases in which the control cost functions satisfy some extra conditions. For the remainder of the section, let an n-person normal form game $\Gamma = (\Phi_1,\dots,\Phi_n,R_1,\dots,R_n)$ and an n-tuple of control cost functions $f = (f_1,\dots,f_n)$ be fixed. Furthermore, assume $s \in E(\Gamma)$ is continuously approached by $s(\varepsilon) \in E(\Gamma^{\varepsilon f})$ as ε tends to 0. Let $i \in N$ and assume, without loss of generality, that $s_i^1 > 0$. Finally, suppose $k,\ell \in \Phi_i$ are such that

$$\text{(4.4.3)}\qquad R_i(s\backslash k) < R_i(s\backslash \ell) < R_i(s\backslash 1)\quad (= \max_{k'\in\Phi_i} R_i(s\backslash k'))\ .$$

To simplify notation, we write,

$$\text{(4.4.4)}\qquad \kappa(\varepsilon) := s_i^k(\varepsilon)\ ,\ \lambda(\varepsilon) := s_i^\ell(\varepsilon)\ ,\ \mu(\varepsilon) := s_i^1(\varepsilon)\ .$$

The proof of (4.4.2) is based on formula (4.2.9). From that formula we see that for every $\varepsilon > 0$

$$\text{(4.4.5)}\qquad \frac{f_i'(\lambda(\varepsilon))}{f_i'(\kappa(\varepsilon))} = \frac{R_i(s(\varepsilon)\backslash 1) - R_i(s(\varepsilon)\backslash \ell) - \varepsilon f_i'(\mu(\varepsilon))}{R_i(s(\varepsilon)\backslash 1) - R_i(s(\varepsilon)\backslash k) - \varepsilon f_i'(\mu(\varepsilon))}\ ,$$

from which it follows, that for every $\varepsilon > 0$

$$(4.4.6)\qquad \frac{\kappa(\varepsilon)}{\lambda(\varepsilon)} = \frac{\kappa(\varepsilon)f_i'(\kappa(\varepsilon))\,[R_i(s(\varepsilon)\backslash 1) - R_i(s(\varepsilon)\backslash \ell) - \varepsilon f_i'(\mu(\varepsilon))]}{\lambda(\varepsilon)f_i'(\lambda(\varepsilon))\,[R_i(s(\varepsilon)\backslash 1) - R_i(s(\varepsilon)\backslash k) - \varepsilon f_i'(\mu(\varepsilon))]}\ .$$

Since both k and ℓ are not a best reply against s, we have that $\kappa(\varepsilon)$ and $\lambda(\varepsilon)$ converge to 0 as ε tends to 0. Since, furthermore, $\mu(\varepsilon)$ tends to $s_i^1 > 0$, we immediately deduce from (4.4.6)

<u>THEOREM 4.4.1</u>. If $\lim_{x\downarrow 0} x\, f_i'(x)$ exists and is finite and unequal to 0, then

$$\lim_{\varepsilon\downarrow 0} \frac{s_i^k(\varepsilon)}{s_i^\ell(\varepsilon)} = \frac{R_i(s\backslash 1) - R_i(s\backslash \ell)}{R_i(s\backslash 1) - R_i(s\backslash k)}\ .$$

Loosely speaking, Theorem 4.4.1 says that, if the condition of the theorem is satisfied, a pure strategy which is not a best reply is chosen with a probability which is inversely proportional to the loss the player incurs, when he plays this strategy. In Theorem 4.4.2, we show that a similar property holds in case $\lim_{x\downarrow 0} x\, f_i'(x) = -\infty$.

<u>THEOREM 4.4.2</u>. If $\lim_{x\downarrow 0} x\, f_i'(x) = -\infty$, then

$$\limsup_{\varepsilon\downarrow 0} \frac{s_i^k(\varepsilon)}{s_i^\ell(\varepsilon)} \geq \frac{R_i(s\backslash 1) - R_i(s\backslash \ell)}{R_i(s\backslash 1) - R_i(s\backslash k)}\ .$$

<u>PROOF</u>. The theorem immediately follows from (4.4.6), if there exists a sequence $\{\varepsilon_t\}_{t\in\mathbb{N}}$ converging to 0 such that

$$\kappa(\varepsilon_t)f_i'(\kappa(\varepsilon_t)) \leq \lambda(\varepsilon_t)f_i'(\lambda(\varepsilon_t)) \qquad \text{for all } t.$$

Assume such a sequence does not exist and let $\varepsilon_1 > 0$ be such that

$$(4.4.7)\qquad \kappa(\varepsilon)f_i'(\kappa(\varepsilon)) > \lambda(\varepsilon)f_i'(\lambda(\varepsilon)) \qquad \text{for all } \varepsilon \in (0,\varepsilon_1], \text{ and}$$

$$(4.4.8)\qquad \kappa(\varepsilon) < \lambda(\varepsilon) \qquad \text{for all } \varepsilon \in (0,\varepsilon_1].$$

Note that such ε_1 can be found, because of Corollary 4.2.4. Since $\lambda(\varepsilon)$ depends continuously on ε and converges to 0 as ε tends to 0, we can define a sequence $\{\varepsilon_t\}_{t\in\mathbb{N}}$ by

$$(4.4.9)\qquad \varepsilon_{t+1} := \min\{\varepsilon \in (0,\varepsilon_t)\ ;\ \lambda(\varepsilon) = \kappa(\varepsilon_t)\}\ .$$

Let us write κ_t (resp. λ_t) for $\kappa(\varepsilon_t)$ (resp. $\lambda(\varepsilon_t)$). Since ε_t converges to 0 as t tends to infinity, λ_t converges also to 0. Furthermore, we have

$$\lambda_{t+1} f_i'(\lambda_{t+1}) = \kappa_t f_i'(\kappa_t) > \lambda_t f_i'(\lambda_t) \qquad \text{for all } t \in \mathbb{N},$$

which contradicts the condition of the theorem. □

Before proving (4.4.2), we consider another special case in which a similar result as in Theorem 4.4.2 holds.

THEOREM 4.4.3. If the limit in formula (4.4.10) exists, then

$$\text{(4.4.10)} \qquad \lim_{\varepsilon \downarrow 0} \frac{s_i^k(\varepsilon)}{s_i^\ell(\varepsilon)} \geq \frac{R_i(s\backslash 1) - R_i(s\backslash \ell)}{R_i(s\backslash 1) - R_i(s\backslash k)} .$$

PROOF. Assume that the limit in (4.4.10) exists, but that the inequality in this formula is not valid. Let ε_1 be such that (4.4.8) is satisfied, define $\{\varepsilon_t\}_{t \in \mathbb{N}}$ as in (4.4.9) and let κ_t and $\lambda_t (t \in \mathbb{N})$ be defined as above. Our assumptions imply that

$$\lim_{t\to\infty} \frac{\lambda_t - \lambda_{t+1}}{\lambda_{t-1} - \lambda_t} = \lim_{t\to\infty} \frac{\lambda_t}{\lambda_{t-1}} < \frac{R_i(s\backslash 1) - R_i(s\backslash \ell)}{R_i(s\backslash 1) - R_i(s\backslash k)} ,$$

which, when combined with (4.4.5), yields

$$\lim_{t\to\infty} \frac{(\lambda_t - \lambda_{t+1}) f_i'(\lambda_{t+1})}{(\lambda_{t-1} - \lambda_t) f_i'(\lambda_t)} < 1,$$

which in turn implies that

$$\sum_t (\lambda_t - \lambda_{t+1}) f_i'(\lambda_{t+1}) > -\infty .$$

Therefore we have, since f_i' is increasing

$$\int_0^{\lambda_1} f_i'(x)dx = \sum_t \int_{\lambda_{t+1}}^{\lambda_t} f_i'(x)dx \geq \sum_t (\lambda_t - \lambda_{t+1}) f_i'(\lambda_{t+1}) > -\infty ,$$

which contradicts the fact that $f_i(0) = \infty$. □

As an immediate consequence of Theorem 4.4.3, we have

COROLLARY 4.4.4. The basic assumption underlying the (weakly) properness concept cannot be justified by the control cost approach (i.e. the statement in (4.4.2) is correct).

4.5. PERFECT EQUILIBRIA

In section 4.3, we saw that f-approachable equilibria need not be perfect: the perfect equilibrium of the game of figure 4.3.1 is f-approachable only if the control costs have considerable influence on the strategy choice of player 2, i.e. only if $\lim_{x \downarrow 0} x\, f_2'(x) = -\infty$. By reversing the roles of the players in this game, it is clear that also $\lim_{x \downarrow 0} x\, f_1'(x) = -\infty$ is necessary to enforce that, for every bimatrix game, only perfect equilibria will be f-approachable. In the next theorem we show that these conditions are also sufficient to guarantee perfectness for bimatrix games.

THEOREM 4.5.1. Let $f = (f_1, f_2)$ be a pair of control cost functions, such that

$$\lim_{x \downarrow 0} x\, f_i'(x) = -\infty \qquad \text{for } i = 1,2 .$$

Then, for every bimatrix game, every weakly f-approachable equilibrium is perfect.

PROOF. Let $\Gamma = (\Phi_1, \Phi_2, R_1, R_2)$ be a bimatrix game. We will prove that every f-approachable equilibrium is perfect (the general case can be proved by the same methods). Hence, let s be an f-approachable equilibrium of Γ and, for $\varepsilon > 0$, let $s(\varepsilon) \in E(\Gamma^{\varepsilon f})$ be such that $s(\varepsilon)$ converges to s as ε tends to 0. In view of Theorem 3.2.2, if suffices to show that s is undominated. Assume, to the contrary, that s_1 is dominated by $\bar{s}_1$. We distinguish two cases:

Case I: $C(\bar{s}_1) \not\subset C(s_1)$. Since every $s_2(\varepsilon)$ is completely mixed, we have

$$R_1(\bar{s}_1, s_2(\varepsilon)) > R_1(s_1, s_2(\varepsilon)) \qquad \text{for all } \varepsilon > 0,$$

and, therefore, for every $\varepsilon > 0$, there exist $k_\varepsilon \in C(s_1)$ and $\bar{k}_\varepsilon \in C(\bar{s}_1) \backslash C(s_1)$, such that

$$R_1(\bar{k}_\varepsilon, s_2(\varepsilon)) > R_1(k_\varepsilon, s_2(\varepsilon)) .$$

Therefore, Corollary 4.2.4 leads to the conclusion, that

$$0 = \lim_{\varepsilon \downarrow 0} s_1^{\bar{k}_\varepsilon}(\varepsilon) \geq \liminf_{\varepsilon \downarrow 0} s_1^{k_\varepsilon}(\varepsilon) \geq \min_{k \in C(s_1)} s_1^k > 0 .$$

The contradiction shows that Case I cannot occur.

Case II: $C(\bar{s}_1) \subset C(s_1)$. Since $\frac{1}{2}(s_1 + \bar{s}_1)$ dominates s_1, we can assume $C(\bar{s}_1) = C(s_1)$. Let $\ell \in \Phi_2$ be such that

$$(4.5.1) \qquad R_1(\bar{s}_1,\ell) > R_1(s_1,\ell) .$$

Then $\ell \notin C(s_2)$. Without loss of generality, assume $1 \in C(s_2)$. From (4.2.9) we obtain that for every $\varepsilon > 0$

$$(4.5.2) \qquad \frac{1}{\varepsilon}[R_2(s_1(\varepsilon),1) - R_2(s_1(\varepsilon),\ell)] = f_2'(s_2^1(\varepsilon)) - f_2'(s_2^\ell(\varepsilon)) .$$

Multiplying both sides of (4.5.2) with $s_2^\ell(\varepsilon)$ and using the condition of the theorem, together with the fact that $s_2^\ell(\varepsilon)$ converges to 0 as ε tends to 0, yields

$$(4.5.3) \qquad \lim_{\varepsilon \downarrow 0} \frac{s_2^\ell(\varepsilon)}{\varepsilon} = \infty.$$

Applying (4.2.9) with respect to player 1 yields, that for all $k,\bar{k} \in C(s_1)$ and all $\varepsilon > 0$

$$\frac{1}{\varepsilon}[R_1(\bar{k},s_2(\varepsilon)) - R_1(k,s_2(\varepsilon))] = f_1'(s_1^{\bar{k}}(\varepsilon)) - f_1'(s_1^k(\varepsilon)),$$

from which it follows, by multiplying both sides with $\bar{s}_1^{\bar{k}} s_1^k$ and summing over all $\bar{k},k \in C(s_1)$, that

$$(4.5.4) \qquad \frac{1}{\varepsilon}[R_1(\bar{s}_1,s_2(\varepsilon)) - R_1(s_1,s_2(\varepsilon))] = \sum_{\bar{k}\in C(s_1)} \bar{s}_1^{\bar{k}}\, f_1'(s_1^{\bar{k}}(\varepsilon)) - \sum_{k\in C(s_1)} s_1^k\, f_1'(s_1^k(\varepsilon)).$$

The limit, as ε goes to 0, of the right hand side of (4.5.4) is finite. For the left hand side we have, since $\bar{s}_1$ dominates s_1 and because of (4.5.1) and (4.5.3):

$$\lim_{\varepsilon \downarrow 0} \frac{1}{\varepsilon}[R_1(\bar{s}_1,s_2(\varepsilon)) - R_1(s_1,s_2(\varepsilon))] \geq \lim_{\varepsilon \downarrow 0} \frac{s_2^\ell(\varepsilon)}{\varepsilon}[R_1(\bar{s}_1,\ell) - R_1(s_1,\ell)] = \infty,$$

The contradiction shows that s_1 cannot be dominated. Similarly it can be shown, that s_2 is undominated and, therefore, s is a perfect equilibrium of Γ. □

The reader might wonder whether Theorem 4.5.1 can be generalized to n-person games. A simple example can serve to show that, in order to guarantee perfectness in this case, the control costs have to satisfy more stringent conditions. Namely, consider the game Γ described by the following rules:

(i) There are n players, every one of them having 2 pure strategies.

(ii) Each player $i \in \{2,\dots,n\}$ receives 1 if he plays his first strategy and 0 if he plays his second strategy.

(iii) The first strategy of player 1 yields him 1 if all players play 1 or if all other players play 2 and 0 otherwise; his second strategy yields 1 if all other players play 1 and 0 otherwise.

Γ can be considered as an n-person analogon of the game of figure 4.3.1.
Let $f = (f_1,\dots,f_1)$ be an n-tuple of identical control cost functions. Then, in the same way as in section 4.3, it is seen that the perfect equilibrium of Γ (in which all players choose their first strategy) is f-approachable if and only if $\lim_{x\downarrow 0} x^{n-1} f_1'(x) = -\infty$. Hence, in order to obtain perfectness for n-person games, the control costs have to go to infinity very fast. It is unknown to the author, whether, for an n-tuple of control cost functions $f = (f_1,\dots,f_n)$ which is such that $\lim_{x\downarrow 0} x^{n-1} f_i'(x) = -\infty$ for all $i \in N$, only perfect equilibria of an n-person game are f-approachable.

The results obtained in this section are of some relevance with respect to the Harsanyi/Selten solution theory for noncooperative games (HARSANYI [1978], HARSANYI AND SELTEN [1980, 1982]). An essential element in this theory is the tracing procedure (or more precisely the logarithmic tracing procedure, HARSANYI [1975]), which is a mathematical procedure to determine a unique solution of a noncooperative game, once one has given for each player i a probability distribution p_i, representing the other players' initial expectations about player i's likely strategy choice (how these p_i's should be determined is another important element of the theory).
To determine the Harsanyi/Selten solution of a noncooperative game Γ, however, one cannot apply the theory directly to Γ, but rather one has to apply the theory to a sequence of perturbed games $\{(\Gamma,\eta)\}_{\eta\downarrow 0}$ (this is necessary to ensure that the solution is a perfect equilibrium). If it would be the case that the tracing procedure would always (no matter which prior is chosen) end up with a perfect equilibrium, then one could circumvent this circuitious way and apply the theory directly to Γ (which would simplify the theory considerably). Unfortunately, the tracing procedure may yield a non-perfect equilibrium for some priors. Namely, the logarithmic tracing procedure involves approximating a normal form game with games with logarithmic control costs and since logarithmic functions do not satisfy the condition of Theorem 4.5.1, one may expect non-perfect equilibria. A simple example where this occurs is the game of figure 4.3.1, but this example is not really convincing, since Harsanyi argues that one should first eliminate all dominated pure strategies, before applying the tracing procedure (HARSANYI [1975], p.69).
However, also examples without dominated pure strategies, in which, nevertheless, the tracing procedure yields a non-perfect equilibrium can be constructed.

4.6. REGULAR EQUILIBRIA

In section 4.3, we saw that, for a given game Γ, the set of equilibria of Γ which are weakly f-approachable may depend upon the choice of f and, that there does not necessarily exist an equilibrium of Γ which is weakly f-approachable for every possible choice of f. This raises the question which conditions an equilibrium has to satisfy, in order to be weakly f-approachable for every possible choice of the control cost functions f. This question is answered in Theorem 4.6.1, the proof of which is the subject of this section.

THEOREM 4.6.1. A regular equilibrium is f-approachable for every possible choice of f.

PROOF. Assume s is a regular equilibrium of an n-person normal form game $\Gamma = (\Phi_1,\ldots,\Phi_n,R_1,\ldots,R_n)$ and let $f = (f_1,\ldots,f_n)$ be an n-tuple of control cost functions. We have to construct, for every sufficiently small $\varepsilon > 0$, an equilibrium $s(\varepsilon)$ of $\Gamma^{\varepsilon f}$, such that $s(\varepsilon)$ converges to s as ε tends to 0. This desired $s(\varepsilon)$ will be constructed by using the implicit function theorem in combination with Brouwer's fixed point theorem.
Let us first fix our notation. We write

$$\Psi_i := \Phi_i \backslash C(s_i) \qquad \Psi := \prod_{i=1}^{n} \Psi_i\ ,$$

$$X_i := \mathcal{F}(\Phi_i, \mathbb{R}) \qquad X := \prod_{i=1}^{n} X_i\ ,$$

$$Y_i := \mathcal{F}(C(s_i), \mathbb{R}) \qquad Y := \prod_{i=1}^{n} Y_i\ ,$$

$$Z_i := \mathcal{F}(\Psi_i, \mathbb{R}) \qquad Z := \prod_{i=1}^{n} Z_i\ .$$

A generic element of X_i is denoted by x_i, etc. If $x \in X$, then we write $x = (y,z)$ where $y \in Y$ and $z \in Z$. The equilibrium s is viewed both as an element of X and as an element of Y. The restriction of $x \in X$ to Z is denoted by ζx and $b(x,\varepsilon)$ denotes the best reply against x in the game $\Gamma^{\varepsilon f}$. Finally, without loss of generality, it is assumed that $(1,\ldots,1) \in C(s)$.
Since s is a quasi-strong equilibrium of Γ (Corollary 2.5.3), there exists a neighborhood $\mathcal{X}$ of s in X, such that

$$x_i^k > 0 \qquad \text{for all } x \in \mathcal{X},\ i \in N \text{ and } k \in C(s_i),$$

$$R_i(x\backslash k) < R_i(x\backslash 1) \qquad \text{for all } x \in \mathcal{X},\ i \in N \text{ and } k \in \Psi_i,$$

from which it follows, as in the proof of Theorem 4.3.1, that

$$\lim_{\varepsilon \downarrow 0} \zeta b(x,\varepsilon) = 0 \qquad \text{for all } x \in \mathcal{X}\ . \tag{4.6.1}$$

Next, consider the mapping $F: \mathcal{X} \times \mathbb{R} \to Y$ defined by

$$(4.6.2) \qquad F_i^k(x,\varepsilon) := R_i(x\backslash k) - R_i(x\backslash 1) - \varepsilon[f_i'(x_i^k) - f_i'(x_i^1)] \quad \text{for } i \in N, k \in C(s_i), k \neq 1,$$

$$(4.6.3) \qquad F_i^{k_i}(x,\varepsilon) := \sum_k x_i^k - 1 \qquad \text{for } i \in N.$$

F is a differentiable mapping and, since s is a regular equilibrium of Γ, we have

$$\left.\frac{\partial F(x,\varepsilon)}{\partial y}\right|_{(s,0)} \quad \text{is nonsingular.}$$

Hence, by the implicit function theorem (DIEUDONNÉ [1960], p.268) there exist neighborhoods $\mathcal{Y}$ of s in Y, $\mathcal{Z}$ of $0 = \zeta s$ in Z and $\mathcal{E}$ of 0 in $\mathbb{R}_+$, as well as a differentiable mapping y: $\mathcal{Z} \times \mathcal{E} \to \mathcal{Y}$, such that

$$(4.6.4) \qquad \{(y,z,\varepsilon) \in \mathcal{Y} \times \mathcal{Z} \times \mathcal{E}\ ;\ F(y,z,\varepsilon) = 0\} = \{(y(z,\varepsilon),z,\varepsilon);\ z \in \mathcal{Z},\ \varepsilon \in \mathcal{E}\}.$$

Since every open neighborhood contains a closed neighborhood (i.e. closed set with nonempty interior), we can choose $\mathcal{Y}$ and $\mathcal{Z}$ such that

$$(4.6.5) \qquad \mathcal{Y} \times \mathcal{Z} \subset \mathcal{X} \text{ and } \mathcal{Z} \text{ is compact and convex.}$$

Define mappings χ and z with domain $\mathcal{Z} \times \mathcal{E}$, by

$$\chi(z,\varepsilon) := (y(z,\varepsilon),z) \quad , \quad z(z,\varepsilon) := \zeta b(\chi(z,\varepsilon),\varepsilon).$$

Note that both mappings are continuous, because of Lemma 4.2.2. In view of (4.6.1) and (4.6.3), we can choose $\mathcal{E}$ so small that

$$(4.6.6) \qquad z(z,\varepsilon) \in \mathcal{Z} \qquad \text{for all } z \in \mathcal{Z} \text{ and } \varepsilon \in \mathcal{E}.$$

Let $\mathcal{E}$ be such that (4.6.6) is satisfied and let $\varepsilon \in \mathcal{E}$. The mapping $z \to z(z,\varepsilon)$ is a continuous mapping from the nonempty compact and convex set $\mathcal{Z}$ into itself and, hence, by Brouwer's Fixed Point Theorem (LEFSCHETZ [1949], p.117) this mapping has a fixed point. Let $z(\varepsilon)$ be a fixed point of this mapping and let us write $x(\varepsilon)$ for $\chi(z(\varepsilon),\varepsilon)$. From (4.6.4) we can conclude that

$$(4.6.7) \qquad R_i(x(\varepsilon)\backslash k) - R_i(x(\varepsilon)\backslash 1) = \varepsilon[f_i'(x_i^k(\varepsilon)) - f_i'(x_i^1(\varepsilon))] \quad \text{for } i \in N,\ k \in C(s_i) \text{ and}$$

$$(4.6.8) \qquad \sum_k x_i^k(\varepsilon) = 1 \qquad \text{for } i \in N.$$

Furthermore, since $z(\varepsilon)$ is a fixed point of the mapping $z \to \zeta b(X(z,\varepsilon),\varepsilon)$, we have

(4.6.9) $\zeta x(\varepsilon) = z(\varepsilon) = \zeta b(x(\varepsilon),\varepsilon)$.

From (4.6.7)-(4.6.9) it follows, by applying Lemma 4.2.5, that $x(\varepsilon)$ is an equilibrium of $\Gamma^{\varepsilon f}$. This completes the proof, since $x(\varepsilon)$ converges to s as ε tends to 0. □

CHAPTER 5

INCOMPLETE INFORMATION

Games with incomplete information are games in which some of the data are unknown to some of the players. In this chapter, a particular class of games with incomplete information, the class of disturbed games, is studied. A disturbed game is a normal form game in which each player, although knowing his own payoff function exactly, has only imprecise information about the payoff functions of his opponents. We study such games, since we feel that it is more realistic to assume that each player always has some slight uncertainty about the payoffs of his opponents, rather than to assume that he knows these payoffs exactly. Our objective in this chapter is to study what the consequences are of this more realistic point of view.

Disturbed games are introduced informally in section 5.1 and formally in section 5.2. In this latter section it is also shown that every disturbed game possesses an equilibrium, provided that some continuity condition is satisfied.

In section 5.3, it is shown that equilibria of disturbed games converge to equilibria of undisturbed games as the disturbances go to 0. Equilibria which can be approximated in this way are called $\mathcal{P}$-stable equilibria, where $\mathcal{P}$ summerizes the characteristics of the disturbances (i.e. of the uncertainty the players have). Since there exist equilibria which fail to be $\mathcal{P}$-stable whatever $\mathcal{P}$ is, not every equilibrium of a normal form game is viable, when the slight uncertainty which each player has about his opponents' payoffs is taken into account.

The main result of section 5.4 states that, if the uncertainty about the payoffs is of a special kind, this uncertainty will force the players to play a perfect equilibrium. Hence, under some conditions on $\mathcal{P}$, every $\mathcal{P}$-stable equilibrium is perfect. However, there exist perfect equilibria which fail to be $\mathcal{P}$-stable for every choice of $\mathcal{P}$. If the uncertainty about the payoffs is of a very special kind, the players will be forced to play a weakly proper equilibrium, as is shown in section 5.5. This implies that the assumption that a considerably worse mistake is chosen with a considerably smaller probability than a less costly mistake is justifiable. The properness concept, however, cannot be justified by the approach of this chapter.

In general, the set of equilibria which are $\mathcal{P}$-stable may depend upon the choice of $\mathcal{P}$

(i.e. upon the exact characteristics of the disturbances). However, in section 5.6, it is shown that every strictly proper equilibrium of a normal form game Γ is P-stable for all disturbances P which occur only with a small probability and that every regular equilibrium is P-stable for all disturbances P.
Finally, section 5.7 is devoted to the (technical) proofs of the results of section 5.5.

5.1. INTRODUCTION

In the preceding chapters we have assumed that each participating player in a game knows the payoff functions (utility functions) of the other players exactly. This assumption, however, is questionable, due to the subjective character of the utility concept. It is more realistic to assume that each player, although knowing his own payoff function exactly, has only somewhat imprecise information about the payoffs of the other players. In this chapter, the consequences of this more realistic point of view will be investigated. Hence, we will examine which influence inexact information about the payoffs has on the strategy choices in a normal form game.
To get a feeling for what these consequences might be, consider the game Γ of figure 5.1.1.

	1	2
1	1, 1	0, 0
2	0, 0	0, 0

Figure 5.1.1. The influences of incomplete information on the strategy choices.

Γ has two equilibria, viz(1,1) and (2,2). Next, let us suppose that each player only knows that his own payoffs are as in Γ and that the payoffs of his opponent are approximately as described by Γ. In this case, is it still sensible for player 1 to play his second strategy? It is only sensible for him to do so, if he is absolutely sure that player 2 will play his second strategy. However, since he is not sure that the payoffs of player 2 are actually as prescribed by Γ, he cannot be sure of this. Namely, the actual payoffs of player 2 might be such that his first strategy strictly dominates his second, in which case player 2 will certainly play his first strategy. Hence, there is a positive probability that player 2 will play his first strategy, which implies that the only rational choice for player 1 is to play his first strategy.

Similarly, it is seen that also player 2 has to play his first strategy and, hence, only the equilibrium (1,1) is viable when each player has somewhat imprecise information about the other player's payoffs.

The example shows that there exist equilibria which are not viable when the slight uncertainty each player has about the other players' payoffs is taken into account. Our aim in this chapter is to investigate which equilibria are still viable in this case. To model the situation in which each player is uncertain about the payoffs of the other players, we will follow the approach as proposed in HARSANYI [1968, 1973a]. The basic assumption underlying this approach is, that this uncertainty is caused by the fact that each player's utility function is subject to small random fluctuations as a result of changes in this player's mood or taste, the precise effects of which will be known only to this player himself. Hence, we will consider games with randomly fluctuating payoffs (which will be called <u>disturbed games</u>) rather than games with a priori fixed and constant payoffs. According to this model, a game in which each player has exact knowledge of the payoff functions of the other players corresponds to the limiting situation in which the random disturbances are 0. Therefore, to model the situation in which each player has <u>slight</u> uncertainty about the payoffs of the other players, we will consider sequences of disturbed games in which the disturbances go to 0. Hence, in order to answer the question of which equilibria are still viable in the case where each player has some slight uncertainty about the payoffs of his opponents, we will investigate which equilibria are approximated by equilibria of such disturbed games. Such equilibria will be called <u>stable equilibria</u>.

In the game of figure 5.1.1, only the perfect equilibrium (1,1) is stable. This is not really surprising since for each player the situation in which he is slightly uncertain about the payoffs of his opponent is equivalent to the situation in which he knows that his opponent with a small probability makes mistakes. Since something similar is true for an arbitrary game (at least if Assumption 5.3.3. is satisfied), the disturbed game model can be viewed as a model in which the mistake probabilities are endogenously determined. This makes it interesting to look at the relations between stable equilibria on the one side and perfect (resp. weakly proper, resp. proper) equilibria on the other side. We will see that, under some conditions on the disturbances, a stable equilibrium is perfect, but that the converse is not true. Hence, the approach of this chapter yields (for normal form games) a refinement of the perfectness concept. Moreover, we will see that, under stronger conditions on the disturbances, every stable equilibrium is weakly proper. This implies that the assumption of a considerably worse mistake being chosen with an order smaller probability than a less costly mistake is justifiable. However, since stable equilibria possess more monotonicity properties than arbitrary weakly proper equilibria, not every weakly proper equilibrium is stable and so our approach yields a refinement of the weak properness concept. Finally, we will see that the assumption that also a little bit more costly mistake will be chosen with a probability of smaller order cannot be justified by the disturbed game approach and, consequently, a stable equilibrium need to be proper.

To conclude this section, let us say something about the terminology which is used throughout the chapter.
We consider a fixed class of n-person normal form games $G(\Phi_1,\ldots,\Phi_n)$. A game in this class is completely determined by its payoff vector $r = (r_1,\ldots,r_n)$, where $r_i \in \mathbb{R}^{m^*}$ is given by (2.1.13). We assume $\mathbb{R}^{m^*}$ is endowed with its Borel σ-field $\mathcal{B}$ and whenever we speak of measurable, we mean Borel measurable. In order to have a consistent framework for our probability calculations, we assume a basic probability space $(\Omega,\mathcal{A},\mathbb{P})$ is given. All random variables to be considered are defined on this space. If X_i is a random vector with values in $\mathbb{R}^{m^*}$, then $X_i(\varphi)$ is the component of X_i corresponding to $\varphi \in \Phi$. Futhermore, for $s \in S$, the random variable $X_i(s)$ is defined by $X_i(s) := \sum_{\varphi} s(\varphi)X_i(\varphi)$.
We use standard measure theoretic terminology. Standard results from measure theory will be used without giving references. For proofs as well as for definitions of measure theoretic concepts, we refer to HALMOS [1950] or KINGMAN AND TAYLOR [1966].

5.2. DISTURBED GAMES

In this section, we introduce the model (the disturbed game $\Gamma(\mu)$) by means of which we will investigate what the consequences are of each player not knowing the payoff functions of the other players exactly. This model is a generalization of the model introduced in HARSANYI [1973a]. Furthermore, it is shown that every disturbed game which satisfies some continuity condition possesses at least one equilibrium.

DEFINITION 5.2.1. Let $\Gamma = (\Phi_1,\ldots,\Phi_n,R_1,\ldots,R_n)$ be an n-person normal form game and let $\mu = (\mu_1,\ldots,\mu_n)$ be an n-tuple of probability measures on $\mathbb{R}^{m^*}$. For $i \in N$, let X_i be a random vector with distribution μ_i. The *disturbed game* $\Gamma(\mu)$ is described by the following rules:

(i) Chance chooses an outcome x of $X := (X_1,\ldots,X_n)$.

(ii) Player i ($i \in N$) gets to hear the outcome x_i of X_i (and nothing more).

(iii) Player i ($i \in N$) chooses an element $s_i \in S_i$.

(iv) If the outcome $x = (x_1,\ldots,x_n)$ resulted in (i) and if $s = (s_1,\ldots,s_n)$ has been chosen in (iii), then player i receives the expected payoff $R_i^{x_i}(s) := R_i(s) + x_i(s)$.

It is assumed that the basic characteristics of $\Gamma(\mu)$, i.e. the game Γ itself and the distributions $(\mu_1,\ldots,\mu_n)$ are known to all players; the outcome of X_i, however, is only known to player i. The probability distribution μ_i represents the information which every player different from i has about the disturbances in the payoffs of player i; the precise effects of the disturbances are known only to the player himself. The disturbed game $\Gamma(\mu)$ is a (possibly infinite) extensive form game with perfect recall (cf. Assumption 6.1.7) and, therefore, the players can restrict themselves to behavior strategies in $\Gamma(\mu)$ (AUMANN [1964]), a *behavior strategy* of player i being a measurable function σ_i from $\mathbb{R}^{m^*}$ to S_i. Two behavior strategies of player i are said to be *equivalent* if they differ only at a set of μ_i-measure zero. If σ_i is a behavior strategy of player i, then σ_i induces an element s_i of S_i defined by $s_i := \int \sigma_i d\mu_i$. We call s_i the *aggregate* of σ_i. If player i plays σ_i, then to an outside observer (and to a player $j \neq i$) it will look as if i plays the aggregate s_i of σ_i. For $i \in N$, $k \in \Phi_i$, $x_i \in \mathbb{R}^{m^*}$ and $s \in S$, we define

$$(5.2.1) \qquad B_i(s|x_i) := \{k \in \Phi_i;\ R_i^{x_i}(s\backslash k) = \max_{\ell \in \Phi_i} R_i^{x_i}(s\backslash \ell)\}, \text{ and}$$

$$(5.2.2) \qquad X_i^k(s) := \{x_i \in \mathbb{R}^{m^*};\ k \in B_i(s|x_i)\}\ .$$

$B_i(s|x_i)$ is the set of all pure best replies of player i against a behavior strategy combination with aggregate s, if the realization of X_i is x_i. We say that a behavior strategy combination σ is an equilibrium of $\Gamma(\mu)$ if each player i always (i.e. for all realizations of X_i) chooses a best reply. Hence, a strategy combination σ with aggregate s is an *equilibrium* of $\Gamma(\mu)$ if we have

$$(5.2.3) \qquad \text{if } \sigma_i^k(x_i) > 0, \text{ then } k \in B_i(s|x_i) \qquad \text{for all } i \in N,\ k \in \Phi_i \text{ and } x_i \in \mathbb{R}^{m^*},$$

or equivalently

$$(5.2.4) \qquad \text{if } \sigma_i^k(x_i) > 0, \text{ then } x_i \in X_i^k(s) \qquad \text{for all } i \in N,\ k \in \Phi_i \text{ and } x_i \in \mathbb{R}^{m^*}.$$

The disturbed game $\Gamma(\mu)$ can be expected to possess an equilibrium only if some continuity conditions are satisfied. Therefore, throughout the chapter, we will assume:

ASSUMPTION 5.2.2. Every μ_i can be written as $\mu_i = \alpha_i \mu_i^d + (1 - \alpha_i)\mu_i^{ac}$ with $\alpha_i \in [0,1)$, where μ_i^d is a discrete probability measure with only finitely many atoms and where μ_i^{ac} is a probability measure which is absolutely continuous with respect to Lebesgue measure, such that the associated density f_i is continuous.

Next, we will show that the disturbed game $\Gamma(\mu)$ possesses an equilibrium, if μ satisfies Assumption 5.2.2. For related (and, in fact, stronger) existence results, we refer to MILGROM AND WEBER [1981] and to RADNER AND ROSENTHAL [1982]. Our proof, which follows the ideas outlined in HARSANYI [1973a], proceeds by constructing a correspondence B from S to S whose fixed points induce equilibria in $\Gamma(\mu)$. Let us first show how B comes about. Let $\Gamma(\mu)$ be such that Assumption 5.2.2 is satisfied and, for $i \in N$ and $s \in S$, define $b_i^{ac}(s)$ as the vector of which the kth component is given by

$$(5.2.5) \qquad b_i^{ac,k}(s) := \mu_i^{ac}(X_i^k(s)) \qquad \text{for } k \in \Phi_i.$$

As a consequence of the fact that

$$(5.2.6) \qquad X_i^k(s) \cap X_i^\ell(s) \subset \{x_i \in \mathbb{R}^{m^*} ; R_i^{x_i}(s\backslash k) = R_i^{x_i}(s\backslash \ell)\} ,$$

and since, if $k \neq \ell$, the set in the right hand side of (5.2.6) is a hyperplane with Lebesgue measure 0, we have

$$(5.2.7) \qquad \mu_i^{ac}(X_i^k(s) \cap X_i^\ell(s)) = 0 \qquad \text{if } k \neq \ell.$$

Formula (5.2.7) implies that $b_i^{ac}(s) \in S_i$ for all $i \in N$, $s \in S$. Another important consequence of (5.2.7) is, that $s \in S$ is the aggregate of an equilibrium σ of $\Gamma(\mu)$ if and only if every component s_i of s can be written as

$$(5.2.8) \qquad s_i = \alpha_i \sum_{x_i \in A_i} \mu_i^d(x_i) b_i(s|x_i) + (1-\alpha_i) b_i^{ac}(s) \qquad \text{with } b_i(s|x_i) \in \operatorname{conv} B_i(s|x_i) \text{ for all } x_i \in A_i,$$

where A_i denotes the set of atoms of μ_i and where "conv" stands for "convex hull", hence $\operatorname{conv} B_i(s|x_i)$ is the set of all mixed strategies of player i with Carrier $B_i(s|x_i)$. Namely, it immediately follows from (5.2.3)-(5.2.4) that the aggregate s of an equilibrium σ of $\Gamma(\mu)$ satisfies (5.2.8) and, conversely, if $s \in S$ satisfies (5.2.8), then every behavior strategy combination σ, defined by

$$\begin{aligned} \sigma_i(x_i) &= b_i(s|x_i) && \text{if } x_i \in A_i, \\ \sigma_i(x_i) &\in \operatorname{conv} B_i(s|x_i) && \text{otherwise,} \end{aligned} \qquad \text{for } i \in N,$$

is an equilibrium of $\Gamma(\mu)$. Hence, to prove that $\Gamma(\mu)$ possesses an equilibrium, it suffices to show that there exists some $s \in S$ for which (5.2.8) is satisfied for every $i \in N$. Now, for $i \in N$ and $s \in S$, define the subset $B_i(s)$ of S_i by

$$B_i(s) := \alpha_i \sum_{x_i \in A_i} \mu_i^d(x_i) \operatorname{conv} B_i(s|x_i) + (1-\alpha_i)\{b_i^{ac}(s)\} ,$$

and let $B(s) := (B_1(s),\ldots,B_n(s))$. Then the fixed points of B correspond to the solutions of (5.2.8), hence, $\Gamma(\mu)$ has an equilibrium if B possesses a fixed point. This, however, follows from the Kakutani Fixed Point Theorem (KAKUTANI [1941]): Since A_i is finite, $B_i(s)$ is nonempty compact and convex, for every $s \in S$, while the finiteness of A_i and the continuity of the density of μ_i^{ac} imply that the correspondence B_i is upper semi continuous. Hence, we have proved

<u>THEOREM 5.2.3</u>. Every disturbed game possesses at least one equilibrium.

Note that it follows from (5.2.7) that, if every μ_i is atomless (the case which is considered in HARSANYI [1973a]), then, in every equilibrium of $\Gamma(\mu)$, each player will choose a pure strategy (an element of Φ_i) almost everywhere. Moreover, in this case, there exists for every equilibrium σ of $\Gamma(\mu)$ another equilibrium σ' of $\Gamma(\mu)$ such that σ' is equivalent to σ and such that $\sigma'_i(x_i) \in \Phi_i$ for all $i \in N$ and $x_i \in \mathbb{R}^{m^*}$. Such σ' is called a *purification* of σ. Hence, we have

<u>THEOREM 5.2.4</u>. (HARSANYI [1973a]). If every μ_i is atomless, then every equilibrium of $\Gamma(\mu)$ has a purification.

For more results on purification we refer to MILGROM AND WEBER [1980], AUMANN et al. [1981] and to RADNER AND ROSENTHAL [1982]. We will return to this subject in section 5.6.
Above, we have seen that there is a one-to-one correspondence between equivalence classes of equilibria of $\Gamma(\mu)$ and elements $s \in S$ for which (5.2.8) is satisfied. Therefore, in the remainder of this chapter, when we speak of an *equilibrium* of $\Gamma(\mu)$, we will mean an element $s \in S$ for which 5.2.8 is satisfied. The set of equilibria of $\Gamma(\mu)$ will be denoted by $E(\Gamma(\mu))$.

5.3. STABLE EQUILIBRIA

In order to investigate which equilibria of an ordinary normal form game are still viable in the case where each player has some slight uncertainty about the exact payoffs of the other players, we will approximate a normal form game Γ with disturbed games $\{\Gamma(\mu^\varepsilon)\}_{\varepsilon \downarrow 0}$ in which the disturbances go to 0 as ε tends to 0.
We will first consider the case in which μ^ε <u>converges weakly</u> to 0 as ε tends to 0 or more precisely the case in which μ^ε converges weakly to the probability distribution which assigns all mass to 0 (cf. BILLINGSLEY [1968]). We say that μ^ε *converges weakly* to 0 as ε tends to 0 (which we denote by $\mu^\varepsilon \overset{w}{\to} 0 (\varepsilon \to 0)$) if

$$\lim_{\varepsilon \downarrow 0} \mu_i^\varepsilon(A) = 1 \text{ for all neighborhoods } A \text{ of } 0 \text{ in } \mathbb{R}^{m^*} \text{ and all } i \in N.$$

If $\mu^\varepsilon \overset{w}{\to} 0$ $(\varepsilon \to 0)$, then for small ε the players are almost sure that the payoffs in $\Gamma(\mu^\varepsilon)$ are very close to the payoffs in Γ. Note that, if μ^ε is the distribution of the random vector X^ε, then $\mu^\varepsilon \overset{w}{\to} 0$ $(\varepsilon \to 0)$ corresponds to X^ε <u>converges in probability</u> to 0 as ε tends to 0.

THEOREM 5.3.1. Let $\Gamma = (\Phi_1,\ldots,\Phi_n,R_1,\ldots,R_n)$ be a normal form game and, for $\varepsilon > 0$, let $\mu^\varepsilon = (\mu_1^\varepsilon,\ldots,\mu_n^\varepsilon)$ be an n-tuple of probability distributions such that $\mu^\varepsilon \overset{w}{\to} 0$ $(\varepsilon \to 0)$. Let $s \in S$ and assume that, for $\varepsilon > 0$, there exists $s(\varepsilon) \in E(\Gamma(\mu^\varepsilon))$ such that $s = \lim_{\varepsilon \downarrow 0} s(\varepsilon)$. Then $s \in E(\Gamma)$.

PROOF. Let $i \in N$ and assume $k,\ell \in \Phi_i$ are such that $R_i(s\backslash k) < R_i(s\backslash \ell)$. We have to show that $s_i^k = \lim_{\varepsilon \downarrow 0} s_i^k(\varepsilon) = 0$. It follows from our assumption, that there exist neighborhoods U of s in $\mathbb{R}^m$ and V of 0 in $\mathbb{R}^{m^*}$, such that, for all $\bar{s} \in U$ and $x_i \in V$

$$R_i^{x_i}(\bar{s}\backslash k) < R_i^{x_i}(\bar{s}\backslash \ell).$$

If ε is sufficiently small, then $s(\varepsilon) \in U$ and $X_i^k(s(\varepsilon)) \cap V = \emptyset$, which implies that

$$\mu_i^\varepsilon[X_i^k(s(\varepsilon))] \le \mu_i^\varepsilon[\mathbb{R}^{m^*}\backslash V],$$

from which we see that indeed $\lim_{\varepsilon \downarrow 0} s_i^k(\varepsilon) = 0$. □

In the introduction of the chapter, we have seen that, in general, not all equilibria of a normal form game can be obtained as a limit in the way of Theorem 5.3.1. This observation motivates the following definition.

DEFINITION 5.3.2. Let Γ be a normal form game and let $P = \{\mu^\varepsilon ; \varepsilon > 0\}$ be a collection probability distributions such that $\mu^\varepsilon \overset{w}{\to} 0$ $(\varepsilon \to 0)$. An equilibrium s of Γ is said to be *P-stable* if $s = \lim_{\varepsilon \downarrow 0} s(\varepsilon)$, where $s(\varepsilon) \in E(\Gamma(\mu^\varepsilon))$ for all $\varepsilon > 0$.

Similarly as in the previous chapter (Definition 4.3.2), one can also define the notions weakly P-stable and continuously P-stable. In this chapter, however, we will restrict our attention to P-stable equilibria (although various results can be generalized either to weakly stable equilibria or to continuously stable equilibria).

A main topic in this chapter is to investigate whether a P-stable equilibrium is perfect. A simple example can already show that, to establish perfectness, P has to have some additional properties. Namely, consider the game Γ of figure 4.3.1 and, for $\varepsilon > 0$, let $\mu^\varepsilon = (\mu_1^\varepsilon,\mu_2^\varepsilon)$ be such that $\mu_1^\varepsilon = \mu_2^\varepsilon$ is the uniform distribution on the sphere (in $\mathbb{R}^4$) with radius ε and centre 0. If ε is small, player 2 will play his first strategy with probability 1 in $\Gamma(\mu^\varepsilon)$ and, so, due to symmetry, player 1 will play both his pure strategies with probability ½. This shows that, if $P := \{\mu^\varepsilon;\ \varepsilon > 0\}$, then only the non-perfect equilibrium in which player 1 chooses both strategies with the same probability is P-stable.
Obviously, the reason that in this example the perfect equilibrium is not obtained, is the fact that μ^ε has a bounded support. One can reasonably expect every P-stable

equilibrium to be perfect only in the case in which $\mathcal{P} = \{\mu^\varepsilon : \varepsilon > 0\}$ is such that every equilibrium of $\Gamma(\mu^\varepsilon)$ is completely mixed. This is assured by the following assumption, which <u>we assume throughout the remainder of the chapter</u>.

<u>ASSUMPTION 5.3.3</u>. For every $i \in N$ we have that Lebesgue measure on $\mathbb{R}^{m^*}$ is absolutely continuous with respect to μ_i (i.e. if $\lambda(A) > 0$, then $\mu_i(A) > 0$ for every $A \in \mathcal{B}$).

Let $\Gamma(\mu)$ be a disturbed game. Since the set $X_i^k(s)$ has positive Lebesgue measure, for all i,k and s, this set also has positive μ_i-measure (and, hence, positive μ_i^{ac}-measure) if Assumption 5.3.3 is satisfied. Hence, from (5.2.8) and Assumption 5.2.2, we see

<u>COROLLARY 5.3.4</u>. If Assumption 5.3.3 is satisfied, every equilibrium of $\Gamma(\mu)$ is completely mixed.

We will also assume that a player does not know one component of another player's payoff vector better than another component of this player's payoff vector. Hence, <u>throughout the remainder of the chapter, we assume</u>:

<u>ASSUMPTION 5.3.5</u>. For every $i \in N$, the distribution μ_i is invariant with respect to coordinate permutations of $\mathbb{R}^{m^*}$, i.e. for every permutation π of $\{1,\ldots,m^*\}$ and for every $A \in \mathcal{B}$, we have $\mu_i(A) = \mu_i(\tilde{\pi}A)$, where $\tilde{\pi}$ is the transformation of $\mathbb{R}^{m^*}$ which permutes the coordinates according to π.

As a consequence of this symmetry assumption, equilibria of $\Gamma(\mu)$ possess a natural monotonicity property:

<u>THEOREM 5.3.6</u>. Let $\Gamma = (\Phi_1,\ldots,\Phi_n,R_1,\ldots,R_n)$ be a normal form game and let $\mu = (\mu_1,\ldots,\mu_n)$ be such that Assumption 5.3.5 is satisfied. Then, for $s \in E(\Gamma(\mu))$, $i \in N$ and $k,\ell \in \Phi_i$, we have

(5.3.1) $\quad$ if $R_i(s\backslash k) < R_i(s\backslash \ell)$, then $s_i^k < s_i^\ell$.

<u>PROOF</u>. Assume $s \in E(\Gamma(\mu))$ is such that the condition of (5.3.1) is satisfied. Let $\text{int}X_i^\ell(s)$ be the interior of $X_i^\ell(s)$, i.e. $\text{int}X_i^\ell(s)$ is the set of all x_i where ℓ is the unique best reply of player i against s and let $\tilde{\pi}$ be the transformation of $\mathbb{R}^{m^*}$ which interchanges, for every $\varphi \in \Phi$, the $(\varphi\backslash k)^{th}$ and $(\varphi\backslash \ell)^{th}$ coordinate. Under this mapping $X_i^k(s)$ is mapped into a strict subset of $\text{int}X_i^\ell(s)$ and, therefore,

$$s_i^k \le \mu_i(X_i^k(s)) = \mu_i(\tilde{\pi}X_i^k(s)) < \mu_i(\text{int}X_i^\ell(s)) \le s_i^\ell . \qquad \Box$$

5.4. PERFECT EQUILIBRIA

In this section, it is investigated under which conditions on P only perfect equilibria are P-stable. First it is shown that a P-stable equilibrium may be imperfect if $P = \{\mu^{\varepsilon};\ \varepsilon > 0\}$ is such that μ^{ε} converges weakly to 0 as ε tends to 0. After that it is shown that a stronger mode of convergence leads to perfect equilibria.

EXAMPLE 5.4.1. A P-stable equilibrium is not necessarily perfect if $P = \{\mu^{\varepsilon};\ \varepsilon > 0\}$ is such that μ^{ε} converges weakly to 0 as ε tends to 0.

Let Γ be the game of figure 4.3.1, let X be a continuous random variable with a positive density and let $P = \{\mu^{\varepsilon};\ \varepsilon > 0\}$ be such that μ_i^{ε} is the product measure on $\mathbb{R}^4$ of the distribution of εX, for every $i \in \{1,2\}$ and $\varepsilon > 0$. Note that indeed μ^{ε} converges weakly to 0 as ε tends to 0. We will, however, show that the perfect equilibrium of Γ is not P-stable if the expectation of X exists.
For $\varepsilon > 0$, let $s(\varepsilon)$ be an equilibrium of $\Gamma(\mu^{\varepsilon})$. Write $p(\varepsilon) = s_1^2(\varepsilon)$ and $q(\varepsilon) = s_2^2(\varepsilon)$. Since μ^{ε} is nonatomic, we have

$$(5.4.1) \qquad p(\varepsilon) = \mu_1^{\varepsilon}[X_1^2(s(\varepsilon))] \qquad q(\varepsilon) = \mu_2^{\varepsilon}[X_2^2(s(\varepsilon))] .$$

Let Y be a random variable which is distributed as the difference of two independent random variables which are both distributed as X, and let Z be independent from Y and having the same distribution as Y. Then (5.4.1) is equivalent to

$$(5.4.2) \qquad p(\varepsilon) = \mathbb{P}[(1-q(\varepsilon))Y + q(\varepsilon)Z \le -q(\varepsilon)/\varepsilon], \text{ and}$$

$$(5.4.3) \qquad q(\varepsilon) = \mathbb{P}[(1-p(\varepsilon))Y + p(\varepsilon)Z \le -1/\varepsilon] .$$

Let F (resp. f) be the common distribution (resp. density) function of Y and Z. From (5.4.2), we see

$$p(\varepsilon) \ge \mathbb{P}[Y \le \frac{-q(\varepsilon)}{\varepsilon} \text{ and } Z \le \frac{-q(\varepsilon)}{\varepsilon}] = \mathbb{P}[Y \le \frac{-q(\varepsilon)}{\varepsilon}]\mathbb{P}[Z \le \frac{-q(\varepsilon)}{\varepsilon}] = (F(\frac{-q(\varepsilon)}{\varepsilon}))^2,$$

which shows that $\lim_{\varepsilon \downarrow 0} p(\varepsilon) = 0$ (in which case the perfect equilibrium of Γ is P-stable) only if

$$(5.4.4) \qquad \lim_{\varepsilon \downarrow 0} \frac{q(\varepsilon)}{\varepsilon} = \infty .$$

By (5.4.3), we have

$$q(\varepsilon) \le \mathbb{P}[Y \le -1/\varepsilon \text{ or } Z \le -1/\varepsilon] \le \mathbb{P}[Y \le -1/\varepsilon] + \mathbb{P}[Z \le -1/\varepsilon] = 2F(-1/\varepsilon),$$

from which we see that (5.4.4) is fulfilled only if

$$(5.4.5) \qquad \lim_{x\downarrow-\infty} x\bar{F}(x) = -\infty .$$

However, if (5.4.5) is satisfied, then

$$\int_{-\infty}^{0} tf(t)dt \le \lim_{x\downarrow-\infty} \int_{-\infty}^{x} tf(t)dt \le \lim_{x\downarrow-\infty} x \int_{-\infty}^{x} f(t)dt = \lim_{x\downarrow-\infty} xF(x) = -\infty ,$$

which means that the expectation of Y (and, hence, of X) does not exist. Hence, every P-stable equilibrium of Γ is imperfect, if the expectation of X exists, which leads to the conclusion that, in general, weak convergence is not sufficient to establish perfectness.

The actual reason why the perfect equilibrium is not obtained in the example above is the following. From (5.4.2), we see that player 1's strategy choice in $\Gamma(\mu^{\varepsilon})$ is determined by two factors:

(i) his a priori uncertainty about his own payoffs, represented by ε, and

(ii) his uncertainty about the exact payoffs of player 2, represented by $q(\varepsilon)$.

Now, our aim in this chapter is to model the situation in which player 1's strategy choice is determined by his own payoff in Γ and by his slight uncertainty about the payoffs of player 2 (and not by his a priori uncertainty about his own payoffs). Hence, we actually want our model to be such that $q(\varepsilon)$ is much larger than ε (i.e. we want that (5.4.4) is satisfied). But, as we have seen above, this property cannot be expected if μ^{ε} converges only weakly to 0. Hence, a collection $\{\Gamma(\mu^{\varepsilon})\}_{\varepsilon\downarrow 0}$ of disturbed games for which μ^{ε} converges weakly to 0 as ε tends to 0 is not a good model for the situation we want to describe.

To obtain a model which fills our needs, we have to decrease a player's a priori uncertainty about his own payoffs. This can be accomplished by looking at collections of disturbed games $\{\Gamma(\mu^{\varepsilon})\}_{\varepsilon\downarrow 0}$ for which $\mu_i^{\varepsilon}(0)$ converges to 1 as ε tends to 0, for every $i \in N$. In this case, if ε is small, the players are almost certain that the payoffs in $\Gamma(\mu^{\varepsilon})$ are the same as the payoffs in Γ and, moreover, each player's strategy choice in $\Gamma(\mu^{\varepsilon})$ is almost solely determined by his own payoffs in Γ and by his uncertainty about the payoffs of the other players. We will prove that, if the uncertainty is of this kind, only perfect equilibria can be obtained.

THEOREM 5.4.2. Every P-stable equilibrium is perfect if $P = \{\mu^{\varepsilon};\ \varepsilon > 0\}$ is such that $\lim_{\varepsilon\downarrow 0} \mu_i^{\varepsilon}(0) = 1$ for all $i \in N$.

PROOF. Let Γ be a normal form game and let P satisfy the condition of the theorem. For $\varepsilon > 0$, let $s(\varepsilon) \in E(\Gamma(\mu^{\varepsilon}))$ be such that $s(\varepsilon)$ converges to $s \in E(\Gamma)$ as ε tends to 0. By rewriting (5.2.8) a little, we see that for every $i \in N$ and $\varepsilon > 0$

(5.4.6) $s_i(\varepsilon) = \mu_i^{\varepsilon}(0)\bar{s}_i(\varepsilon) + (1 - \mu_i^{\varepsilon}(0))\bar{\bar{s}}_i(\varepsilon)$ with $\bar{s}_i(\varepsilon) \in \text{conv } B_i(s(\varepsilon)|0)$

which, since $B_i(s(\varepsilon)|0)$ is nothing else than the set of pure best replies of player i against $s(\varepsilon)$ in Γ, is equivalent to

(5.4.7) $s_i(\varepsilon) = \mu_i^{\varepsilon}(0)\bar{s}_i(\varepsilon) + (1 - \mu_i^{\varepsilon}(0))\bar{\bar{s}}_i(\varepsilon)$ with $\bar{s}_i(\varepsilon)$ a best reply against $s(\varepsilon)$ in Γ.

Since $\mu_i^{\varepsilon}(0)$ converges to 1 as ε tends to 0, we have that $\bar{s}_i(\varepsilon)$ converges to s_i as ε tends to 0 and, therefore,every s_i is a best reply against $s(\varepsilon)$ for all sufficiently small ε. Since, furthermore, every $s(\varepsilon)$ is completely mixed by Corollary 5.3.4, s is a perfect equilibrium. □

Theoreom 5.4.2 shows that, in order to justify the restriction to perfect equilibria for normal form games, one does not have to rely on the assumption that the players with a small probability make mistakes. Rather one can refer to the fact that a player always has some slight uncertainty about the payoffs of the other players. However, note that perfect equilibria are obtained only if this uncertainty is of a very special kind. Note, furthermore, that the converse of Theorem 5.4.2 is not correct: there exist perfect equilibria which for every choice of $\mathcal{P}$ fail to be $\mathcal{P}$-stable. Namely, because of the monotonicity property of equilibria of disturbed games (Theorem 5.3.6) the unreasonable perfect equilibria in which a player assigns a greater probability to a more costly mistake than to a less costly one can never be $\mathcal{P}$-stable. So, for instance, in the game of figure 3.1.1 with $M = 1$, the perfect equilibrium in which player 1 plays his second strategy can never be $\mathcal{P}$-stable.

<u>THEOREM 5.4.3</u>. There exist perfect equilibria which fail to be $\mathcal{P}$-stable whatever $\mathcal{P}$ is.

In the next section, it will be investigated whether the result of Theorem 5.4.2 can be strenghtened in the sense that every $\mathcal{P}$-stable equilibrium is proper (or weakly proper) if $\mathcal{P}$ satisfies the condition of the Theorem. For the sake of a clear exposition, we will restrict ourselves to disturbed games $\Gamma(\mu)$ in which every μ_i has no atoms except possibly at 0. Hence, <u>throughout the remainder of the chapter, we will assume</u>

<u>ASSUMPTION 5.4.4</u>. For every $i \in N$ the distribution μ_i has at most an atom at 0.

It should, however, be stressed that our results hold also in the case in which this assumption is not satisfied. If $\Gamma(\mu)$ is a disturbed game for which Assumption 5.4.4 is satisfied, then we see from (5.2.8) that s is an equilibrium of $\Gamma(\mu^{\varepsilon})$ if and only if every s_i can be written as

$$(5.4.8) \qquad s_i = \mu_i(0)\bar{s}_i + (1 - \mu_i(0))b_i^{ac}(s) \qquad \text{with } \bar{s}_i \text{ a best reply against } s \text{ in } \Gamma,$$

where $b_i^{ac}(s)$ is as in (5.2.5).

5.5. WEAKLY PROPER EQUILIBRIA

In this section, it is investigated under which conditions on P every P-stable equilibrium is weakly proper. We start by showing that a P-stable equilibrium is not necessarily weakly proper if $P = \{\mu^\varepsilon; \varepsilon > 0\}$ is such that $\mu_i^\varepsilon(0)$ converges to 1 as ε tends to 0. The example used to demonstrate this fact (Example 5.5.1), however, suggests that some stronger mode of convergence (which we will call strong convergence) might lead to weakly proper equilibria. It will then be investigated whether this is indeed the case.

EXAMPLE 5.5.1. A P-stable equilibrium need not be weakly proper if $P = \{\mu^\varepsilon;\ \varepsilon > 0\}$ is such that $\lim_{\varepsilon \downarrow 0} \mu_i^\varepsilon(0) = 1$ for all $i \in N$.

Let Γ be the game of figure 4.1.1 and let $P = \{\mu^\varepsilon;\ \varepsilon > 0\}$ be such that, for $i \in \{1,2\}$ and $\varepsilon > 0$, the distribution μ_i^ε is given by $\mu_i^\varepsilon = (1-\varepsilon)\delta + \varepsilon\nu$, where δ is the probability measure which assigns all mass to 0 and where ν is an arbitrary nonatomic probability measure on $\mathbb{R}^6$.
We claim that, for M sufficiently large, only the non-weakly proper equilibrium in which player 1 uses his second pure strategy is P-stable. Namely, for $\varepsilon > 0$, let $s(\varepsilon)$ be an equilibrium of $\Gamma(\mu^\varepsilon)$. Since player 2 will play his first pure strategy, if his exact payoff is as in Γ, we have

$$s_2^k(\varepsilon) = \varepsilon\nu[X_2^k(s(\varepsilon))] \qquad \text{for } k \in \{2,3\},$$

hence, we have

$$(5.5.1) \qquad \frac{s_2^3(\varepsilon)}{s_2^2(\varepsilon)} = \frac{\nu[X_2^3(s(\varepsilon))]}{\nu[X_2^2(s(\varepsilon))]} \qquad \text{for all } \varepsilon > 0.$$

Now, for all $s \in S$, we have

$$\nu[X_2^3(s)] \geq \nu[\{x_2;\ \min\{x_2(\varphi);\varphi_2 = 3\} \geq 2 + \max\{x_2(\varphi);\varphi_2 \neq 3\}\}] > 0,$$

from which it follows that, if M is sufficiently large

$$(5.5.2) \qquad \frac{s_2^3(\varepsilon)}{s_2^2(\varepsilon)} > \nu[X_2^3(s(\varepsilon))] > \frac{1}{M} \qquad \text{for all } \varepsilon > 0.$$

If (5.5.2) is satisfied, then player 1 will play his second pure strategy in $\Gamma(\mu^\varepsilon)$ if he gets to hear that his actual payoff is as described by Γ. This shows that, if M is sufficiently large, only the non-weakly proper equilibrium in which player 1 plays his second strategy is P-stable.

The actual reason why, in the example above, the weakly proper equilibrium is not obtained, is the fact that the ratio in (5.5.1) does not directly depend on ε but only indirectly via $s(\varepsilon)$. In the example above, the measure ν represents the beliefs player 1 has about the payoffs of player 2 in $\Gamma(\mu^\varepsilon)$, once he knows that these payoffs are not as in Γ. More precisely if X_2^ε generates μ_2^ε, then

$$\nu(A) = \mathbb{P}(X_2^\varepsilon \in A \mid X_2^\varepsilon \neq 0) \qquad \text{for all } A \in \mathcal{B} \text{ and } \varepsilon > 0,$$

and, hence, these beliefs are independent of ε. But if a player has only slight uncertainty about the payoffs of another player, then in the case in which he knows that this player's payoffs are not as in Γ, he will still think that these payoffs are close to those of Γ. This idea leads to the notion of strong convergence. For $\varepsilon > 0$, let $\mu^\varepsilon = (\mu_1^\varepsilon,\dots,\mu_n^\varepsilon)$ be an n-tuple of probability distributions on $\mathbb{R}^{m^*}$ for which Assumption 5.4.4 is satisfied. We say that μ^ε *converges strongly* to 0 as ε tends to 0 (which is denoted by $\mu^\varepsilon \overset{s}{\to} 0$ $(\varepsilon \to 0)$) if the following two conditions are satisfied:

(5.5.3) $\mu_i^\varepsilon(0)$ converges to 1 as ε tends to 0, for all $i \in N$,

(5.5.4) $\nu^\varepsilon := \mu^{\varepsilon,ac}$ (the absolute continuous component of μ^ε) converges weakly to 0 as ε tends to 0.

If $\mu^\varepsilon \overset{s}{\to} 0$ $(\varepsilon \to 0)$ and if X_i^ε is a random vector generating μ_i^ε, then

$$X_i^\varepsilon = \begin{cases} 0 \text{ with probability } \mu_i^\varepsilon(0) & \text{(which tends to 1 as } \varepsilon \text{ tends to 0),} \\ Y_i^\varepsilon \text{ with probability } 1-\mu_i^\varepsilon(0), & \text{where } Y_i^\varepsilon \text{ converges in probability} \\ & \text{to 0 as } \varepsilon \text{ tends to 0.} \end{cases}$$

Hence, strong convergence expresses that the disturbances occur with a small probability and that disturbances are small.

For the remainder of the section, let $P = \{\mu^\varepsilon;\ \varepsilon > 0\}$ be such that $\mu^\varepsilon \overset{s}{\to} 0$ $(\varepsilon \to 0)$ and let us investigate whether, for every game Γ, every P-stable equilibrium is proper or weakly proper. Let us first consider weakly proper equilibria. Assume s is a P-stable equilibrium of a game Γ and, for $\varepsilon > 0$, let $s(\varepsilon) \in E(\Gamma(\mu^\varepsilon))$ be such that $s(\varepsilon)$ converges to s as ε tends to 0. In the proof of Theorem 5.4.2, we have seen that every $s(\varepsilon)$ is completely mixed and that s is a best reply against $s(\varepsilon)$ if ε is sufficiently small. Hence, s is weakly proper whenever $s(\varepsilon)$ satisfies condition (2.3.2). Let $i \in N$ and $k,\ell \in \Phi_i$ be such that $R_i(s\backslash k) < R_i(s\backslash \ell)$. In this case, if ε is small, $X_i^k(s(\varepsilon))$ is much further away from 0 than $X_i^\ell(s(\varepsilon))$ is and, therefore, if ν_i^ε is tightly concentrated around 0, one may expect that $s_i^k(\varepsilon)$ will be of smaller order than $s_i^\ell(\varepsilon)$. An example of a measure which is tightly concentrated is a measure with a normal (Gaussian) density and, in fact, we have:

<u>THEOREM 5.5.2</u>. Let $\mathcal{P} = \{\mu^\varepsilon;\ \varepsilon > 0\}$ be such that μ^ε converges strongly to 0 as ε tends to 0 and such that, for $i \in N$ and $\varepsilon > 0$, the distribution ν_i^ε (as in (5.5.4)) is the product measure of a measure on $\mathbb{R}$ with a normal density with parameters 0 and ε (see section 5.7.). Then every $\mathcal{P}$-stable equilibrium is weakly proper.

The proof of this theorem is postponed till section 5.7, since it is rather technical.

Another extreme case is the one in which ν_i^ε is widespread (has a density with a heavy tail). In this case, if $R_i(s\backslash k) < R_i(s\backslash \ell)$, it might occur that $s_i^k(\varepsilon)$ is not of smaller order than $s_i^\ell(\varepsilon)$. Namely, if ν_i^ε is widespread, then there is a relatively large probability of the actual payoffs of player i in $\Gamma(\mu^\varepsilon)$ being far away from his payoffs in Γ, which implies that his payoffs in Γ will have only a relatively small influence on the probabilities associated with any of his equilibrium strategies in $\Gamma(\mu^\varepsilon)$. An example of a measure which is widespread is a measure with a Cauchy density and, in fact, we have

<u>THEOREM 5.5.3</u>. Let $\mathcal{P} = \{\mu^\varepsilon;\ \varepsilon > 0\}$ be such that μ^ε converges strongly to 0 $(\varepsilon \to 0)$ and such that, for $i \in N$ and $\varepsilon > 0$, the distribution ν_i^ε (as in (5.5.4) is the product measure of a measure on $\mathbb{R}$ with a Cauchy density with parameters 0 and ε (see section 5.7.). Then there exists a game for which every $\mathcal{P}$-stable equilibrium fails to be weakly proper.

Again, we refer to section 5.7 for the proof.

Next, let us turn to proper equilibria and let us investigate whether Theorem 5.5.2 can be strengthened to yield that every $\mathcal{P}$-stable equilibrium is proper, if $\mathcal{P}$ is as in that theorem. This will be the case if every equilibrium $s(\varepsilon)$ of $\Gamma(\mu^\varepsilon)$ satisfies condition (2.3.1). However, this cannot be expected. Namely, if the pure strategy k of player i is only a little bit worse than the pure strategy ℓ against $s(\varepsilon)$, then $X_i^k(s(\varepsilon))$ is only a little bit smaller than $X_i^\ell(s(\varepsilon))$, which implies, by Assumption 5.3.5, that $s_i^k(\varepsilon)$ will not be of smaller order than $s_i^\ell(\varepsilon)$. Hence, we have the following theorem, which is proved in section 5.7.

THEOREM 5.5.4. Under the conditions of Theorem 5.5.2, there exists a game for which every $\mathcal{P}$-stable equilibrium fails to be proper.

5.6. STRICTLY PROPER EQUILIBRIA AND REGULAR EQUILIBRIA

We have already seen that the set of equilibria of a normal form game which are $\mathcal{P}$-stable may depend upon the choice of $\mathcal{P}$ (cf. Theorem 5.4.2 and Example 5.4.1). This raises the question of which equilibria are $\mathcal{P}$-stable for every choice of $\mathcal{P}$. In this section, it is shown that the answer to this question is related to strictly proper equilibria and to regular equilibria.
As a first result, we have:

THEOREM 5.6.1. A strictly proper equilibrium is $\mathcal{P}$-stable for all $\mathcal{P} = \{\mu^\varepsilon;\ \varepsilon > 0\}$ which are such that $\lim_{\varepsilon \downarrow 0} \mu_i^\varepsilon(0) = 1$ for all $i \in N$.

PROOF. Let Γ be an n-person normal form game and let $\mathcal{P} = \{\mu^\varepsilon;\ \varepsilon > 0\}$ satisfy the condition of the Theorem. For $s \in S$ and $\varepsilon > 0$, define $\eta(s,\varepsilon)$ by

$$\eta_i(s,\varepsilon) := (1 - \mu_i^\varepsilon(0))b_i^\varepsilon(s) \qquad \text{for } i \in N,$$

where $b_i^\varepsilon(s)$ is the vector with k^{th} component

$$b_i^{\varepsilon,k}(s) := \nu_i^\varepsilon[X_i^k(s)] \qquad \text{for } k \in \Phi_i\ .$$

From (5.4.8) we see that s is an equilibrium of $\Gamma(\mu^\varepsilon)$ if and only if every s_i can be written as

$$\text{(5.6.1)} \qquad s_i = \mu_i^\varepsilon(0)\bar{s}_i + \eta_i(s,\varepsilon) \qquad \text{with } \bar{s}_i \text{ a best reply against } s \text{ in } \Gamma,$$

from which it follows, by means of (2.2.3), that

$$s \in E(\Gamma(\mu^\varepsilon)) \text{ if and only if } s \in E(\Gamma,\eta(s,\varepsilon)),$$

where the perturbed game $(\Gamma,\eta(s,\varepsilon))$ is as in Definition 2.2.1. Next, assume $\hat{s}$ is a strictly proper equilibrium of Γ and let $\hat{\eta}$ be as in Definition 2.3.7. If ε is sufficiently small, then $\eta(s,\varepsilon) < \hat{\eta}$ for all $s \in S$ (since $\lim_{\varepsilon \downarrow 0} \mu_i^\varepsilon(0) = 1$) and in this case there exists for every $s \in S$ an equilibrium $\hat{s}(\eta(s,\varepsilon))$ of $(\Gamma,\eta(s,\varepsilon))$ which is close to $\hat{s}$ and which depends continuously on $\eta(s,\varepsilon)$. Consider the mapping $s \to \hat{s}(\eta(s,\varepsilon))$. Since μ_i^{ac} has a continuous density (by Assumption 5.2.2), this mapping is continuous, which implies (by Brouwer's Fixed Point Theorem, SMART [1974]) that it has a fixed point $\hat{s}(\varepsilon)$. Hence, we have that $\hat{s}(\varepsilon)$ is an equilibrium of $(\Gamma,\eta(\hat{s}(\varepsilon),\varepsilon)$, which implies (by 5.6.1), that $\hat{s}(\varepsilon)$ is an equilibrium of $\Gamma(\mu^\varepsilon)$. This shows that $\hat{s}$ is a P-stable equilibrium of Γ, since $\hat{s}(\varepsilon)$ converges to $\hat{s}$ as ε tends to 0. □

A simple example can show that the statement in Theorem 5.6.1 is incorrect if the condition of the Theorem is replaced by "μ^ε converges weakly to 0 as ε tends to 0". Namely, consider the 2-person normal form game in which both players have 2 pure strategies and in which all payoffs are 1. Then all equilibria are strictly proper, but, due to the symmetry assumption 5.3.5 only the symmetric equilibrium in which both players play $(\frac{1}{2},\frac{1}{2})$ is P-stable, if $P = \{\mu^\varepsilon;\ \varepsilon > 0\}$ is such that every μ^ε is atomless and such that $\mu^\varepsilon \overset{w}{\to} 0$ $(\varepsilon \to 0)$.
Next, we will show that every regular equilibrium is P-stable for all $P = \{\mu^\varepsilon;\ \varepsilon > 0\}$ for which $\mu^\varepsilon \overset{w}{\to} 0$ $(\varepsilon \to 0)$ and which are such that μ^ε depends continuously on ε (this latter assumption is made only to keep the analysis tractable, as the reader will see from the proof of Theorem 5.6.2). The proof of Theorem 5.6.2 has the same structure as the proof of Theorem 4.6.1: it is an application of the Implicit Function Theorem in combination with Brouwer's Fixed Point Theorem. The proof is a generalization of the proof of Theorem 7 of HARSANYI [1973a]. Presenting it gives us the opportunity to correct a mathematical error in Harsanyi's proof (which occurs in his Lemma 7).

THEOREM 5.6.2. A regular equilibrium is P-stable for all collections $P = \{\mu^\varepsilon;\ \varepsilon > 0\}$ for which there exists a random vector $X = (X_1,\ldots,X_n)$ such that ν_i^ε (as in (5.5.4)) is the distribution of εX_i, for every $i \in N$ and $\varepsilon > 0$.

PROOF. Let $\Gamma = (\Phi_1,\ldots,\Phi_n,R_1,\ldots,R_n)$ be a normal form game and let P and X be as in the theorem. We will restrict ourselves to the case in which μ_i^ε is atomless, for every i and ε. Hence, we have $\mu_i^\varepsilon = \nu_i^\varepsilon$. The reader can easily adjust the proof to the situation in which there are atoms. Assume $\hat{s}$ is a regular equilibrium of Γ and, without loss of generality, assume $(1,\ldots,1) \in C(\hat{s})$. Let $\varepsilon > 0$. From (5.2.8), we see that s is an equilibrium of $\Gamma(\mu^\varepsilon)$ if and only if

$$(5.6.2) \qquad s_i^k = \mu_i^\varepsilon[X_i^k(s)] \qquad \text{for all } i,k,$$

which, by the condition of the theorem, is equivalent to

$$(5.6.3) \qquad s_i^k = \mathbb{P}\,[R_i(s\backslash k) + \varepsilon X_i(s\backslash k) \geq R_i(s\backslash \ell) + \varepsilon X_i(s\backslash \ell) \text{ for all } \ell \in \Phi_i] \quad \text{for all } i,k.$$

In order to facilitate the application of the Implicit Function Theorem, we will rewrite (5.6.3) in a way which at first sight looks rather cumbersome. Let us write

$$A_i := \{\alpha_i,\ \alpha_i \in F(C(\hat{s}_i),\mathbb{R}) \text{ with } \alpha_i^1 = 0\} \quad \text{and} \quad A := \prod_{i=1}^{n} A_i ,$$

and for $s \in S$ and $\alpha \in A$, define $F(s,\alpha)$ by

$$F_i^k(s,\alpha) := \mathbb{P}\,[\alpha_i^k - \alpha_i^\ell \geq X_i(s\backslash \ell) - X_i(s\backslash k) \text{ for all } \ell \in C(\hat{s}_i)] \quad (i \in N, k \in C(\hat{s}_i)).$$

Then we see from (5.6.3) that s is an equilibrium of $\Gamma(\mu^\varepsilon)$ if and only if there exist $\alpha,\beta \in A$ such that

(5.6.4) $\quad s_i^1 = 1 - \sum_{k\neq 1} s_i^k \qquad$ for $i \in N$,

(5.6.5) $\quad s_i^k = F_i^k(s,\alpha) - \beta_i^k \qquad$ for $i \in N$, $k \in C(\hat{s}_i)$, $k \neq 1$,

(5.6.6) $\quad \alpha_i^k = \frac{1}{\varepsilon}[R_i(s\backslash k) - R_i(s\backslash 1)] \qquad$ for $i \in N$, $k \in C(\hat{s}_i)$, $k \neq 1$,

(5.6.7) $\quad \beta_i^k = F_i^k(s,\alpha) - \mu_i^\varepsilon[X_i^k(s)] \qquad$ for $i \in N$, $k \in C(\hat{s}_i)$, $k \neq 1$, and

(5.6.8) $\quad s_i^k = \mu_i^\varepsilon[X_i^k(s)] \qquad$ for $i \in N$, $k \notin C(\hat{s}_i)$.

Note that, if $\hat{s}$ is completely mixed, then s is an equilibrium of $\Gamma(\mu^\varepsilon)$ if and only if there exists some $\alpha \in A$ such that (5.6.4)-(5.6.6) are satisfied with $\beta = 0$. The application of the implicit function theorem can already be seen by comparing (5.6.4) and (5.6.6) with (4.6.2) and (4.6.3). To apply this theorem we need some $\hat{\alpha} \in A$ for which $F_i^k(\hat{s},\hat{\alpha}) = \hat{s}_i^k$ for all $i \in N$ and $k \in C(\hat{s}_i)$ with $k \neq 1$. We claim that such $\hat{\alpha}$ exists. Namely, consider the mapping $E\colon A \to A$ defined by

$$E_i^k(\alpha) := \begin{cases} \alpha_i^k - \max(0,F_i^k(\hat{s},\alpha) - \hat{s}_i^k) + \max(0,F_i^1(\hat{s},\alpha) - \hat{s}_i^1) & (i \in N, k \in C(\hat{s}_i), k \neq 1), \\ 0 & (i \in N, k = 1). \end{cases}$$

By using that $\alpha_i^1 = 0$ for all $\alpha_i \in A_i$, the reader can verify that for all $k \neq 1$

$$\lim_{\alpha_i^k \downarrow -\infty} F_i^k(\hat{s},\alpha) = 0 \qquad \text{and} \qquad \lim_{\alpha_i^k \uparrow \infty} F_i^1(\hat{s},\alpha) = 0,$$

which implies that there exists a nonempty, compact and convex set K in A such that $E(K) \subset K$. Since E is continuous, there exists a fixed point $\hat{\alpha}$ of E, as follows from Brouwer's Fixed Point Theorem (SMART [1974]). For every $i \in N$ and $k \in C(\hat{s}_i)$ with $k \neq 1$, we have

$$\max(0,F_i^k(\hat{s},\hat{\alpha}) - \hat{s}_i^k) = \max\,(0,F_i^1(\hat{s},\hat{\alpha}) - \hat{s}_i^1),$$

from which it follows, by using

$$\sum_{k\in C(\hat{s}_i)} F_i^k(\hat{s},\hat{\alpha}) = \sum_{k\in C(\hat{s}_i)} \hat{s}_i^k = 1,$$

that indeed $F_i^k(\hat{s},\hat{\alpha}) = \hat{s}_i^k$ for all $i \in N$ and $k \in C(\hat{s}_i)$.
Next, consider the mappings G and H defined by

$$G_i^1(s,\alpha,\beta,\varepsilon) := \sum_k s_i^k - 1 \qquad \text{for } i \in N,$$

$$G_i^k(s,\alpha,\beta,\varepsilon) := R_i(s\backslash k) - R_i(s\backslash 1) - \varepsilon\alpha_i^k \qquad \text{for } i \in N,\ k \in C(\hat{s}_i),\ k \neq 1,$$

$$H_i^k(s,\alpha,\beta,\varepsilon) := s_i^k - F_i^k(s,\alpha) + \beta_i^k \qquad \text{for } i \in N,\ k \in C(\hat{s}_i),\ k \neq 1.$$

Note that the definitions of these mappings are motivated by (5.6.4)-(5.6.6). Since X has a continuous density by Assumption (5.2.2), the mappings G and H are differentiable. For $s \in S$, let us write $s = (\sigma,\tau)$, where σ is the restriction of s to $C(\hat{s})$ and where τ is the vector consisting of the remaining components of s. Since $\hat{s}$ is a regular equilibrium of Γ and since the density of X is positive everywhere (by Assumption 5.3.3), we have that

$$\left.\frac{\partial(G,H)}{\partial(\sigma,\alpha)}\right|_{(\hat{s},\hat{\alpha},0,0)} \quad \text{is nonsingular.}$$

Therefore, it follows from the Implicit Function Theorem (DIEUDONNÉ [1960], p.268), that there exist neighborhoods U of $\tau = 0$, V of $\beta = 0$ and W of $\varepsilon = 0$ and, for every $(\tau,\beta,\varepsilon) \in U \times V \times W$, some $\sigma(\tau,\beta,\varepsilon)$ close to $\hat{s}$ and $\alpha(\tau,\beta,\varepsilon)$ close to $\hat{\alpha}$ such that

(5.6.9) $\quad (\sigma(\tau,\beta,\varepsilon),\ \tau,\ \alpha(\tau,\beta,\varepsilon),\ \beta,\varepsilon)$ is a solution of (5.6.4)-(5.6.5)

Let us write $s(\tau,\beta,\varepsilon)$ for $(\sigma(\tau,\beta,\varepsilon),\tau)$ and let $\varepsilon \in W$. Motivated by (5.6.7)-(5.6.8), define mappings M and N with domain $U \times V$ by

(5.6.10) $\quad M_i^k(\tau,\beta) := \mu_i^\varepsilon[X_i^k(s(\tau,\beta,\varepsilon))] \qquad$ for $i \in N, k \notin \Phi_i$, and

(5.6.11) $\quad N_i^k(\tau,\beta) := F_i^k(s(\tau,\beta,\varepsilon),\alpha(\tau,\beta,\varepsilon)) - \mu_i^\varepsilon[X_i^k(s(\tau,\beta,\varepsilon))] \quad$ for $i \in N, k \in \Phi_i, k \neq 1$.

Since $\hat{s}$ is a quasi-strong equilibrium (Corollary 2.5.3), it follows that for sufficiently small ε

$$(M(\tau,\beta),N(\tau,\beta)) \in U \times V \quad \text{for all } (\tau,\beta) \in U \times V .$$

Since U and V can be chosen compact and convex and since M and N are continuous, we can conclude from Brouwer's Fixed Point Theorem (SMART [1974]) that there exists a fixed point $(\tau(\varepsilon),\beta(\varepsilon))$ of (M,N). Let us write $s(\varepsilon)$ for $s(\tau(\varepsilon),\beta(\varepsilon),\varepsilon)$ and $\alpha(\varepsilon)$ for $\alpha(\tau(\varepsilon),\beta(\varepsilon),\varepsilon)$. Then it follows from (5.6.9)-(5.6.11) and the fixed point property of $(\tau(\varepsilon),\beta(\varepsilon))$, that $(s(\varepsilon),\alpha(\varepsilon),\beta(\varepsilon))$ is a solution to (5.6.4)-(5.6.8), which shows that $s(\varepsilon)$ is an equilibrium of $\Gamma(\mu^{\varepsilon})$. This completes the proof, since $s(\varepsilon)$ converges to $\hat{s}$ as ε tends to 0. □

Next, let us return to the instability of mixed strategy equilibria which was considered in section 1.6. In that section, we said that this instability is only a seeming instability. This view is justified by the Theorems 2.6.2, 5.2.4 and 5.6.2: For almost all equilibria (viz. for the regular ones) this instability disappears if the slight uncertainty which each player has about the other players' payoffs is taken into account.

5.7. PROOFS OF THE THEOREMS OF SECTION 5.5

In this section, we write f_{α}^{β} (resp. F_{α}^{β}) for the normal density function (resp. normal distribution function) with parameters α and β, hence

$$(5.7.1) \qquad f_0^1(x) := \frac{1}{\sqrt{2\pi}} e^{-x^2/2} \; ; \; f_{\alpha}^{\beta}(x) := \frac{1}{\beta} f_0^1\left(\frac{x-\alpha}{\beta}\right) \; ; \; F_{\alpha}^{\beta}(x) := \int_{-\infty}^{x} f_{\alpha}^{\beta}(t)dt.$$

Furthermore, we write g_{α}^{β} (resp. G_{α}^{β}) for the Cauchy density (resp. distribution) function with parameters α and β, i.e.

$$(5.7.2) \qquad g_0^1(x) := \frac{1}{\pi(1+x^2)} \; ; \; g_{\alpha}^{\beta}(x) := \frac{1}{\beta} g_0^1\left(\frac{x-\alpha}{\beta}\right) \; ; \; G_{\alpha}^{\beta}(x) := \int_{-\infty}^{x} g_{\alpha}^{\beta}(t)dt.$$

We use $\sim$ to denote asymptotic equivalence, i.e. for $a \in \mathbb{R} \cup \{-\infty\} \cup \{\infty\}$ and functions f and g, we write

$$f(x) \sim g(x) \quad (x \to a) \quad \text{if} \quad \lim_{x \to a} \frac{f(x)}{g(x)} = 1.$$

We need the following standard results from asymptotic analysis (cf. DE BRUYN [1958]), which can be proved by elementary methods.

$$(5.7.3) \qquad F_0^1(x) \sim \frac{-f_0^1(x)}{x} \qquad (x \downarrow -\infty), \text{ and}$$

$$(5.7.4) \qquad G_0^1(x) \sim \frac{-1}{\pi x} \qquad (x \downarrow -\infty) .$$

Now, we are ready to prove our theorems.

PROOF OF THEOREM 5.5.2. Let $\Gamma = (\Phi_1,\dots,\Phi_n,R_1,\dots,R_n)$ be an n-person normal form game, let $P = \{\mu^\varepsilon;\ \varepsilon > 0\}$ satisfy the condition of Theorem 5.5.2, let $\hat{s}$ be P-stable and, for $\varepsilon > 0$, let $s(\varepsilon) \in E(\Gamma(\mu^\varepsilon))$ be such that $s(\varepsilon)$ converges to $\hat{s}$ as ε tends to 0. Since $s(\varepsilon)$ is completely mixed, for every $\varepsilon > 0$ and since $\hat{s}$ is a best reply against $s(\varepsilon)$ for all sufficiently small ε, it suffices to show that

$$(5.7.5)\qquad \lim_{\varepsilon\downarrow 0} \frac{s_i^k(\varepsilon)}{s_i^\ell(\varepsilon)} = 0 \quad \text{if } R_i(\hat{s}\backslash k) < R_i(\hat{s}\backslash \ell)\ , \quad \text{for all } i,k,\ell\ .$$

Assume $i \in N$, $k,\ell \in \Phi_i$ are such that the condition of (5.7.5) is satisfied and let ν^ε be as in (5.5.4). For $\varepsilon > 0$, we have

$$s_i^k(\varepsilon) = (1-\mu_i^\varepsilon(0))\nu_i^\varepsilon[X_i^k(s(\varepsilon))] \qquad s_i^\ell(\varepsilon) \geq (1-\mu_i^\varepsilon(0))\nu_i^\varepsilon[X_i^\ell(s(\varepsilon))],$$

hence, it suffices to show that

$$(5.7.6)\qquad \lim_{\varepsilon\downarrow 0} \frac{\nu_i^\varepsilon[X_i^k(s(\varepsilon))]}{\nu_i^\varepsilon[X_i^\ell(s(\varepsilon))]} = 0.$$

For $\varepsilon > 0$, let Y_i^ε be a random vector with distribution ν_i^ε and for $s \in S$, let $Z_i^\varepsilon(s) := R_i(s) + Y_i^\varepsilon(s)$. For every $k' \in \Phi_i$, we have

$$\nu_i^\varepsilon[X_i^{k'}(s(\varepsilon))] = \mathbb{P}[Z_i^\varepsilon(s(\varepsilon)\backslash k') = \max_{\ell'\in\Phi_i} Z_i^\varepsilon(s(\varepsilon)\backslash \ell')]\ .$$

Now, $Z_i^\varepsilon(s(\varepsilon)\backslash k')$ has a normal distribution with parameters $R_i(s(\varepsilon)\backslash k)$ and $\sigma_i(\varepsilon)$, where $\sigma_i(\varepsilon)$ is given by

$$(5.7.7)\qquad \sigma_i(\varepsilon) := \varepsilon\left(\sum_{\varphi_{-i}\in\Phi_{-i}} (s_{-i}(\varepsilon,\varphi_{-i}))^2\right)^{\frac{1}{2}}\ ,$$

in which $s_{-i}(\varepsilon,\varphi_{-i})$ denotes the probability which $s_{-i}(\varepsilon) := (s_1(\varepsilon),\dots,s_{i-1}(\varepsilon),s_{i+1}(\varepsilon),\dots,s_n(\varepsilon))$ assigns to $\varphi_i \in \Phi_{-i} := \prod_{j\neq i}\Phi_j$. Note that $\sigma_i(\varepsilon)$ converges to 0 as ε tends to 0 and, therefore, after suitable transformations, (5.7.6) follows the following Lemma.

LEMMA 5.7.1. For $\varepsilon > 0$, let $(Z_1^\varepsilon,\dots,Z_m^\varepsilon)$ be an m-tuple of independent random variables, each Z_i^ε having a normal distribution with parameters α_i and ε, such that $\alpha_1 < \alpha_2$. Then

$$(5.7.8)\qquad \lim_{\varepsilon\downarrow 0} \frac{\mathbb{P}[Z_1^\varepsilon = \max_k Z_k^\varepsilon]}{\mathbb{P}[Z_2^\varepsilon = \max_k Z_k^\varepsilon]} = 0.$$

PROOF. (5.7.8) follows easily if $\alpha_2 = \max_k \alpha_k$. Therefore assume, without loss of generality, that $\alpha_3 > \alpha_2$. Furthermore, assume, without loss of generality that $\alpha_1 = 0$. Define Z^ε by

$$Z^\varepsilon := \max_{k\geq 3} Z_k^\varepsilon$$

The reader can verify that, in order to prove (5.7.8), it suffices to show that

$$\lim_{\varepsilon\downarrow 0} \frac{\mathbb{P}[Z_1^\varepsilon \geq Z^\varepsilon]}{\mathbb{P}[Z_2^\varepsilon \geq Z^\varepsilon]} = 0.$$

For $i \in \{1,2\}$, we have

$$\text{(5.7.9)} \qquad \mathbb{P}[Z_i^\varepsilon \geq Z^\varepsilon] = \int_{-\infty}^{\infty} F^\varepsilon(x) f_{\alpha_i}^\varepsilon(x)\,dx\ ,$$

where the distribution function F^ε of Z^ε is given by:

$$F^\varepsilon(x) = \prod_{k=3}^{m} F_{\alpha_k}^\varepsilon(x).$$

For $\varepsilon > 0$, define

$$c(\varepsilon) := e^{-\alpha_2(\alpha_3 - \alpha_2)/2\varepsilon^2}\ ,$$

then the reader can verify that

$$\text{(5.7.10)} \qquad F_{\alpha_3}^\varepsilon(x) \leq c(\varepsilon) F_{\alpha_3}^\varepsilon(x + \alpha_2) \qquad \text{if } 2x \leq \alpha_3, \text{ and}$$

$$\text{(5.7.11)} \qquad f_{\alpha_1}^\varepsilon(x) \leq c(\varepsilon) f_{\alpha_2}^\varepsilon(x) \qquad \text{if } 2x \geq \alpha_3.$$

By using the monotonicity of $F_{\alpha_k}^\varepsilon$, it follows from (5.7.10) that

$$\text{(5.7.12)} \qquad F^\varepsilon(x) \leq c(\varepsilon) F^\varepsilon(x + \alpha_2) \qquad \text{if } 2x \leq \alpha_3.$$

By splitting the integral of (5.7.9) for $i = 1$ into two parts and by using (5.7.11)-(5.7.12), it follows that

$$\mathbb{P}[Z_1^\varepsilon \geq Z^\varepsilon] \leq 2c(\varepsilon)\mathbb{P}[Z_2^\varepsilon \geq Z^\varepsilon]\ .$$

Since $c(\varepsilon)$ converges to 0 as ε tends to 0, this completes the proof of the Lemma and, hence, the proof of Theorem 5.5.2. □

PROOF OF THEOREM 5.5.3. Let Γ be the game of figure 4.1.1 and let P be as in Theorem 5.5.3. We will show that, for sufficiently large M, only the equilibrium in which player 1 plays his second strategy is P-stable. For $\varepsilon > 0$, let $s(\varepsilon)$ be an equilibrium of $\Gamma(\mu^\varepsilon)$. Since player 2 will play his first strategy if his payoff is as in Γ, we have

$$s_2^k(\varepsilon) = (1 - \mu_2^\varepsilon(0))\nu_2^\varepsilon[X_2^k(s(\varepsilon))] \qquad \text{for } k \in \{2,3\} . \tag{5.7.13}$$

For $\varepsilon > 0$ and $s \in S$, let Y_2^ε be a random vector with distribution ν_2^ε and let $Z_2^\varepsilon(s) := R_2(s) + Y_2^\varepsilon(s)$. Then (5.7.13) is equivalent to

$$s_2^k(\varepsilon) = (1 - \mu_2^\varepsilon(0))\mathbb{P}[Z_2^\varepsilon(s(\varepsilon)\backslash k) = \max_{\ell\in\{1,2,3\}} Z_2^\varepsilon(s(\varepsilon)\backslash \ell)] \qquad \text{for } k \in \{2,3\}. \tag{5.7.14}$$

Since $Z_2^\varepsilon(s\backslash\ell)$ has a Cauchy distribution with parameters $R_2(s\backslash\ell)$ and $\sigma = \sigma_1(\varepsilon)$ given by (5.7.7), it follows from (5.7.14), that

$$s_2^3(\varepsilon) \doteq (1 - \mu_2^\varepsilon(0)) \int_{-\infty}^{\infty} G_2^\sigma(x)G_1^\sigma(x)g_0^\sigma(x)dx .$$

If ε is small, σ is close to 0, in which case

$$G_2^\sigma(x)G_1^\sigma(x) \geq \tfrac{1}{2} \qquad \text{for all } x \geq 3,$$

With the consequence that

$$s_2^3(\varepsilon) \geq (1 - \mu_2^\varepsilon(0)) \int_3^{\infty} \tfrac{1}{2}g_0^\sigma(x)dx = \tfrac{1}{2}(1 - \mu_2^\varepsilon(0))G_0^\sigma(-3) . \tag{5.7.15}$$

On the other hand we have

$$s_2^2(\varepsilon) \leq (1 - \mu_2^\varepsilon(0))\mathbb{P}[Z_2^\varepsilon(s(\varepsilon)\backslash 2) \geq Z_2^\varepsilon(s(\varepsilon)\backslash 1)] ,$$

hence, since the difference of two random variables, both having a Cauchy distribution, again has a Cauchy distribution

$$s_2^2(\varepsilon) \leq (1 - \mu_2^\varepsilon(0)) F_0^{\sqrt{2}\sigma}(-1) . \tag{5.7.16}$$

By combining (5.7.15), (5.7.16) and (5.7.4) we see that

$$\lim_{\varepsilon\downarrow 0} \frac{s_2^3(\varepsilon)}{s_2^2(\varepsilon)} \geq \frac{1}{12}\sqrt{2} ,$$

hence, if $M > 6\sqrt{2}$, then only the non-weakly proper equilibrium in which player 2 plays his second strategy is P-stable. □

<u>PROOF OF THEOREM 5.5.4</u>. Let Γ be the game of figure 2.3.2 and let P be as in Theorem 5.5.4. We claim that, if $s(\varepsilon)$ is an equilibrium of $\Gamma(\mu^{\varepsilon})$, then

$$(5.7.17) \qquad s_2^3(\varepsilon) \sim s_2^2(\varepsilon) \qquad (\varepsilon \downarrow 0) .$$

Obviously, (5.7.17) has the consequence that player 1 will play his second strategy if his payoff is as in Γ and if ε is small, which implies that the unique proper equilibrium of Γ (which has player 1 playing his first strategy) is not P-stable. Formula (5.7.17) can be proved by using the same methods as in the proof of Theorem 5.5.2. Let us give a more instructive proof of the slightly weaker result

$$(5.7.18) \qquad \mathbb{P}[Z_2^{\varepsilon}(s(\varepsilon)\backslash 3) \geq Z_2^{\varepsilon}(s(\varepsilon)\backslash 1)] \sim \mathbb{P}[Z_2^{\varepsilon}(s(\varepsilon)\backslash 2) \geq Z_2^{\varepsilon}(s(\varepsilon)\backslash 1)] \quad (\varepsilon \downarrow 0) ,$$

where $Z_2^{\varepsilon}(s)$, for $\varepsilon > 0$ and $s \in S$, is as in the proof of Theorem 5.5.2. Let us write σ for $\sigma_1(\varepsilon)$ as defined in (5.7.7). Then

$$(5.7.19) \qquad \mathbb{P}[Z_2^{\varepsilon}(s(\varepsilon)\backslash 3) \geq Z_2^{\varepsilon}(s(\varepsilon)\backslash 1)] = F_0^{\sqrt{2}\sigma}(-1 - s_1^3(\varepsilon)) \text{ , and}$$

$$(5.7.20) \qquad \mathbb{P}[Z_2^{\varepsilon}(s(\varepsilon)\backslash 2) \geq Z_2^{\varepsilon}(s(\varepsilon)\backslash 1)] = F_0^{\sqrt{2}\sigma}(-1) .$$

Now, if we write $\bar{\sigma}$ for $\sigma_2(\varepsilon)$ as defined in (5.7.7), then

$$s_1^3(\varepsilon) \leq \mathbb{P}[Z_1^{\varepsilon}(s(\varepsilon)\backslash 3) \geq Z_1^{\varepsilon}(s(\varepsilon)\backslash 1)] \leq F_0^{\sqrt{2}\bar{\sigma}}(-1),$$

which implies that $s_1^3(\varepsilon)$ is of smaller order than $\bar{\sigma}$, hence, also of smaller order than σ, since $\sigma \sim \bar{\sigma} \sim \varepsilon$ $(\varepsilon \downarrow 0)$. From this fact it follows, by combining (5.7.19)-(5.7.20) with (5.7.3), that (5.7.18) is indeed correct. □

CHAPTER 6

EXTENSIVE FORM GAMES

The most profound reason why the Nash equilibrium concept has to be refined lies in the fact that a Nash equilibrium of an extensive form game may prescribe irrational behavior at unreached parts of the game tree. Until now, however, we have mainly studied games in normal form. This comprehensive study yielded a deeper insight into the relations between various refinements of the Nash equilibrium concept. Our goal in this chapter is to investigate to what extend this study has yielded results which are also relevant for extensive form games. It will turn out that the insights we obtained are valuable, but that many results we proved for normal form games cannot be generalized to extensive form games.

The discussion in this chapter is confined to finite extensive form games having perfect recall. In section 1, the formal definition of such a game is given and several notions related to it are introduced.

Section 2 considers equilibria and subgame perfect equilibria. It is shown that an equilibrium has to prescribe rational behavior only at those information sets which can be reached when the equilibrium is played. Furthermore, it is shown that every game possesses at least one subgame perfect equilibrium.

The concept of sequential equilibria is the subject of section 3. The formal definition of this concept is given and some basic properties of it are derived.

Section 4 contains a discussion concerning perfect equilibria. It is shown that every game possesses at least one perfect equilibrium and the relation with the sequential equilibrium concept is studied. Also the difference between perfectness in the normal form and perfectness in the extensive form is stressed.

Proper equilibria are considered in section 5. Every proper equilibrium is sequential, but many sequential equilibria fail to be proper. Furthermore, it is demonstrated that there is a close connection between equilibria which are proper in the extensive form of a game and equilibria which are proper in the normal form of this game. It is shown that although some intuitively unreasonable sequential equilibria can be eliminated by restricting oneself to proper equilibria, not all such equilibria are eliminated by this concept.

Extensive form games with control costs are studied in section 6. It is shown that, if control costs are present, the players will play a sequential equilibrium. In section 7, it is investigated what the influence is of incomplete knowledge of the payoff functions on the strategy choices in an extensive form game. It is demonstrated that only very specific uncertainty will force the players to play a sequential equilibrium. It should, however, be noted that many challenging problems concerning the incomplete information approach are still unsolved.
The results in this chapter are based on VAN DAMME [1980c], KREPS AND WILSON [1981a] and SELTEN [1975].

6.1. DEFINITIONS

In this section, the formal definition of a (finite) game in extensive form is given. Furthermore, several concepts which are related to such a game are introduced. The exposition follows SELTEN [1975].

The extensive form representation of a game is the representation which explicitly displays the rules of the game, i.e. it specifies the following data (cf. the examples in the sections 1.2 - 1.4):

(i) the order of the moves in the game,
(ii) for every decision point, which player has to move there,
(iii) the information a player has, whenever it is his turn to move,
(iv) the choices available to a player, when he has to move,
(v) the probabilities associated with the chance moves, and
(vi) the payoffs for all players.

Mathematically, this specification is provided by a sextuple (K,P,U,C,p,r) of which K specifies the order of the moves, P specifies the player who has to move, etc. Formally, a *(finite) n-person game in extensive form* is defined as a sextuple Γ = (K,P,U,C,p,r) of which the constituents are as follows:

(6.1.1) *The game tree* K:
The game tree K is a finite tree with a distinguished node *0*, the *origin* (or root) of K. The unique sequence of nodes and branches connecting the root *0* with a node x of K is called the *path* to x, and we say that x *comes before* y (to be denoted by $x < y$) if x is on the path to y and different from y. Note that $<$ is a partial ordering. The terminology which will be used with respect to K is summarized in Table 6.1.1. The interpretation of K is as follows: the game starts at the root *0* and proceeds along a path from node to immediate successor until an endpoint is reached. The various paths give the "plays" that might occur.

Notation	Definition	Terminology
$x < y$	x on the path to y and $x \neq y$	y comes after x, x comes before y
$P(x)$	$\max \{y;\ y < x\}$ $(x \neq 0)$	the immediate predecessor of x
$S(x)$	$\{y;\ x \in P(Y)\}$	the immediate successors of x
Z	$\{x;\ S(x) = \emptyset\}$	the endpoints of the tree
X	the complement of Z	the decision points
$Z(x)$	$\{y \in Z;\ x < y\}$	the terminal successors of x.

Table 6.1.1. The terminology used with respect to the game tree.

(6.1.2) *The player partition* P:

The player partition P is a partition of X into n + 1 sets $P_0, P_1, \ldots, P_n$. The set P_i is the set of decision points of player i. Player 0 is the *chance player* responsible for the random moves occurring in the game.

(6.1.3) *The information partition* U:

The information partition U is an n-tuple $(U_1, \ldots, U_n)$ where U_i is a partition of P_i (into so called *information sets* of player i) such that for every information set the following two conditions are satisfied

(i) every path intersects the information set at most once, and

(ii) all nodes in the information set have the same number of immediate successors.

The information set $u \in U_i$ which contains $x \in P_i$ represents the set of nodes player i cannot distinguish from x based on the information he has when he has to move at x. In our figures we depict information sets by connecting the nodes in this set by a dotted line and we label the set with i whenever it is an information set of player i.

(6.1.4) *The choice partition* C:

The choice partition C is a collection $C = \{C_u;\ u \in \bigcup_{i=1}^{n} U_i\}$, where C_u is a partition of $\bigcup_{x \in u} S(x)$ into so called *choices* at u, such that every choice contains exactly one element of $S(x)$ for every $x \in u$ (note that this is possible because of condition (6.1.3)(ii)).

The interpretation is that, if player i takes the choice $c \in C_u$ at the information set $u \in U_i$, then, if he is actually at $x \in u$, the next node reached by the play is that element of $S(x)$ which is contained in c. We identify the choice c at u with the collection of branches leading out of u and having an element in c as endpoint and in our graphical representations we label the choices along these branches. So, in the game of figure 1.4.2, the choice L_2 of player 2 consists of the two left-hand branches leading out at the information set of player 2.

(6.1.5) *The probability assignment* p:

The probability assignment p specifies for every $x \in P_0$ a completely mixed probability distribution p_x on S(x).

The interpretation is that, if x is reached, then $y \in S(x)$ is reached with the (positive) probability $p_x(y)$. In the figures the probabilities are depicted along the branches.

(6.1.6) *The payoff function r:*

The payoff function r is an n-tuple $(r_1,\dots,r_n)$ where r_i is a real valued function with domain Z.

If the endpoint z is reached, then player i receives the payoff $r_i(z)$. We depict the vector r(z) at the endpoint z, first the payoff of player 1, etc.

Throughout the chapter, we will restrict ourselves to extensive form games in which every player never forgets anything, i.e. at every point where a player has to make a decision, he knows what he previously has known (i.e. which of his information sets have been reached) and what he previously has done (i.e. which choices he has taken). To formalize this, let us say that a choice c comes before a node x (or $c < x$) if one of the branches in c is on the path to x. Throughout the chapter, we will assume:

ASSUMPTION 6.1.7. The game Γ is a game with *perfect recall* (KUHN [1953]), i.e. for all $i \in \{1,\dots,n\}$, $u,v \in U_i$, $c \in C_u$ and $x,y \in v$, we have that c comes before x if and only if c comes before y.

For a discussion of Assumption 6.1.7 we refer to SELTEN [1975]. As a consequence of this assumption it makes sense to say that the choice c comes before the information set v ($c < v$) and that the information set $u \in U_i$ comes before $v \in U_i$ (to be denoted by $u < v$). Note that the relation < is a partial ordering on U_i, from which it follows that player i can represent his decision problem by means of a decision tree, once he knows the strategies chosen by his opponents (see WILSON [1972]).

Another important consequence of Assumption 6.1.7 is that a player does not have to correlate his choices at different information sets, but that he can restrict himself to behavior strategies (KUHN [1953], see (6.1.11)).

In the remainder of this section, we introduce several concepts which are related to an extensive form game Γ.

(6.1.8) Strategies.

A *pure strategy* φ_i of player i is a mapping which assigns a choice $c \in C_u$ to every information set $u \in U_i$. The set of all pure strategies of player i is denoted by Φ_i.
A *mixed strategy* s_i of player i is a probability distribution on Φ_i and the set of

all such strategies is denoted by S_i. A *behavior strategy* of player i assigns a probability distribution on C_u to every information set $u \in U_i$. The set of all these strategies is B_i. Mixed strategies correspond to prior randomization, behavior strategies to local randomization. A *strategy combination* is an n-tuple of strategies, one for each player. B denotes the set of all behavior strategy combinations, the ones which are relevant for games with perfect recall (see (6.1.11). If $b_i \in B_i$ and $c \in C_u$ with $u \in U_i$, then $b_i\backslash c$ denotes the strategy b_i changed so that c is taken with certainty at u. For $b \in B$ and $b_i' \in B_i$, we denote by $b\backslash b_i'$ that strategy combination in which all players play in accordance to b, except player i who plays b_i'. Finally, if c is a choice of player i, then $b\backslash c = b\backslash b_i'$ where $b_i' := b_i\backslash c$.

(6.1.9) Realization probabilities.

If $b \in B$, then for every $z \in Z$ one can compute the probability $\mathbb{P}^b(z)$ that z will be reached when b is played. Hence, every $b \in B$ induces a probability distribution $\mathbb{P}^b$ on Z. If A is an arbitrary set of nodes, then we write $\mathbb{P}^b(A)$ for $\mathbb{P}^b(Z(A))$ where Z(A) denotes the set of endpoints coming after A. Hence, $\mathbb{P}^b(A)$ is the probability that A will be reached when b is played.

A node x is said to be *possible* when playing $b_i \in B_i$ if there exists some $b \in B$ with i^{th} component b_i such that $\mathbb{P}^b(x) > 0$. An information set u is said to be *relevant* when playing b_i if some node in u is possible when playing b_i. Poss(b_i) (resp. Rel(b_i)) denotes the set of all nodes of the tree (resp. $u \in U_i$) which are possible (resp. relevant) when playing b_i. The following lemma is an immediate corollary of Assumption 6.1.7.

LEMMA 6.1.10.

(i) If $u \in U_i$ is relevant when playing b_i, then every node is possible when playing b_i.

(ii) If $x \in u$ and $b_i', b_i'' \in \text{Rel}(u)$, then $\mathbb{P}^{b\backslash b_i'}(x|u) = \mathbb{P}^{b\backslash b_i''}(x|u)$ for every $b \in B$ for which these conditional probabilities are well-defined.

(6.1.11) The restriction to behavior strategies.

If player i uses the mixed strategy s_i, then if $u \in U_i$ is reached, he will take the choice $c \in C_u$ with the probability

$$(6.1.12) \qquad b_{iu}(c) = \sum_{\varphi_i \in \text{Rel}(c)} s_i(\varphi_i) \Big/ \sum_{\varphi_i \in \text{Rel}(u)} s_i(\varphi_i) \; ,$$

where Rel(u) denotes the set of all pure strategies for which u is relevant and Rel(c) is the subset of Rel(u) consisting of those strategies which choose c at u. Let b_i be a behavior strategy defined by (6.1.12) whenever this quantity is well-defined and defined arbitrary for those u which cannot be reached when s_i is played. In KUHN [1953] it is shown that such a behavior strategy b_i is *realization equivalent* to s_i, i.e. that

(6.1.13) $\mathbb{P}^{\pi\backslash s_i} = \mathbb{P}^{\pi\backslash b_i}$

for any (mixed or behavior) strategy combination π. This shows that whatever can be achieved by using a mixed strategy can also be achieved by using a behavior strategy. Hence , since there is no reason whatever for a player to use a strategy more general than a behavior strategy, we will restrict ourselves to this class of strategies.

(6.1.14) Expected payoffs and the normal form.
If b is played, then the expected payoff $R_i(b)$ to player i is given by $R_i(b) = \Sigma_z \mathbb{P}^b(z) r_i(z)$. The normal form of Γ is the normal form game $N(\Gamma) = (\Phi_1, \ldots, \Phi_n, R_1, \ldots, R_n)$. To compute the expected payoff for a mixed strategy combination, knowledge of the normal form is sufficient, but this is not true for behavior strategy combinations.

(6.1.15) Conditional realization probabilities
Let b be a behavior strategy combination and let $x \in X$. For every $z \in Z$ one can compute the probability $\mathbb{P}^b_x(z)$ that z will be reached if b is played and if the game is started at x. If $\mathbb{P}^b(x) > 0$, then $\mathbb{P}^b_x(z)$ is just the conditional probability $\mathbb{P}^b(z|x)$, but $\mathbb{P}^b_x(z)$ is also well-defined if $\mathbb{P}^b(x) = 0$. (Note that for $\mathbb{P}^b_x$ to be well-defined it is not necessary that the subgame starting at x (see 6.1.16) is well-defined). The expectation of r_i with respect to $\mathbb{P}^b_x$ will be denoted by $R_{ix}(b)$.

(6.1.16) Subgames.
Frequently it is the case that a game naturally decomposes into smaller games. This is formalized by the notion of subgames. Let $x \in X$ and let K_x be the subtree of K rising at x. If it is the case that every information set of Γ either is completely contained in K_x or is disjoint from K_x, then the restriction of Γ to K_x constitutes a game of its own, to be called the *subgame* Γ_x *starting at* x. In this case every behavior strategy combination b decomposes into a pair (b_{-x}, b_x) where b_x is a behavior strategy combination in Γ_x and b_{-x} is a behavior strategy combination for the remaining part of the game (the *truncated game*). If it is known that b_x will be played in Γ_x, then, in order to analyse Γ, it suffices to analyse the truncated game $\Gamma_{-x}(b_x)$ which results from Γ by replacing the subtree K_x by an endpoint with payoff $R_{ix}(b_x)$ for every player i.

6.2. EQUILIBRIA AND SUBGAME PERFECTNESS

Let Γ be an extensive form game and let b be a behavior strategy combination in Γ. We say that $b_i' \in B_i$ is a *best reply* (of player i) against b, if

(6.2.1) $R_i(b\backslash b_i') = \max_{b_i'' \in B_i} R_i(b\backslash b_i'')$, where the expected payoff $R_i(.)$ is as in (6.1.14). The strategy combination b' is said to be a *best reply* against b if every component of b' is a best reply against b and a strategy combination which is a best reply against itself is called a *(Nash) equilibrium* of Γ. Since the normal form of Γ possesses an equilibrium in mixed strategies and since for every mixed strategy there exists an equivalent behavior strategy (see (6.1.11)), Γ has at least one equilibrium.

If an equilibrium is played, then each player uses a strategy which maximizes his a priori expected payoff. However, once the information set $u \in U_i$ is reached, only the payoffs after u are relevant to player i and, therefore, in the remainder of the game, player i will use a strategy which is a *best reply at* u, i.e. a strategy b_i' which satisfies

(6.2.2) $$R_{iu}(b\backslash b_i') = \max_{b_i'' \in B_i} R_{iu}(b\backslash b_i'') ,$$

where the conditional expected payoff $R_{iu}(b)$ is defined by

(6.2.3) $$R_{iu}(b) = \sum_{z \in Z} \mathbb{P}^b(z\,|\,u)r_i(z) = \sum_{x \in u} \mathbb{P}^b(x\,|\,u)R_{ix}(b) \qquad \text{if } \mathbb{P}^b(u) > 0.$$

Note that it follows from Lemma 6.1.10 that $R_{iu}(b\backslash b_i')$ depends only on what b_i' prescribes at the information sets v with $v \geq u$.

In the following theorem the two "best reply" concepts which have been introduced are related to each other.

THEOREM 6.2.1. b_i' is a best reply against b if and only if b_i' is a best reply against b at all information sets $u \in U_i$ which are reached with positive probability when $b\backslash b_i'$ is played.

PROOF. Let $\{u_\alpha;\ \alpha \in A\}$ be a collection of information sets of player i such that $\{Z(u_\alpha);\ \alpha \in A\}$ is a partition of $Z(P_i)$, where P_i is the set of decision points of player i. Then, for every $b \in B$, we have

$$R_i(b) = \sum_{\alpha} \mathbb{P}^b(u_\alpha)R_{iu_\alpha}(b) + \sum_{z \notin Z(P_i)} \mathbb{P}^b(z)r_i(z),$$

where the summation ranges over all α for which $\mathbb{P}^b(u_\alpha) > 0$.
From this the statement of the theorem follows immediately. □

Theorem 6.2.1 shows that for a strategy combination to be an equilibrium it is only necessary that rational behavior is prescribed at every information set which might be reached when the equilibrium is played; at every other information set the behavior may be more or less arbitrary. This is the cause for the existence of unreasonable equilibria of extensive form games as we have seen in chapter 1 and the reason why the Nash equilibrium concept has to be refined. For extensive form games, the need to refine the equilibrium concept is much more severe than for normal form games, since there are "many" extensive form games with unreasonable equilibria , whereas we have seen that for almost all normal form games all equilibria are nice (Theorem 2.6.2). To demonstrate this, consider the game of figure 1.2.1. All games close to this game have two equilibria, of which only (R_1,R_2) is reasonable. Hence, for extensive form games, it is definitely not true that for almost all games all equilibria are nice. Note, furthermore, that, since all games close to the game of figure 1.2.1 have (L_1,L_2) as an equilibrium, (L_1,L_2) is an essential equilibrium of this game (where essentiality is defined similarly as in Definition 2.4.1). Hence, for extensive form games an essential equilibrium need not be nice and Theorem 2.4.3 cannot be generalized to extensive form games. In fact, by using the methods of the proof of Theorem 2 of KREPS AND WILSON [1982a], one can show:

THEOREM 6.2.2. For almost all extensive form games all equilibria are essential.

This theorem shows that many essential equilibria are unreasonable and, therefore, we will not consider the concept of essential equilibria any more.

The first concept we considered in chapter 1 to eliminate Nash equilibria which prescribe irrational behavior at unreached information sets was the subgame perfectness concept (SELTEN [1965]). An equilibrium b of Γ is said to be a *subgame perfect equilibrium* of Γ if, for every subgame Γ_x of Γ, the restriction b_x of b to Γ constitutes a Nash equilibrium of Γ_x. The following lemma is essential in establishing that every game possesses at least one subgame perfect equilibrium.

LEMMA 6.2.3. (KUHN [1953]). If b_x is an equilibrium of the subgame Γ_x and b_{-x} is an equilibrium of the truncated game $\Gamma_{-x}(b_x)$, then (b_{-x},b_x) is an equilibrium of Γ.

The proof of Lemma 6.2.3 follows easily from the observation that for every $b \in B$

$$R_i(b) = \mathbb{P}^b(x)R_{ix}(b) + \sum_{z \notin Z(x)} \mathbb{P}^b(z)r_i(z) ,$$

and that, if Γ_x is well-defined, $R_{ix}(b)$ depends only on b_x. Lemma 6.2.3 implies that a subgame perfect equilibrium of Γ can be found by dynamic programming: first one considers all smallest subgames of Γ and then one truncates Γ by assuming that in any such subgame an equilibrium will be played. This procedure is repeated until there are no subgames left. In this way one meets all subgames and lemma 6.2.3 assures that in every subgame an equilibrium results.

THEOREM 6.2.4. Every game possesses at least one subgame perfect equilibrium.

Since there are many games with unreasonable subgame perfect equilibria (e.g. all games close to the game of figure 1.4.1 have this property), the equilibrium concept has to be refined further. One such refinement is considered in the next section.

6.3. SEQUENTIAL EQUILIBRIA

The concept of sequential equilibria has been proposed in KREPS AND WILSON [1982a] in order to exclude the unreasonable Nash equilibria. In this section, we give the formal definition of this concept and derive some elementary properties of it. Throughout the section, we consider a fixed extensive form game Γ. The section contains no results which are not already contained in KREPS AND WILSON [1982a].

Suppose the players have agreed to play the equilibrium b of Γ. It seems reasonable to suppose that player i, upon reaching an information set u with prior probability 0, will try to reconstruct what has happened and will choose a strategy which is a best reply at u against b, with respect to his beliefs about how the game has evolved thus far. The basic assumption underlying the sequential equilibrium concept, is that the players indeed behave in this way (which corresponds to the notion of rationality of SAVAGE [1954]). According to this concept, a rational solution of the game, therefore, not only has to prescribe the strategies used by the players, but also has to prescribe the beliefs the players have. This leads to the following definitions.
A *system of beliefs* is a mapping $\mu: X \to [0,1]$ with $\sum_{x \in u} \mu(x) = 1$ for all information sets u. An *assessment* is a pair (b,μ) where b is a behavior strategy combination and μ is a system of beliefs.
In an assessment (b,μ), the system of beliefs μ represents the beliefs of the players when b is played, i.e. if $x \in u$ with $u \in U_i$, then $\mu(x)$ is the probability player i assigns to being at x if he gets to hear that u is reached. An assessment (b,μ) together with an information set u, determine a probability distribution $\mathbb{P}_u^{b,\mu}$ on Z by

$$\mathbb{P}_u^{b,\mu} := \sum_{x \in u} \mu(x) \mathbb{P}_x^b .$$

The expectation of r_i with respect to $\mathbb{P}_u^{b,\mu}$ will be denoted by $R_{iu}^{\mu}(b)$, hence

$$R_{iu}^{\mu}(b) = \sum_{z \in Z} \mathbb{P}_u^{b,\mu}(z) r_i(z).$$

If player i expects b to be played and if his beliefs are given by μ, then, if $u \in U_i$ is reached, he will choose a strategy b_i' satisfying

$$R^{\mu}_{iu}(b\backslash b'_i) = \max_{b''_i \in B_i} R^{\mu}_{iu}(b\backslash b''_i).$$

Such a strategy is called a *best reply at u against* (b,μ). Obviously, for an assessment (b,μ) to be an equilibrium, it is necessary that b is a *sequential best reply* against (b,μ), i.e. that b prescribes a best reply at every information set, but this is not sufficient, since the beliefs μ also have to be consistent with b. In particular, the beliefs should be determined by b, whenever possible, i.e.

(6.3.1) $$\mu(x) = \mathbb{P}^b(x|u) \qquad \text{if } x \in u \text{ and } \mathbb{P}^b(u) > 0 .$$

Note that (6.3.1) determines μ completely if b is completely mixed. But also if $\mathbb{P}^b(u) = 0$ the beliefs at u cannot be completely arbitrary, since they have to respect the structure of the game. For instance, if the beliefs of player i are given by μ and if b is played, then at an information set $v \geq u$ his beliefs should satisfy.

$$\mu(x) = \mathbb{P}^{b,\mu}_u(x|v) \qquad \text{if } x \in v \text{ and } \mathbb{P}^{b,\mu}_u(v) > 0.$$

To ensure that all such conditions are satisfied, Kreps and Wilson adopt the following definition of consistency which in essence means that the beliefs μ can be explained by small deviations from b, i.e. by means of mistakes.

DEFINITION 6.3.1. An assessment (b,μ) is *consistent* if there exists a sequence $\{b(\varepsilon),\mu(\varepsilon)\}_{\varepsilon\downarrow 0}$ where $b(\varepsilon)$ is a completely mixed behavior strategy combination and $\mu(\varepsilon)$ is the system of beliefs generated by $b(\varepsilon)$ (i.e. is given by (6.3.1)) such that $\lim_{\varepsilon\downarrow 0}(b(\varepsilon),\mu(\varepsilon)) = (b,\mu)$.

A *sequential equilibrium* is a consistent assessment (b,μ) for which b is a sequential best reply against (b,μ).

For an extensive discussion concerning the definition of consistency, we refer to KREPS AND WILSON [1982a]. It is a consequence of the Theorems 6.4.3 and 6.4.4 that every game possesses at least one sequential equilibrium. Sometimes we will abuse terminology a little and call a strategy combination b a sequential equilibrium if some μ can be found for which (b,μ) is a sequential equilibrium. Note that for b to be sequential it is only necessary that b is supported by some system of beliefs; it might very well be the case that another system of beliefs which is also consistent with b completely upsets the equilibrium (this is the case for the equilibrium (A,R_2) in the game of figure 6.5.1).

Recall that the perfect recall assumption 6.1.7 implies that the set of information sets of player i is partially ordered and that it is possible to construct a decision tree for player i once the opponents of i have fixed their strategies. For a choice $c \in C_u$

with $u \in U_i$, let us denote by S(c) the set of all those information sets and endpoints of player i's decision tree which come directly after c, hence

$$S(c) := \{v \in U_i \cup Z;\ c < v \text{ and (if } w \in U_i \cup Z \text{ and } c < w \leq v, \text{ then } w = v)\} .$$

Let (b,μ) be a consistent assessment. Perfect recall implies that the beliefs of player i are not influenced by his own strategy and, therefore, for all $u \in U_i$ and $c \in C_u$, we have

$$\mathbb{P}_u^{b\backslash c,\mu} = \sum_{v \in S(c)} \mathbb{P}_u^{b\backslash c,\mu}(v)\,\mathbb{P}_v^{b,\mu} ,$$

where $\mathbb{P}_z^{b,\mu}$ is the degenerate distribution at z for $z \in Z$. This implies that for all $u \in U_i$ and $c \in C_u$

$$R_{iu}^{\mu}(b\backslash c) = \sum_{v \in S(c)} \mathbb{P}_u^{b\backslash c,\mu}(v)\,R_{iv}^{\mu}(b) . \tag{6.3.2}$$

Let $\tilde{R}_{iu}^{\mu}(b)$ (resp. $\tilde{R}_{ic}^{\mu}(b)$) be the maximum expected payoff player i can get against (b,μ) if u is reached (resp. u is reached and c is played at u). Then it follows from (6.3.2) that these quantities can be iteratively computed by the dynamic programming scheme

$$\tilde{R}_{ic}^{\mu}(b) = \sum_{v \in S(c)} \mathbb{P}_u^{b\backslash c,\mu}(v)\,\tilde{R}_{iv}^{\mu}(b) , \tag{6.3.3}$$

$$\tilde{R}_{iu}^{\mu}(b) = \max_{c \in C_u} \tilde{R}_{ic}^{\mu}(b) , \tag{6.3.4}$$

which is initialized by setting $\tilde{R}_{iz}^{\mu}(b) = r_i(z)$ for $z \in Z$. Therefore, b_i' is a sequential best reply against (b,μ) if and only if for all $u \in U_i$ and $c \in C_i$:

(6.3.5) if $b_{iu}'(c) > 0$, then c attains the maximum in (6.3.4)

and so checking whether a consistent assessment is a sequential equilibrium is very easy. Since, furthermore, verifying whether an assessment is consistent can be executed by an efficient labelling procedure (KREPS AND WILSON [1982a], Appendix 1), it is easy to check whether an assessment is a sequential equilibrium. This is a great advantage of this concept, when compared to Selten's perfectness concept, which will be considered in the next section.

To conclude our preliminary discussion on sequential equilibria, we note that the following theorem can easily be proved by the methods of Theorem 6.2.1.

THEOREM 6.3.2. Every sequential equilibrium is subgame perfect.

In section 5, we will see that not all sequential equilibria are sensible and that, therefore, this concept has to be refined further. The perfectness concept, which will be considered in the next section, is such a refinement, but as we will see, this concept refines the sequential equilibrium concept only slightly.

6.4. PERFECT EQUILIBRIA

The perfectness concept has been proposed in SELTEN [1975] in order to eliminate the equilibria which prescribe irrational behavior at unreached information sets. In this section, we show that every extensive form game possesses at least one perfect equilibrium. The relation between perfect equilibria and sequential equilibria is studied and the difference between perfectness in the normal form and perfectness in the extensive form is illustrated.

An equilibrium strategy can prescribe irrational behavior only at those information sets which cannot be reached when the equilibrium is played. Selten has argued that virtually all information sets are reachable, whatever equilibrium is played, as a consequence of the possibility that mistakes might occur. Each player should incorporate this possibility in choosing his strategy and, therefore, he should prescribe a rational choice at every information set. Mathematically, the idea of mistakes is formalized in the same way as for normal form games, i.e. by a perturbed game. In such a perturbed game, every choice at every information set has to be chosen with a strictly positive (mistake) probability.

DEFINITION 6.4.1. Let Γ be an extensive form game. If η is a mapping which assigns to every choice in Γ a positive number η_c such that $\sum_{c \in C_u} \eta_c < 1$ for every information set u, then the *perturbed game* (Γ,η) is the (infinite) extensive form game with the same structure as Γ, but in which every player i is only allowed to use behavior strategies b_i which satisfy $b_{iu}(c) \geq \eta_c$ for all $u \in U_i$ and $c \in C_u$.

Let (Γ,η) be a perturbed game and let $B(\eta)$ be the set of admissible strategy combinations in (Γ,η). An admissible strategy combination b is said to be an equilibrium of (Γ,η) if it is a best reply against itself, i.e. if it satisfies

$$(6.4.1) \qquad R_i(b) = \max_{b_i' \in B_i(\eta)} R_i(b \backslash b_i') \qquad \text{for all } i \in \{1,\ldots,n\}.$$

From Theorem 6.2.1 it is seen that b is an equilibrium of (Γ,η) if and only if b prescribes a best reply at every information set, i.e.

(6.4.2) $$R_{iu}(b) = \max_{b'_i \in B_i(\eta)} R_{iu}(b \backslash b'_i) \qquad \text{for all } i,\ u\ .$$

An equilibrium of Γ is said to be a perfect equilibrium if it is still sensible to play this equilibrium if slight mistakes are taken into account. Formally

DEFINITION 6.4.2. b is a *perfect equilibrium* of Γ if b is a limit point of a sequence $\{b(\eta)\}_{\eta \downarrow 0}$ where $b(\eta)$ is an equilibrium of (Γ,η).

Assume b is a perfect equilibrium of Γ and, for $t \in \mathbb{N}$, let $b(t)$ be an equilibrium of $(\Gamma,\eta(t))$ such that $\lim_{t\to\infty} b(t) = b$ and $\lim_{t\to\infty} \eta(t) = 0$. For $t \in \mathbb{N}$, let $\mu(t)$ be the system of beliefs generated by $b(t)$ and, without loss of generality, assume $\mu = \lim_{t\to\infty} \mu(t)$ exists. Since for all $i \in U$, $u \in U_i$ and $b'_i \in B_i$

$$\lim_{t\to\infty} R_{iu}(b(t)\backslash b'_i) = R^{\mu}_{iu}(b\backslash b'_i)\ ,$$

it follows from (6.4.2) that

$$R^{\mu}_{iu}(b) = \max_{b'_i \in B_i} R^{\mu}_{iu}(b\backslash b'_i) \qquad \text{for all } i,u,$$

which shows that (b,μ) is a sequential equilibrium. Hence, every perfect equilibrium is sequential. In section 1.4, we have seen that the converse of this statement is not correct. This is also clear by comparing the definitions of sequential equilibria and perfect equilibria: whereas sequential equilibria only have to be optimal with respect to mistakes made in the past, perfect equilibria also have to be optimal with respect to mistakes that might occur in the future. Hence, a perfect equilibrium, in addition to being sequential, also has to satisfy some robustness condition (cf. normal form games, in this case every equilibrium is sequential). As for normal form games, one might expect that almost all sequential equilibria possess this robustness condition and, in fact, we have

THEOREM 6.4.3. (KREPS AND WILSON [1982a]).

(i) Every perfect equilibrium is sequential.

(ii) For almost all extensive form games, almost all sequential equilibria are perfect.

(iii) For almost all games, the set of sequential equilibrium outcomes (i.e. the set of probability distributions over the endpoints resulting from sequential equilibria) coincides with the set of perfect equilibrium outcomes.

(iv) For almost all games, the number of sequential equilibrium outcomes is finite.

In part (iv) of Theorem 6.4.3, finite cannot be replaced by odd as one can see by considering the game of figure 6.5.1: all games close to this one have two sequential equilibrium outcomes, viz. (L_1,L_2) and A. Furthermore, note the difference between the parts (ii) and (iii) of the theorem: Part (iii) states that generically an outside observer cannot conclude whether a perfect or a sequential equilibrium is played, but even for a generic game there may exist some sequential equilibria which are not perfect (however, part (ii) guarantees that there is only a small set of such equilibria).

Theorem 6.4.3 shows that generically there is little difference between the sequential equilibrium concept and the perfectness concept. Kreps and Wilson have shown that exact coincidence can be obtained by slightly modifying Selten's perfectness definition. Namely, define a *weakly perfect equilibrium* of Γ as a strategy combination b which is a limit point of a sequence $\{b(\eta)\}_{\eta \downarrow 0}$ where $b(\eta)$ is an equilibrium of a perturbed game $(\Gamma(\eta),\eta)$ associated with an extensive form game $\Gamma(\eta)$ with payoffs close to those of Γ. Then it can be shown (KREPS AND WILSON [1982a], Proposition 6) that an equilibrium is sequential if and only if it is weakly perfect.

Comparing Theorem 6.4.3 with Theorem 2.6.2, the reader might get the impression that for extensive form games it is not necessary to consider more stringent refinements than sequential equilibria, in the sense that almost always all sequential equilibria have all nice properties one wants equilibria to have. In the next section, it will be shown that this impression is wrong.

We will now show that every extensive form game possesses at least one perfect equilibrium (and, hence, also at least one sequential equilibrium). It suffices to show that every perturbed game possesses at least one quilibrium. It will be clear that in an equilibrium of a perturbed game a choice which is not optimal has to be taken with minimum probability. Hence, for an admissible strategy combination b to be an equilibrium of (Γ,μ), it is necessary that

$$(6.4.3) \qquad \text{if } b_{iu}(c) > \eta_c, \text{ then } R_{iu}(b\backslash c) = \max_{c' \in C_u} R_{iu}(b\backslash c') \qquad \text{for all } i,u,c.$$

By using a dynamic programming argument, one easily sees that (6.4.3) implies (6.4.2), hence, $b \in B(\eta)$ is an equilibrium of (Γ,η) if and only if b satisfies (6.4.3). Notice that, since the choices at u do not influence the payoffs at the information sets $v \in U_i$ which do not come after u, formula (6.4.3) is equivalent to

$$(6.4.4) \qquad \text{if } R_i(b\backslash c) < R_i(b\backslash c'), \text{ then } b_{iu}(c) = \eta_c \qquad \text{for all } i,u,c,c'.$$

Now consider Kuhn's interpretation of how an extensive form game is played (KUHN [1953]). Kuhn views a player as a collection of separated agents, one agent for each information set of this player, each agent having the same payoff as the player to whom he belongs. The normal form game $AN(\Gamma)$ corresponding to this interpretation is called the *agent normal form* of Γ (SELTEN [1975]). The players in $AN(\Gamma)$ are the agents of Γ, agent iu (i.e. the one corresponding to the information set $u \in U_i$) has

C_u as pure strategy set and R_i as payoff. By comparing (6.4.4) with (2.2.3), it is seen that b is an equilibrium of (Γ,η) if and only if b is an equilibrium of $(AN(\Gamma),\eta)$. Therefore, we can conclude from Theorem 2.1.1 that (Γ,η) possesses at least one equilibrium, hence, that Γ has at least one perfect equilibrium.

THEOREM 6.4.4. (SELTEN [1975]). Every extensive form game possesses at least one perfect equilibrium. The set of perfect equilibria of Γ coincides with the set of perfect equilibria of the agent normal form of Γ.

In general, the perfect equilibria of Γ do not coincide with the perfect equilibria of the normal form of Γ, as is illustrated by means of the games of the figures 6.4.1 and 6.4.2.

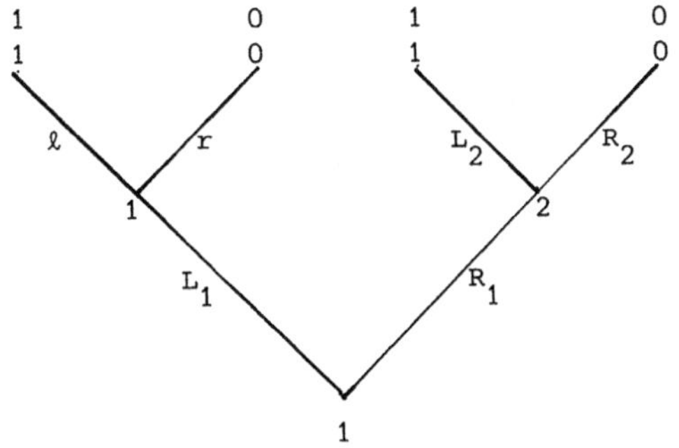

Figure 6.4.1. A perfect equilibrium of Γ need not be a perfect equilibrium of the normal form of Γ.

The unique perfect equilibrium of the normal form of the game of figure 6.4.1 is $(L_1\ell,L_2)$. In the extensive form also the equilibrium $(R_1\ell,L_2)$ is perfect: if player 1 expects that player 2 makes mistakes with a smaller probability than he himself does, then it is indeed rational for him to choose R_1 at his first information set. The game of figure 6.4.1 shows that a perfect equilibrium of an extensive form game may involve dominated strategies. It follows from (6.4.4) that a perfect equilibrium cannot involve dominated choices, but Theorem 3.2.1 cannot be generalized to extensive form games: for 2 person games, an equilibrium which is in undominated choices need not be perfect (caused by the fact that a 2-person extensive form game may have more than 2 agents).

The game of figure 6.4.1 might be called a degenerate game and, in fact, it can be shown that almost always a perfect equilibrium of Γ will also be perfect in the normal form of this game. The game of figure 6.4.2, however, shows that it is frequently the case that a perfect equilibrium of $N(\Gamma)$ is not a perfect equilibrium of Γ (also see SELTEN [1975], section 13).

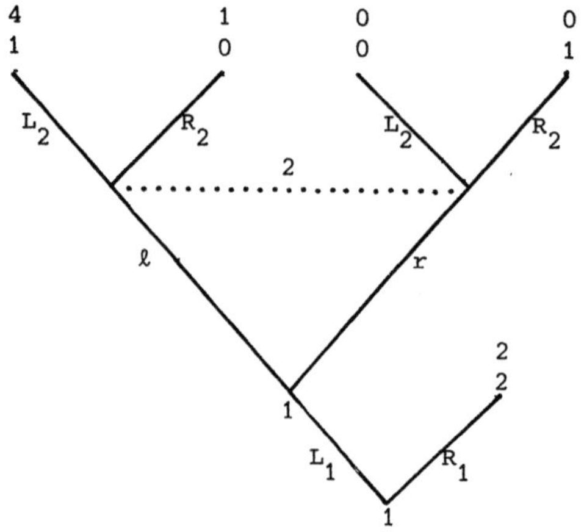

Extensive form game Γ

	L_2	R_2
$L_1\ell$	4, 1	1, 0
L_1r	0, 0	0, 1
$R_1\ell$	2, 2	2, 2
R_1r	2, 2	2, 2

Normal form game $N(\Gamma)$

Figure 6.4.2. A perfect equilibrium of the normal form of Γ is not necessarily a perfect equilibrium of Γ.

The unique subgame perfect equilibrium of Γ is $(L_1\ell, L_2)$. In the normal form of Γ, also $(R_1\ell, R_2)$ is perfect: if player 2 expects player 1 to make the mistake L_1r with a larger probability than the mistake $L_1\ell$, then it is optimal for him to choose R_2, thereby forcing player 1 to choose $R_1\ell$ or R_1r. Note that the perfectness concept for normal form games does not exclude the possibility that L_1r occurs with a larger probability than $L_1\ell$. In Γ, however, player 2 should not think that L_1r occurs with a larger probability than $L_1\ell$: if the second information set of player 1 is reached, then ℓ is better for player 1 than r and, therefore, player 1 will intend to choose ℓ and so ℓ will occur with the largest probability.

Note that the equilibrium $(R_1\ell, R_2)$ is not a proper equilibrium of $N(\Gamma)$. The properness concept prevents player 2 from thinking that L_1r occurs with a greater probability than $L_1\ell$. The only proper equilibrium of $N(\Gamma)$ is $(L_1\ell, L_2)$ and so, in this example, the proper equilibrium of Γ prescribes sensible behavior in Γ. In the next section, it will be shown that this is generally true.

6.5. PROPER EQUILIBRIA

In MYERSON [1978] the properness concept has been introduced for normal form games. In this section, the properness concept for extensive form games is considered. First it is shown that unreasonable sequential equilibria can be eliminated by restricting oneself to proper equilibria of the agent normal form. Next, we show that also proper equilibria of the normal form of Γ induce sequential equilibria in Γ and that the restriction to such equilibria also eliminates unreasonable sequential equilibria. The concluding example of the section shows that not all unreasonable sequential equilibria are eliminated by the properness concept.

Consider the game of figure 6.5.1 which is a slight modification of the game of figure 6.4.2. (We do not claim that these games are equivalent).

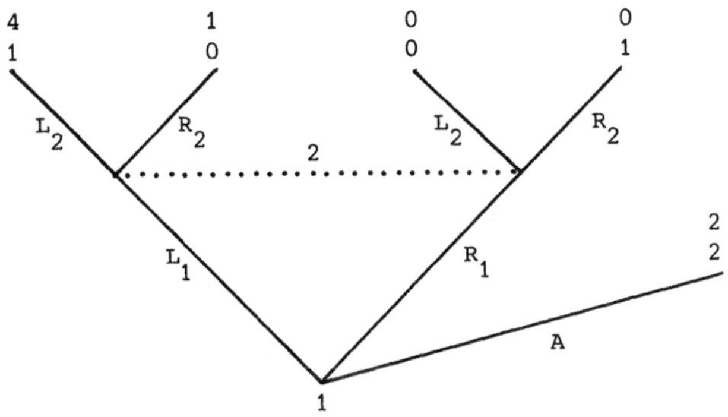

Figure 6.5.1. Not all sequential equilibria are sensible.

A sequential (and perfect) equilibrium of this game is (A,R_2). This equilibrium is supported by the beliefs of player 2 that the mistake R_1 occurs with a larger probability than the mistake L_1. In our view these beliefs are not sensible. Since for player 1 the choice L_1 is better than the choice R_1, player 2 should expect L_1 to occur with the largest probability and, therefore, if his information set is reached, he should play L_2, thereby inducing player 1 to play L_1. Hence, only (L_1,L_2) is a sensible equilibrium. Notice that all games close to the game of figure 6.5.1 have (A,R_2) as a sequential (yet not sensible) equilibrium and so there exists an open set of games for which not all sequential equilibria are sensible, which shows that the sequential equilibrium concept has to be refined further.

In the game Γ of figure 6.5.1, the equilibrium (A,R_2) can be excluded by restricting oneself to proper equilibria of the agent normal form of Γ. A proper equilibrium of $AN(\Gamma)$ is a strategy combination b, which is the limit of a sequence $\{b^{\varepsilon}\}_{\varepsilon \downarrow 0}$ of completely mixed behavior strategy combinations which satisfy

$$\text{(6.5.1)} \qquad \text{if } R_{iu}(b^{\varepsilon}\backslash c) < R_{iu}(b^{\varepsilon}\backslash c') \text{ then } b^{\varepsilon}_{iu}(c) \le \varepsilon b^{\varepsilon}_{iu}(c') \qquad \text{for all } i,u \text{ and } c,c' \in C_u.$$

(cf. Definition 2.3.1). Note that every proper equilibrium of $AN(\Gamma)$ is a perfect equilibrium of Γ (Theorem 6.4.4). The converse is not true as we have seen above. Formule (6.5.1) expresses the idea that if some choice c is worse than a choice c' at the <u>same</u> information set, then c is mistakenly chosen with a much smaller probability than c'. However, the fact that only choices at the same information set of a player are compared has the consequence that not all unreasonable sequential equilibria are excluded by restricting oneself to proper equilibria of $AN(\Gamma)$. This is demonstrated by means of the game of figure 6.5.2, which is a slight modification of the game of figure 6.5.1.

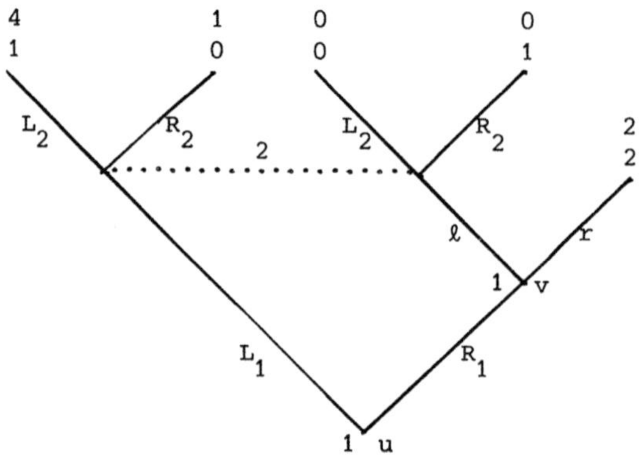

<u>Figure 6.5.2.</u> A proper equilibrium of $AN(\Gamma)$ need not be sensible in Γ.

A perfect equilibrium of the game of figure 6.5.2 is (R_1r,R_2). Since at each information set there are just two choices, every perfect equilibrium of $AN(\Gamma)$ (hence, of Γ) is a proper equilibrium of $AN(\Gamma)$ and so (R_1r,R_2) is a proper equilibrium of $AN(\Gamma)$. We do not consider this equilibrium as being reasonable. Upon reaching his information set, player 2 should realize that for player 1 the choice ℓ at v is worse than his choice L_1 at u. Therefore, he should assign the largest probability to being in the left hand node of his information set and, consequently, he should play L_2, thereby inducing player 1 to play L_1. Hence, the only sensible equilibrium is (L_1r,L_2).

Consider the normal form $N(\Gamma)$ of the game Γ of figure 6.5.2, which is given in figure 6.5.3

	L_2	R_2
$L_1\ell$	4, 1	1, 0
L_1r	4, 1	1, 0
$R_1\ell$	0, 0	0, 1
R_1r	2, 2	2, 2

Figure 6.5.3. The normal form of the game of figure 6.5.2.

The proper equilibria of this game are the equilibria in which player 2 plays L_2 and player 1 plays a combination of $L_1\ell$ and L_1r. Therefore, every proper equilibrium leads to L_1 and L_2 being played in Γ and so yields the unique sensible outcome of Γ. Note, however, that a proper equilibrium of $N(\Gamma)$ may prescribe irrational behavior off the equilibrium path: $(L_1\ell, L_2)$ prescribes irrational behavior at the information set v of player 1. Off the equilibrium path, rational behavior can be obtained by looking at limit points of (behavior strategy combinations induced by) ε-proper equilibria as ε tends to 0. If s^ε is an ε-proper equilibrium of $N(\Gamma)$ close to $(L_1\ell, L_2)$ and if b^ε is the behavior strategy combination induced by s^ε (i.e. b_i^ε is given by (6.1.12) for $i \in \{1,2\}$), then we have that b^ε converges to the unique sensible equilibrium (L_1r, L_2) of Γ, as follows easily from the definition of an ε-proper equilibrium of $N(\Gamma)$ and (6.1.12).

In the game Γ of figure 6.5.2, proper equilibria of $N(\Gamma)$ give rise to sensible outcomes in Γ and limit points of ε-proper equilibria of $N(\Gamma)$ prescribe rational behavior everywhere in the game tree. Next, it will be shown that this is true for any extensive form game Γ. In fact, it will be shown that a behavior strategy combination b^ε induced by an ε-proper equilibrium of $N(\Gamma)$ possesses a property similar to (6.5.1) (see (6.5.5)). Let Γ be an extensive form game and let b be a completely mixed behavior strategy combination. For $c \in C_u$ with $u \in U_i$ define $\tilde{R}_{ic}(b)$ as the maximum payoff player i can get if u is reached, if he plays c at u and if his opponents play b, i.e.

(6.5.2) $$\tilde{R}_{ic}(b) = \max_{b_i' \in B_i} R_{iu}(b \backslash b_i' \backslash c) ,$$

where $b\backslash b_i'\backslash c$ denotes the behavior strategy combination $b\backslash(b_i'\backslash c)$. Note that $\tilde{R}_{ic}(b)$ can be computed by the following dynamic programming scheme (cf. (6.3.3),(6.3.4)):

$$(6.5.3)\qquad \tilde{R}_{ic}(b) = \sum_{v\in S(c)} \mathbb{P}_u^{b\backslash c}(v)\tilde{R}_{iv}(b) \qquad \text{for } c \in C_u,$$

$$(6.5.4)\qquad \tilde{R}_{iu}(b) = \max_{c\in C_u} \tilde{R}_{ic}(b) \ ,$$

which is initialized by setting $\tilde{R}_{iz}(b) = r_i(z)$ for $z \in Z$.
We have (cf. formula (6.5.1)):

<u>LEMMA 6.5.1</u>. If b^ε is a behavior strategy combination in Γ which is induced by an ε-proper equilibrium s^ε of $N(\Gamma)$, then

$$(6.5.5)\qquad \text{if } \tilde{R}_{ic}(b^\varepsilon) < \tilde{R}_{i\hat{c}}(b^\varepsilon), \text{ then } b_{iu}^\varepsilon(c) \le \varepsilon|\mathrm{Rel}(c)|b_{iu}^\varepsilon(\hat{c}) \quad \text{for all } i,u \text{ and } c,\hat{c}\in C_u,$$

where Rel(c) denotes the set of all pure strategies which are relevant for c (see (6.1.12)).

<u>PROOF</u>. Assume $i,u,c,\hat{c}$ are such that the condition of (6.5.5) is satisfied and let $\tilde{\varphi}_i \in \mathrm{Rel}(\hat{c})$ be a pure strategy which satisfies

$$\tilde{R}_{i\hat{c}}(b^\varepsilon) = R_{iu}(b^\varepsilon\backslash\tilde{\varphi}_i) \ .$$

For any strategy $\varphi_i \in \mathrm{Rel}(c)$, we have

$$(6.5.6)\qquad R_{iu}(b^\varepsilon\backslash\varphi_i) < R_{iu}(b^\varepsilon\backslash\tilde{\varphi}_i) \ .$$

For $\varphi_i \in \mathrm{Rel}(c)$, define $\hat{\varphi}_i \in \mathrm{Rel}(\hat{c})$ by

$$\hat{\varphi}_{iv} = \begin{cases} \tilde{\varphi}_{iv} & \text{if } v \ge u \ , \\ \varphi_{iv} & \text{otherwise} \ . \end{cases}$$

Then it follows from (6.5.6) that

$$R_i(b^\varepsilon\backslash\varphi_i) < R_i(b^\varepsilon\backslash\hat{\varphi}_i) \ ,$$

which, since b^ε is induced by s^ε, is equivalent to

$$R_i(s^\varepsilon\backslash\varphi_i) < R_i(s^\varepsilon\backslash\hat{\varphi}_i).$$

Hence, from the definition of an ε-proper equilibrium, we deduce

$$s_i^\varepsilon(\varphi_i) \le \varepsilon s_i^\varepsilon(\hat{\varphi}_i) \ ,$$

which, obviously, implies that

$$(6.5.7) \qquad \sum_{\varphi_i \in \mathrm{Rel}(c)} s_i^{\varepsilon}(\varphi_i) \leq \varepsilon |\mathrm{Rel}(c)| \sum_{\varphi_i \in \mathrm{Rel}(\hat{c})} s_i^{\varepsilon}(\varphi_i) .$$

Dividing both sides of (6.5.7) by $\sum_{\varphi_i \in \mathrm{Rel}(u)} s_i^{\varepsilon}(\varphi_i)$ yields (6.5.5). □

Let s be a proper equilibrium of $N(\Gamma)$, for $\varepsilon > 0$, let s^{ε} be an ε-proper equilibrium of Γ converging to s as ε tends to 0 and let b^{ε} be induced by s^{ε}.
Without loss of generality, assume that $(b,\mu) = \lim_{\varepsilon \downarrow 0}(b^{\varepsilon},\mu^{\varepsilon})$ exists, where μ^{ε} is the system of beliefs generated by b^{ε} (i.e. μ^{ε} is given by (6.3.1)). From (6.5.4) and (6.5.5) we see that

$$\text{if } b_{iu}(c) > 0, \text{ then } \tilde{R}_{ic}(b^{\varepsilon}) = \tilde{R}_{iu}(b^{\varepsilon}) \quad \text{for all sufficiently small } \varepsilon.$$

Therefore, we have

$$\text{if } b_{iu}(c) > 0, \text{ then } \tilde{R}^{\mu}_{ic}(b) = \tilde{R}^{\mu}_{iu}(b) \quad \text{for all } i,u,c,$$

and, so, from the characterization of sequential best replies given in (6.3.5), it follows that (b,μ) is a sequential equilibrium of Γ. Since, furthermore, the behavior strategy induced by s_i coincides with b_i at all information sets which might be reached when s_i is played, we have that b generates the same path as s does, i.e. $\mathbb{P}^s = \mathbb{P}^b$. Hence, we have proved.

<u>THEOREM 6.5.2</u>

(i) If s is a proper equilibrium of $N(\Gamma)$, then $\mathbb{P}^s$ is a sequential equilibrium outcome in Γ.

(ii) If b is a limit point of a sequence $\{b^{\varepsilon}\}_{\varepsilon \downarrow 0}$ where b^{ε} is induced by an ε-proper equilibrium s^{ε} of $N(\Gamma)$, then b is a sequential equilibrium of Γ.

In theorem 6.5.2 "sequential" cannot be replaced by "perfect". Namely, consider the game Γ in which the payoffs are the same as in the game of figure 6.4.1, except for the fact that now player 1 always receives 1 if he plays R_1. The unique perfect equilibrium of this game is $(R_1 \ell, L_2)$. However, since $(L_1 \ell, L_2)$ is a proper equilibrium of the normal form of this game, also this equilibrium can be induced in the way of Theorem 6.5.2. Hence, a strategy induced by a proper equilibrium need not be robust with respect to mistakes made by the player himself.

We have already seen that by restricting oneself to proper equilibria (of the normal form, or of the agent normal form) one can eliminate unreasonable sequential equilibria. By means of the game of figure 6.5.4, which has the same structure as Kohlberg's example in KREPS AND WILSON [1982a] (Figure 14) it is shown that not all intuitively unreasonable sequential equilibria can be eliminated in this way.

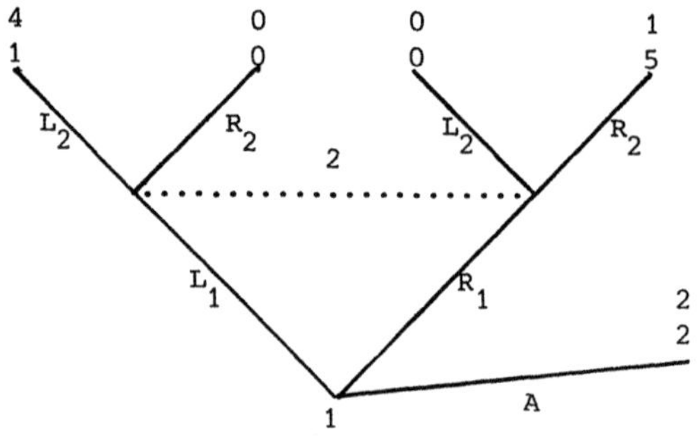

Figure 6.5.4. Not all proper equilibria are sensible.

A proper equilibrium of the game of figure 6.5.4 is (A,R_2): if player 2 expects the mistake R_1 to occur with a larger probability than the mistake L_1, then it is optimal for him to play R_2. However, this equilibrium is not sensible. If the players have agreed to play (A,R_2) and if the information set of player 2 is nevertheless reached, then at the outset player 2 should not conclude that player 1 has made a mistake, but he should ask himself whether player 1 could have had any reason to deviate. Since for rational players only equilibria are sensible, this means that he should check whether player 1 perhaps opts for a different equilibrium. Now, since (L_1,L_2) is the only equilibrium for which the information set of player 2 is reached and since, moreover, player 1 prefers this equilibrium to (A,R_2), he should conclude that indeed player 1 has chosen L_1 and, therefore, he is forced to choose L_2. Hence, only (L_1,L_2) is sensible.

The problem of how to refine the properness concept in order to exclude the unreasonable proper equilibria as in the game of figure 6.5.4 is still unsolved. In the author's view, this is by far the most important remaining problem in this area.

6.6. CONTROL COSTS

A game with control costs models the idea that a player makes mistakes as a consequence of the fact that it is too costly to control his actions completely (see chapter 4). If every player incurs control costs at any of his information sets in an extensive form game, then every choice will be taken with a positive probability and, consequently, every information set will be reached with positive probability. Therefore, one expects that only sequential equilibria can be obtained as limit points of equilibria of games with control costs as these costs go to 0. We will show that this is indeed the case, provided that the control costs are incorporated into the model in the correct way

A naive way to investigate the influence of control costs in an extensive form game would be to investigate the influence in the agent normal form. By means of the game of figure 6.6.1, it will be shown that this is not the correct way of modelling.

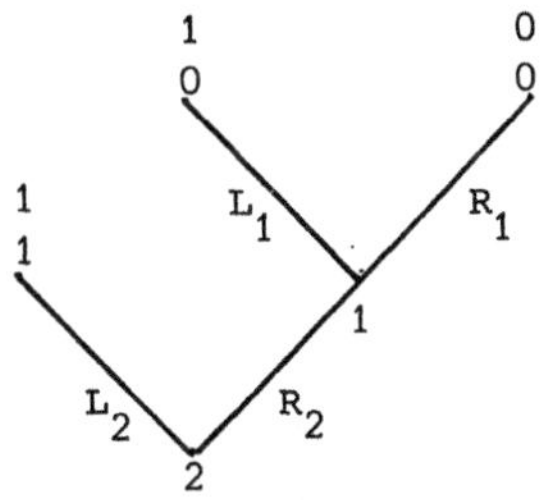

Extensive form game Γ

	L_2	R_2
L_1	1, 1	1, 0
R_1	1, 1	0, 0

Agent normal form $AN(\Gamma)$

Figure 6.6.1. The influence of control costs cannot be investigated by means of the agent normal form.

From the viewpoint of player 1, the game Γ is much different from $AN(\Gamma)$. In $AN(\Gamma)$ player 1 always has to move (no matter what player 2 does) and his choice R_1 is not much worse than L_1 (since player 2 will intend to play L_2). Therefore, if he incurs control costs, he will not spend much effort in trying to prevent R_1, in fact, the control costs may force him to choose R_1 with a positive probability (see section 4.3). In Γ, however, player 1 has to move only if player 2 has chosen R_2 and in this case R_1 is much worse than L_1. Therefore, if his information set is reached, player 1 will try very hard to prevent R_1 and even if he incurs control costs he will choose R_1 with a very small probability.

The reason that the influence of control costs cannot be investigated by means of the agent normal form is that in the agent normal form one always has to move and, hence, always incurs control costs, whereas in the extensive form one incurs control costs only if an information set is actually reached. This motivates the following definition.

DEFINITION 6.6.1. Let Γ be an n-person extensive form game and let $f = (f_1, \ldots, f_n)$ be an n-tuple of control cost functions (see section 4.1). The game Γ^f, which is called a *game with control costs*, is the extensive form game with the same structure as Γ, but in which the payoff to player i if b is played is given by

$$(6.6.1) \qquad R_i^f(b) := R_i(b) - \sum_{u\in U_i} \sum_{c\in C_u} \mathbb{P}^b(u) f_i(b_{iu}(c)) .$$

The game Γ^f models the idea that each player i incurs control costs as described by f_i at any of his information sets. One could also allow the possibility of different control costs at different information sets (in this case one just has to replace f_i by f_u in formula (6.6.1)), in fact, one can even allow different control costs for different choices (in this case (6.6.1) contains a term f_c). We will not consider these extensions. Note that the term $\mathbb{P}^b(u)$ in formula (6.6.1) ensures that player i incurs a cost at u only if u is actually reached when b is played.
The reader should have no difficulty in proving the following generalization of Theorem 4.2.6.

THEOREM 6.6.2. The game Γ^f possesses at least one equilibrium. All equilibria of Γ^f are completely mixed.

Similarly as in the proof of Lemma 4.2.3, it is seen that a completely mixed strategy combination b is an equilibrium of Γ^f if and only if

$$(6.6.2) \qquad R_i(b\backslash c) - R_i(b\backslash \hat{c}) = \mathbb{P}^b(u)[f_i'(b_{iu}(c)) - f_i'(b_{iu}(\hat{c}))] \quad \text{for all } i,u,c,\hat{c} .$$

Since, for every $u \in U_i$ and $c \in C_u$

$$R_i(b\backslash c) = \mathbb{P}^b(u) R_{iu}(b\backslash c) + \sum_{z\notin Z(u)} \mathbb{P}^b(z) r_i(z),$$

we can conclude from (6.6.2) that b is an equilibrium of Γ^f if and only if

$$(6.6.3) \qquad R_{iu}(b\backslash c) - R_{iu}(b\backslash \hat{c}) = f_i'(b_{iu}(c)) - f_i'(b_{iu}(\hat{c})) \quad \text{for all } i,u,c,\hat{c} .$$

From formula (6.6.3) we can conclude:

THEOREM 6.6.3. Let Γ be an n-person extensive form game and let f be an n-tuple of control cost functions. If b is a limit point of a sequence $\{b^\varepsilon\}_{\varepsilon\downarrow 0}$, where b^ε is an equilibrium of $\Gamma^{\varepsilon f}$, then b is a sequential equilibrium of Γ.

PROOF. Without loss of generality, assume b is the limit of $\{b^\varepsilon\}$. For $\varepsilon > 0$, let μ^ε be the system of beliefs generated by b^ε and, without loss of generality, assume $\mu = \lim_{\varepsilon\downarrow 0} \mu^\varepsilon$ exists. From (6.6.3) we can deduce

$$R_{iu}(b^\varepsilon\backslash c) - R_{iu}(b^\varepsilon\backslash \hat{c}) = \varepsilon[f_i'(b_{iu}^\varepsilon(c)) - f_i'(b_{iu}^\varepsilon(\hat{c}))] \quad \text{for all } i,u,c,\hat{c} .$$

Since, furthermore

$$\lim_{\varepsilon \downarrow 0} R_{iu}(b^{\varepsilon}\backslash c) = R^{\mu}_{iu}(b\backslash c) \qquad \text{for all } i,u,c,$$

it follows in the same way as in the proof of Theorem 4.3.1, that

$$\text{if } R^{\mu}_{iu}(b\backslash c) < R^{\mu}_{iu}(b\backslash \hat{c}), \text{ then } b_{iu}(c) = 0 \qquad \text{for all } i,u,c,\hat{c},$$

from which one can conclude, e.g. by using a dynamic programming argument, that b is a sequential best reply against (b,μ). □

Since for normal form games every equilibrium is sequential, it follows from our discussion in section 4.3 that not all sequential equilibria can be obtained as a limit in the way of Theorem 6.6.3. Futhermore, it follows from the results in chapter 4 that to obtain perfectness instead of sequentialness the control costs have to satisfy more stringent conditions.

6.7. INCOMPLETE INFORMATION

In this section, it is investigated what the influences are of inexact knowledge of the payoffs on the strategy choices in an extensive form game. To that end, we study disturbed extensive form games, i.e. games in which each player, although knowing his own payoff function exactly, knows the payoff functions of his opponents somewhat imprecisely. One might expect that, under similar conditions as in chapter 5, only sequential equilibria can be obtained as limit points of equilibria of disturbed games as these disturbances go to zero, i.e. if the information about the payoffs becomes better and better. We will indicate that this is the case only if the disturbances are of a special kind, but it should be noted that the results are far from complete and that many challenging problems are still unsolved.

Let us start by giving an informal definition of a disturbed extensive form game (the formal definition is similar to Definition 5.2.1). Let Γ be an ordinary (complete information) n-person extensive form game. The situation we have in mind is the following: the players have to play a game of which it is common knowledge (AUMANN [1976]) that it has the same structure as Γ, but of which the payoffs may be slightly different from those in Γ, since each player's payoff is subject to small random disturbances, the precise effects of which are only known to the player himself. It is assumed that the distribution μ_i of the disturbances of player i's payoff is k n to all players. The game with these rules is denoted by $\Gamma(\mu)$, where μ is the n-tuple $(\mu_1,\ldots,\mu_n)$. As in chapter 5, it is assumed that μ satisfies the Assumptions 5.2.2 and 5.3.5. Since we are interested in the case in which the players are only slightly uncertain about each other's payoffs, we will investigate what happens if the disturbances go to 0, i.e. which equilibria of Γ can be approximated by equilibria of disturbed games $\Gamma(\mu^{\varepsilon})$ for which μ^{ε} converges weakly to 0 as ε tends to 0 (see section 5.3).

The first question which has to be answered is: how should an equilibrium of $\Gamma(\mu)$ be defined? First of all, a strategy of player i in $\Gamma(\mu)$ is a mechanism which tells him what to do for every payoff he might have, i.e. it is a mapping $\sigma_i : \mathbb{R}^Z \to B_i$, where Z is the set of endpoints of K and B_i is the set of behavior strategies of player i in Γ. We will restrict ourselves to strategies which satisfy:

(6.7.1) $$\text{if } r_i(z) > \max_{z' \neq z} r_i(z'), \text{ then } z \in \mathrm{Poss}(\sigma_i(r_i)) ,$$

where $\mathrm{Poss}(\sigma_i(r_i))$ is the set of nodes in the tree which might be reached when $\sigma_i(r_i)$ is played (see (6.1.9)). Obviously, every sensible strategy satisfies (6.7.1). Suppose the strategy combination $\sigma = (\sigma_1, \ldots, \sigma_n)$ is played in $\Gamma(\mu)$ and let u be an information set of player i. If player i gets to hear that u is reached, then he can deduce that the payoff of player j must be in the set.

(6.7.2) $$R_j(u,\sigma) := \{r_j \in \mathbb{R}^Z ; \mathrm{Poss}(\sigma_j(r_j)) \cap u \neq \emptyset\}$$

and, in this case, he will think that the disturbances in the payoffs of player j have the distribution

(6.7.3) $$\mu_j^{u,\sigma} := \mu_j(.|R_j(u,\sigma)) .$$

Note that $\mu_j^{u,\sigma}$ is well-defined for every u and σ by (6.7.1) and Assumption 5.3.3. Also note that this distribution depends only on the component σ_j of σ. Based on the observation that u is reached, player i will predict that player j will choose c at the information set v with the probability

(6.7.4) $$\int \sigma_{jv}(c) \, d\mu_j^{u,\sigma}(.|R_j(v,\sigma)),$$

where $\sigma_{jv}(c)$ is the mapping which assigns to each payoff r_j the probability $\sigma_{jv}(c,r_j)$ that player j chooses c at v if the payoff is r_j. Note that (6.7.4) is well-defined for all v which might be reached when u is reached (i.e. $Z(u) \cap Z(v) \neq \emptyset$). Let $b_j^{u,\sigma}$ be a behavior strategy which is defined as in (6.7.4) whenever possible and which is arbitrarily defined elsewhere. Let $b^{u,\sigma}$ be a behavior strategy combination in which every player j plays $b_j^{u,\sigma}$. If player i gets to hear that u is reached, he will predict the behavior of his opponents by $b^{u,\sigma}$. For the strategy combination σ to be an equilibrium of $\Gamma(\mu)$, we should have that every player at any information set u chooses a best reply against the strategies he expects the others to follow, based on the observation that u is reached. Therefore, we define

DEFINITION 6.7.1. A strategy combination σ is an *equilibrium* of $\Gamma(\mu)$ if for all $i \in N$, $u \in U_i$ and $r_i \in \mathbb{R}^Z$

$$(6.7.5) \qquad R_{iu}(b^{u,\sigma}\backslash\sigma_i(r_i)) = \max_{b_i' \in B_i} R_{iu}(b^{u,\sigma}\backslash b_i') ,$$

where $R_{iu}(.)$ denotes the expected payoff for player i after u if his actual payoff vector in $\Gamma(\mu)$ is r_i.

Note that the conditional expected payoff in (6.7.5) is well-defined, since u is reached if $b^{u,\sigma}$ is played (Assumption 5.3.3 and (6.7.1)) and since $b^{u,\sigma}$ is defined by (6.7.4) in all those parts of the game tree which can effect the expected payoff $R_{iu}(.)$. We conjecture that a disturbed extensive form game always (i.e. whenever Assumption 5.2.2 is satisfied) possesses an equilibrium, but a proof is not yet on paper. Instead of studying the existence problem, let us consider the question of which equilibria of Γ can be approximated by equilibria of $\Gamma(\mu^\varepsilon)$ if μ^ε converges weakly to 0 as ε tends to 0. To be more precise: if the strategy combination σ is played in $\Gamma(\mu)$, then to an outside observer it will look as if the behavior strategy combination b defined by

$$(6.7.6) \qquad b_{iu} = b_{iu}^{u,\sigma} \qquad \text{for all } i,u$$

is played, where $b_{iu}^{u,\sigma}$ is as in (6.7.4). b is called the behavior strategy combination *induced* by σ. We will investigate which equilibria of Γ can be obtained as limit points of a sequence $\{b^\varepsilon\}_{\varepsilon\downarrow 0}$ where b^ε is induced by an equilibrium σ^ε of $\Gamma(\mu^\varepsilon)$. Such equilibria will be called *P-stable* equilibria (where $P = \{\mu^\varepsilon;\ \varepsilon > 0\}$).
The game of figure 6.7.1 illustrates that in general non-sequential equilibria might be obtained as limit points.

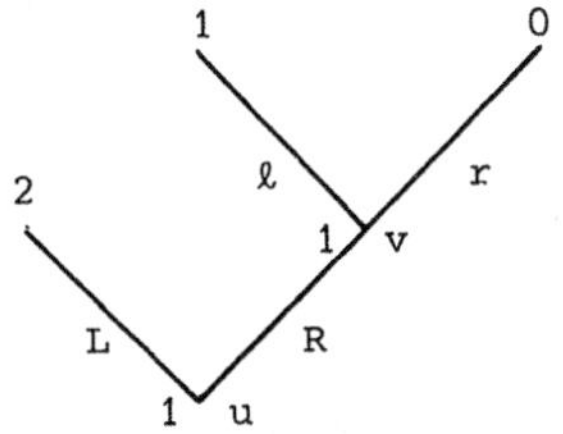

Figure 6.7.1. Uncertainty about the payoffs does not necessarily lead to a sequential equilibrium being played.

Assume the payoffs of player 1 fluctuate around (2,1,0). Let the random variable X_i^ε represent the payoff at he i^{th} endpoint of the tree (counting from left to right). If ε is close to 0, then an outside observer will see player 1 playing L with a probability close to 1, but at v he does not necessarily observe ℓ being played with a probability close to 1. If b^ε is induced by an equilibrium of the ε-disturbed game, then

$$b_{1v}^{\varepsilon}(r) = \mathbb{P}[X_3^\varepsilon > X_2^\varepsilon | \max(X_2^\varepsilon, X_3^\varepsilon) > X_1^\varepsilon]$$

and although $\mathbb{P}[X_3^\varepsilon > X_2^\varepsilon]$ tends to 0 as ε tends to 0, the limit of $b_{1v}^\varepsilon(r)$ may be positive. This, for instance, will be true if X_i^ε has a Cauchy distribution (cf. the proof of Theorem 5.5.3). Hence, non-sequential equilibria may be $\mathcal{P}$-stable.

The reason why a non-sequential equilibrium may be $\mathcal{P}$-stable in the game of figure 6.7.1 is that, if v is actually reached, then the payoffs after v may be quite different from those displayed in figure 6.7.1. Hence, in the disturbed game the subgame starting at v may be quite different from this subgame in the undisturbed game. The game of figure 6.7.2 is another example to demonstrate this. By means of this game we illustrate the difference between the incomplete rationality (perfectness) approach and the incomplete information approach.

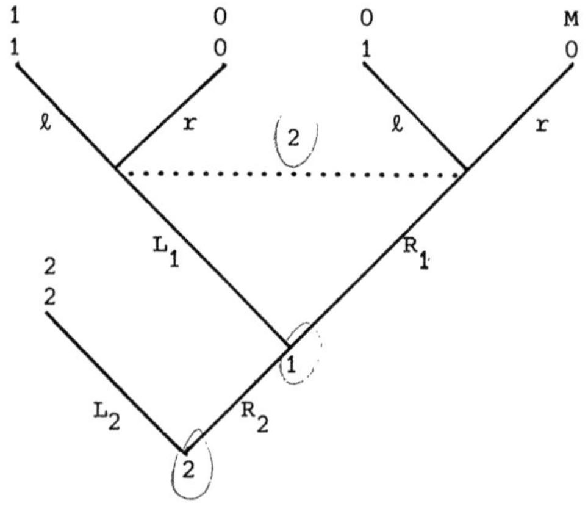

Figure 6.7.2. The difference between the incomplete information approach and the incomplete rationality approach (M is some real number).

Consider first the case in which there are no random disturbances in the payoffs, but in which the players might be slightly irrational. In this case, if the information set of player 1 is reached, this player concludes that player 2 has made a mistake. Yet, player 1 will think that player 2 will make mistakes only with a small probability at his second information set and, therefore, player 1 will play L_1.

Next, consider the case in which there are random disturbances in the payoffs. A priori, player 1 thinks that the payoffs of player 2 are as displayed in Γ and, therefore, he expects his information set not to be reached. If his information set is reached, then player 1 has to revise his priors and he might as well come to the conclusion that the payoffs of player 2 in the subgame are quite different from those displayed in figure 6.7.2. Therefore, he might assign a positive probability to player 2 playing r in the subgame and, consequently, it might be optimal to choose R_1 if M is large. To make the latter statement more precise, note that the normal form of the game of figure 6.7.2 is the game of figure 4.1.1 and in Theorem 5.5.3 we showed that it is optimal for player 1 to choose R_1 in the case in which the disturbances have a Cauchy distribution.

In both examples, the reason why a non-sequential equilibrium of Γ might be $\mathcal{P}$-stable is that, upon unexpectedly reaching an information set $u \in U_i$, player i might conclude that the payoffs after u are completely different from those in Γ. Hence, to obtain that only sequential equilibria will be $\mathcal{P}$-stable, it is necessary that a player does not have to revise his beliefs about the payoffs after u, if u is reached. More precisely, let σ be a strategy combination in $\Gamma(\mu^{\varepsilon})$, let $\mu^{\varepsilon,u,\sigma}$ be defined as in (6.7.3) and let $\bar{\mu}_i^{\varepsilon,u,\sigma}$ be the conditional distribution of $\mu_i^{\varepsilon,u,\sigma}$ on Z(u), i.e.

$$(6.7.7) \qquad \bar{\mu}_i^{\varepsilon,u,\sigma}(B) := \mu_i^{\varepsilon,u,\sigma}(B \times \mathbb{R}^{Z \setminus Z(u)}) \qquad \text{for a Borel subset B of } \mathbb{R}^{Z(u)}.$$

If σ is played in $\Gamma(\mu^{\varepsilon})$, then, if u is reached, the beliefs about the payoffs of player i after u are described by $\bar{\mu}_i^{\varepsilon,u,\sigma}$. The condition that a player, upon reaching u, should still think that the payoffs of player i after u in $\Gamma(\mu^{\varepsilon})$ are close to the payoff in Γ amounts to requiring that

$$(6.7.8) \qquad \bar{\mu}_i^{\varepsilon,u,\sigma} \text{ converges weakly to 0 as } \varepsilon \text{ tends to 0} \qquad \text{for all } i,u,\sigma.$$

We conjecture that (6.7.8) is fulfilled if the disturbances at the different endpoints of the game are independent and have a normal distribution with parameters 0 and ε (cf. Lemma 5.7.1). Furthermore, we conjecture that only sequential equilibria are $\mathcal{P}$-stable if $\mathcal{P} = \{\mu^{\varepsilon};\ \varepsilon > 0\}$ is such that (6.7.8) is satisfied.

We conclude this section by noting that not all sequential equilibria can be $\mathcal{P}$-stable. Consider the game Γ of figure 6.5.1 and let $\mathcal{P} = \{\mu^{\varepsilon};\ \varepsilon > 0\}$ be such that every μ_i^{ε} is the product distribution on $\mathbb{R}^5$ of a normal distribution on $\mathbb{R}$ with parameters 0 and ε. By (6.7.8) player 2, when he has to make a choice, believes that the payoffs of player 1 after this player's choices L_1 and R_1 are close to those of Γ (he cannot conclude anything about the payoffs of player 1 after A). Therefore, he will conclude that player 1 has chosen L_1 and, consequently, he will choose L_2. Hence, only the equilibrium (L_1, L_2) is $\mathcal{P}$-stable (cf. the discussions in the sections 5.5 and 6.5). Note that, if (6.7.8) is satisfied, the disturbed game approach in essence means that player 2 analyses the game Γ of figure 6.5.1 by means of the game Γ' which is obtained from Γ by deleting the choice A of player 1: since the unique equilibrium Γ' is (L_1, L_2) player 2 has to choose L_2.

REFERENCES

AUMANN, R.J. [1959]. Acceptable points in general cooperative n-person games, pp. 287-324 in A.W. Tucker and R.D. Luce (eds.). Contributions to the theory of games IV, (Annals of Mathematics Studies 40), Princeton University Press, Princeton.

AUMANN, R.J. [1964]. Mixed and behavior strategies in infinite extensive games, pp. 627-650 in M. Dresher, L.S. Shapley and A.W. Tucker (eds.), Advances in Game Theory (Annals of Mathematics Studies 52), Princeton University Press, Princeton.

AUMANN, R.J. [1974]. Subjectivity and correlation in randomized strategies. J. Math. Econ. 1, 67-96.

AUMANN, R.J. [1976]. Agreeing to disagree. The Annals of Statistics 4, 1236-1239.

AUMANN, R.J. AND M. MASCHLER [1972]. Some thoughts on the minimax principle. Management Science 18, 54-63.

BALINSKI, M.L.[1961]. An algorithm for finding all vertices of a convex set. J. Soc. Ind. Appl. Math. 9, 72-88.

BELLMAN, R. [1957]. Dynamic programming. Princeton University Press, Princeton.

BILLINGSLEY, P. [1968]. Convergence of probability measures. John Wiley and Sons, New York.

BOHNENBLUST, H.F., S. KARLIN AND L.S. SHAPLEY [1950]. Solutions of discrete two-person games, pp. 51-72 in H.W. Kuhn and A.W. Tucker (eds.), contributions to the theory of games I (Annals of Mathematics Studies 24), Princeton University Press, Princeton.

BRUYN, N.G. de [1958]. Asymptotic methods in analysis. North Holland, Amsterdam.

CHIN, H.H., T. PARTHASARATHY AND T.E.S. RAGHAVAN [1974]. Structure of equilibria in n-person non-cooperative games. Int. J. Game Theory 3, 1-19.

DAMME, E.E.C. van [1980a]. Some comments on Harsanyi's postulates for rational behavior in game situations. Methods of Operations Research 38, 189-205.

DAMME, E.E.C. van [1980b]. A characterization of perfect and proper equilibria in zero-sum games. Memorandum Cosor 80-18. Eindhoven University of Technology, Eindhoven. (to appear in Int.J. Game Theory).

DAMME, E.E.C. van [1980c]. A relation between perfect equilibria in extensive form games and proper equilibria in normal form games. Memorandum COSOR 80-19, Eindhoven University of Technology, Eindhoven. (To appear in Int. J. Game Theory).

DAMME, E.E.C. van [1981a]. History-dependent equilibrium points in dynamic games, pp. 27-38 in O. Moeschlin and D. Pallaschke (eds.), Game Theory and Mathematical Economics, North-Holland, Amsterdam.

DAMME, E.E.C. van [1981b]. Refinements of the Nash equilibrium concept for bimatrix games. Memorandum COSOR 81-08, Eindhoven University of Technology, Eindhoven.

DAMME, E.E.C. van [1981c]. Regular equilibrium points of n-person games in normal form. Memorandum COSOR 81-12, Eindhoven University of Technology, Eindhoven.

DAMME, E.E.C. van [1982]. Refining the equilibrium concept for bimatrix games via control costs. Memorandum COSOR 82-02, Eindhoven University of Technology, Eindhoven.

DEBREU, G. [1970]. Economies with a finite set of equilibria. Econometrica, 38, 387-392.

DIEUDONNÉ, J. [1969]. Foundations of modern analysis. Academic Press, New York.

DRESHER, M. [1961]. Games of strategy. Prentice-Hall, Englewood Cliffs, New Jersey.

FORT, M.K. [1950]. Essential and non-essential fixed points. Am. J. Math. 72, 315-322.

FUDENBERG, D. AND D. LEVINE [1981]. Perfect equilibria of finite and infinite horizon games. Working paper No. 216, Department of Economics, UCLA.

FUDENBERG, D. AND J. TIROLE [1981]. Sequential bargaining with incomplete information. Mimeo M.I.T.

GALE, D. AND S. SHERMAN [1950]. Solutions of finite two-person games, pp. 37-49 in H.W. Kuhn and A.W.Tucker (eds.). Contributions to the theory of games I (Annals of Mathematics Studies 24), Princeton University Press, Princeton.

HALMOS, P.R. [1950]. Measure theory, Van Nostrand, Princeton, New Jersey.

HARSANYI, J.C. [1968]. Games with incomplete information played by "Bayesian" players, Parts I, II and III. Management Science 14, 159-182, 320-332, 468-502.

HARSANYI, J.C. [1973a]. Games with randomly disturbed payoffs: a new rationale for mixed strategy equilibrium points. Int. J. Game Theory 2, 1-23.

HARSANYI, J.C. [1973b]. Oddness of the number of equilibrium points: a new proof. Int. J. Game Theory 2, 235-250.

HARSANYI, J.C. [1975]. The tracing procedure: a Bayesian approach to defining a solution for n-person noncooperative games. Int. J. Game Theory 4, 61-94.

HARSANYI, J.C. [1976]. A solution concept for n-person noncooperative games. Int. J. Game Theory 5, 211-225.

HARSANYI, J.C. [1977]. Rational behavior and bargaining equilibrium in games and social situations. Cambridge University Press.

HARSANYI, J.C. AND R. SELTEN [1980]. A general theory of equilibrium selection in games. Chapters 1, 2 and 3. Working Papers nos 91, 92 and 105 of the Institute of Mathematical Economics, University of Bielefeld.

HARSANYI, J.C. AND R. SELTEN [1982]. A general theory of equilibrium selection in games, revised version of chapter 2. Working paper no. 114 of the Institute of Mathematical Economics, University of Bielefeld.

HEUER, G.A. AND C.B. MILLHAM [1976]. On Nash subsets and mobility chains in bimatrix games. Naval Res. Logist. Quart. 23, 311-319.

JANSEN, M.J.M. [1981a]. Maximal Nash subsets for bimatrix games. Naval. Res. Logist. Quart. 28, 147-152.

JANSEN, M.J.M. [1981b]. Regularity and stability of equilibrium points of bimatrix games. Mathematics of Operations Research 6, 530-550.

KAKUTANI, S. [1941]. A generalisation of Brouwer's fixed point theorem. Duke Math. J. 8, 457-459.

KALAI, E. [1980]. Preplay negotiations in noncooperative games. Discussion paper no. 421, Northwestern University, Evanston, Illinois.

KALAI, E. AND D. SAMET [1982]. Persistent equilibria in strategic games. Discussion Paper No. 515, Northwestern University, Evanston, Illinois.

KANEKO, M. [1981]. A bilateral monopoly and the Nash cooperative solution. J. Econ. Theory 24, 311-327.

KINGMAN, J.F.C. AND S.J. TAYLOR [1966]. Introduction to measure and probability. Cambridge University Press, London.

KREPS, D.M. AND R. WILSON [1982a]. Sequential equilibria. Econometrica 50, 863-894.

KREPS, D.M. AND R. WILSON [1982b]. Reputation and imperfect information. J. Econ. Theory 27, 253-279.

KUHN, H.W. [1953]. Extensive games and the problem of information. Annals of Mathematics Studies 28, 193-216.

KUHN, H.W. [1961]. An algorithm for equilibrium points in bimatrix games. Proc. Nat. Acad. Sci. U.S.A. 47, 1656-1662.

LEFSCHETZ, S. [1949]. Introduction to topology. Princeton University Press, Princeton.

LEMKE, C.E. AND J.T. HOWSON [1964]. Equilibrium points of bimatrix games. J. Soc. Indust. Appl. Math. 12, 413-423.

LUCE, R.D. AND H. RAIFFA [1957]. Games and decisions. John Wiley, New York.

MILGROM, P. AND R. WEBER [1980]. Distributional strategies for games with incomplete information. Discussion Paper No. 428. Northwestern University, Evanston, Illinois.

MILGROM, P. AND R. WEBER [1981]. Topologies on information and strategies in games with incomplete information, pp. 89-96 in O. Moeschlin and D. Pallaschke (eds.), Game Theory and Mathematical Economics, North Holland, Amsterdam.

MILLHAM, C.B. [1974]. On Nash subsets of bimatrix games. Naval. Res. Logist. Quart. 21, 307-317.

MILLS, H. [1960]. Equilibrium points in finite games. J. Soc. Indust. Appl. Math. 8, 397-402.

MILNOR, J. [1965]. Topology from the differentiable viewpoint. The university press of Virginia, Charlottesville.

MOULIN, H. [1982]. Bargaining and non-cooperative implementation. Laboratoire d'économetrie de l'école polytechnique, Paris.

MYERSON, R.B. [1978]. Refinements of the Nash equilibrium concept. Int. J. Game Theory 7, 73-80.

NASH, J.F. [1950]. Equilibrium points in n-person games. Proc. Nat. Acad. Sci. U.S.A. 36, 48-49.

NASH, J.F. [1951]. Non-cooperative games. Ann. of Math. 54, 286-295.

NEUMANN, J. von [1928]. Zur Theorie der Gesellschaftsspiele. Math. Ann. 100, 295-320.

NEUMANN, J. von and O. MORGENSTERN [1944]. Theory of games and economic behavior. Princeton University Press, Princeton.

OKADA, A. [1981]. On stability of perfect equilibrium points. Int. J. Game Theory, 10, 67-73.

OKADA, A. [1982]. A note on quasi-strong equilibrium points of noncooperative games. Research report No. B-114, Department of Systems Science of the Tokyo institute of technology.

OWEN, G. [1968]. Game theory. W.B. Saunders Company, Philadelphia.

PONSSARD, J.P. [1976]. On the subject of non optimal play in zero sum extensive form games: "the trap phenomenon". Int. J. Game Theory 5, 105-115.

RADNER, R. AND R.W. ROSENTHAL [1982]. Private information and pure strategy equilibria Math. Oper. Res. 7, 401-409.

ROCKEFELLAR, R.T. [1970]. Convex analysis. Princeton University Press, Princeton.

ROSEN, J.B. [1965]. Existence and uniqueness of equilibrium points for concave n-person games. Econometrica 33, 520-534.

ROSENMÜLLER, J. [1971]. On a generalization of the Lemke-Howson algorithm to noncooperative n-person games. Siam J. Appl. Math. 21, 73-79.

ROSENMÜLLER, J. [1981]. The theory of games and markets. North Holland, Amsterdam.

RUBINSTEIN, A. [1980]. Strong perfect equilibrium. Int. J. Game Theory 9, 1-12.

RUBINSTEIN, A. [1982]. Perfect equilibrium in a bargaining model. Econometrica 50, 97-109.

SAVAGE, L.J. [1954]. The foundations of statistics. John Wiley and Sons, New York.

SARD, A. [1942]. The measure of the critical values of differentiable maps. Bulletin of the American Mathematical Society 48, 883-890.

SCHELLING, T.C. [1960]. The strategy of conflict. Harvard University Press, Cambridge, Mass.

SELTEN, R. [1965]. Spieltheoretische Behandlung eines Oligopolmodells mit Nachfragetragheit. Zeitschrift fur die gesamte Staatswissenschaft 12, 301-324.

SELTEN, R. [1973]. A simple model of imperfect competition, where 4 are few and 6 are many. Int. J. Game Theory 3, 141-201.

SELTEN, R. [1975]. Reexamination of the perfectness concept for equilibrium points in extensive games. Int. J. Game Theory 4, 25-55.

SELTEN, R. [1977]. A simple model of kidnapping, pp. 139-156 in R. Henn and O. Moeschlin (eds.), Mathematical Economics and Game Theory. Lecture notes in economics and mathematical system 141, Springer-Verlag, Berlin.

SELTEN, R. [1978]. The chain store paradox. Theory and decision 9, 127-159.

SHAPLEY, L.S. [1974]. A note on the Lemke-Howson algorithm. Math. Programming Study 1, 175-189.

SMART, D.R. [1974]. Fixed point theorems. Cambridge University Press, London.

STÅHL, I [1977]. An n-person bargaining game in the extensive form, pp. 156-173 in R. Henn and O. Moeschlin (eds.), Mathematical Economics and Game Theory. Lecture notes in economics and mathematical system 141, Springer-Verlag, Berlin.

VOROB'EV, N.N. [1958]. Equilibrium points in bimatrix games. Theory Probability Appl. 3, 297-309.

WILSON, R. [1971]. Computing equilibria of n-person games. Siam J. Appl. Math. 21, 80-87.

WILSON, R. [1972]. Computing equilibria of two-person games from the extensive form. Management Science, 18, 448-460.

WINKELS, H.M. [1979]. An algorithm to determine all equilibrium points of a bimatrix game, pp. 137-148 in O. Moeschlin and D. Pallaschke (eds.), Game Theory and related topics, North-Holland, Amsterdam.

WU WEN-TSŪN AND JIANG JIA-HE [1962]. Essential equilibrium points of n-person non-cooperative games. Sci. Sinica 11, 1307-1322.

SURVEY

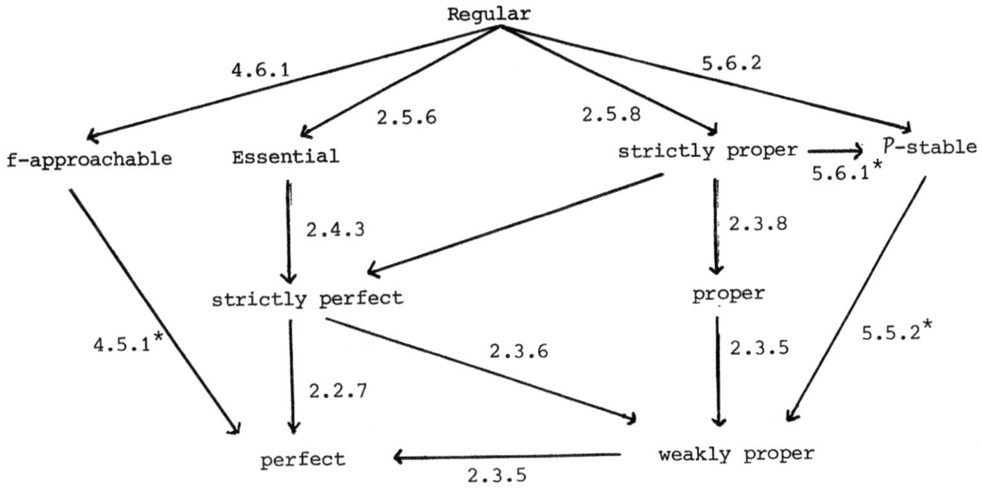

An overview of the relations between refinements of the Nash equilibrium concept for normal form games. Inclusions go in the direction of the arrows. Numbers represent the theorem in which the result is proved. A star denotes that the relation holds only if some additional condition is satisfied. All inclusions displayed are strict, except (possibly) the one which is not numbered.

SUBJECT INDEX

Vol. 214: M. Faber, H. Niemes und G. Stephan, Entropie, Umweltschutz und Rohstoffverbrauch. IX, 181 Seiten. 1983.

Vol. 215: Semi-Infinite Programming and Applications. Proceedings, 1981. Edited by A. V. Fiacco and K. O. Kortanek. XI, 322 pages. 1983.

Vol. 216: H. H. Müller, Fiscal Policies in a General Equilibrium Model with Persistent Unemployment. VI, 92 pages. 1983.

Vol. 217: Ch. Grootaert, The Relation Between Final Demand and Income Distribution. XIV, 105 pages. 1983.

Vol. 218: P. van Loon, A Dynamic Theory of the Firm: Production, Finance and Investment. VII, 191 pages. 1983.

Vol. 219: E. van Damme, Refinements of the Nash Equilibrium Concept. VI, 151 pages. 1983.

Ökonometrie und Unternehmensforschung
Econometrics and Operations Research

Vol. I	Nichtlineare Programmierung. Von H. P. Künzi und W. Krelle unter Mitwirkung von W. Oettli. Vergriffen
Vol. II	Lineare Programmierung und Erweiterungen. Von G. B. Dantzig. Ins Deutsche übertragen und bearbeitet von A. Jaeger. – Mit 103 Abbildungen. XVI, 712 Seiten. 1966. Geb.
Vol. III	Stochastic Processes. By M. Girault. – With 35 figures. XII, 126 pages. 1966. Cloth
Vol. IV	Methoden der Unternehmensforschung im Versicherungswesen. Von K. H. Wolff. – Mit 14 Diagrammen. VIII, 266 Seiten. 1966. Geb.
Vol. V	The Theory of Max-Min and its Application to Weapons Allocation Problems. By John M. Danskin. – With 6 figures. X, 126 pages. 1967. Cloth
Vol. VI	Entscheidungskriterien bei Risiko. Von H. Schneeweiss. – Mit 35 Abbildungen. XII, 215 Seiten. 1967. Geb.
Vol. VII	Boolean Methods in Operations Research and Related Areas. By P. L. Hammer (Ivănescu) and S. Rudeanu. With a preface by R. Bellman. – With 25 figures. XVI, 329 pages. 1968. Cloth
Vol. VIII	Strategy for R & D: Studies in the Microeconomics of Development. By Th. Marschak. Th K. Glennan Jr., and R. Summers. – With 44 figures. XIV, 330 pages. 1967. Cloth
Vol. IX	Dynamic Programming of Economic Decisions. By M. J. Beckmann. – With 9 figures XII, 143 pages. 1968. Cloth
Vol. X	Input-Output-Analyse. Von J. Schumann. – Mit 12 Abbildungen. X, 311 Seiten. 1968. Geb.
Vol. XI	Produktionstheorie. Von W. Wittmann. – Mit 54 Abbildungen. VIII, 177 Seiten. 1968. Geb.
Vol. XII	Sensitivitätsanalysen und parametrische Programmierung. Von W. Dinkelbach. – Mit 20 Abbildungen. XI, 190 Seiten. 1969. Geb.
Vol. XIII	Graphentheoretische Methoden und ihre Anwendungen. Von W. Knödel. – Mit 24 Abbildungen. VIII, 111 Seiten. 1969. Geb.
Vol. XIV	Praktische Studien zur Unternehmensforschung. Von E. Nievergelt, O. Müller, F. E. Schlaepfer und W. H. Landis. – Mit 82 Abbildungen. XII, 240 Seiten. 1970. Geb.
Vol. XV	Optimale Reihenfolgen. Von H. Müller-Merbach. – Mit 45 Abbildungen. IX, 225 Seiten. 1970. Geb.
Vol. XVI	Preispolitik der Mehrproduktenunternehmung in der statischen Theorie. Von R. Selten. – Mit 20 Abbildungen. VIII, 195 Seiten. 1970. Geb.
Vol. XVII	Information Theory for Systems Engineers. By L. P. Hyvärinen. – With 42 figures. VIII, 197 pages. 1970. Cloth
Vol. XVIII	Unternehmensforschung im Bergbau. Von F. L. Wilke. – Mit 29 Abbildungen. VIII, 150 Seiten. 1972. Geb.
Vol. XIX	Anti-Äquilibrium. Von J. Kornai. – Mit 31 Abbildungen. XVI, 382 Seiten. 1975. Geb.
Vol. XX	Mathematische Optimierung. Von E. Blum, W. Oettli. IX, 413 Seiten. (davon 75 Seiten Bibliographie). 1975. Geb.
Vol. XXI	Stochastic Linear Programming. By P. Kall. VI, 95 pages. 1976. Cloth.